Locke

A. J. Pyle

polity

Copyright © A. J. Pyle 2013

The right of A. J. Pyle to be identified as Author of this Work has been asserted in accordance with the UK Copyright, Designs and Patents Act 1988.

First published in 2013 by Polity Press

Polity Press
65 Bridge Street
Cambridge CB2 1UR, UK

Polity Press
350 Main Street
Malden, MA 02148, USA

All rights reserved. Except for the quotation of short passages for the purpose of criticism and review, no part of this publication may be reproduced, stored in a retrieval system, or transmitted, in any form or by any means, electronic, mechanical, photocopying, recording or otherwise, without the prior permission of the publisher.

ISBN-13: 978-0-7456-5066-1
ISBN-13: 978-0-7456-5067-8(pb)

A catalogue record for this book is available from the British Library.

Typeset in 10.5 on 12 pt Palatino
by Toppan Best-set Premedia Limited
Printed and bound in Great Britain by the MPG Books Group

The publisher has used its best endeavours to ensure that the URLs for external websites referred to in this book are correct and active at the time of going to press. However, the publisher has no responsibility for the websites and can make no guarantee that a site will remain live or that the content is or will remain appropriate.

Every effort has been made to trace all copyright holders, but if any have been inadvertently overlooked the publisher will be pleased to include any necessary credits in any subsequent reprint or edition.

For further information on Polity, visit our website: www.politybooks.com

Contents

Abbreviations

C	*The Correspondence of John Locke*
CU	*Of the Conduct of the Understanding*
ECT	*An Essay Concerning Toleration, and Other Writings on Law and Politics, 1667–1683*
EHU	*An Essay Concerning Human Understanding*
ELN	*Essays on the Law of Nature and Other Associated Writings*
LT	*Locke on Toleration*
PW	*Posthumous Works of Mr John Locke*
RC	*The Reasonableness of Christianity, as Delivered in the Scriptures*
STCE	*Some Thoughts Concerning Education*
TTG	*Two Treatises of Government*
WJL	*The Works of John Locke*

Introduction

The Unity of Locke's Thought

John Locke (1632–1704) has been described both as the greatest English philosopher (Hume, of course, was Scottish) and as the father of modern empiricism. Both judgements might be challenged: Ockham, Hobbes, Mill and Russell might vie for the former title, while Bacon and Gassendi clearly played major roles in the development and articulation of empiricism long before Locke. But Locke's place in philosophy's premier league is not in doubt; his influence on subsequent epistemology, metaphysics, religion and politics was enormous; and his philosophical reputation has if anything grown over the last thirty years. No scholar today would endorse Gilbert Ryle's celebrated verdict, delivered in a lecture in 1965, that 'nearly every youthful student of philosophy both can and does in about his second essay refute Locke's entire theory of knowledge'.[1] The scholarship of the past generation has helped to strip away centuries of misunderstanding and misrepresentation, and the real Locke turns out to have been a much more powerful and profound thinker than the caricature still sometimes found – regrettably – in textbook accounts of 'the British empiricists'.

The range of Locke's thought is as impressive as its depth. Here is a man who thought long and hard about natural and revealed theology, metaphysics, epistemology, the natural sciences, medicine, psychology, physical and human geography, semantics, ethics, politics, education and economics, and made significant original contributions to several of these disciplines. This presents an obvious problem for commentators and authors of textbooks. Does one attempt an overview of Locke's thought as a whole, or does one choose to focus on the *Essay Concerning Human Understanding*, or the *Two Treatises of Government*, or the *Reasonableness of Christianity*? Does one sacrifice depth for breadth or vice versa? In accordance with the stated aims of this series, this book aims to be fairly comprehensive in its scope, covering at least Locke's metaphysics, religion, epistemology and politics, while glancing briefly at his views on other subjects. But the danger then looms that the book will simply fall apart into a series of entirely distinct chapters, one on each key text or each aspect of Locke's multifaceted thought. To avoid this peril, a leading idea or guiding thread is clearly needed.

At this point, some recent scholars might ask whether it is right even to attempt to find such a leading idea. Each of Locke's main works, it has been argued, is written as a response to some definite problem of his day, and cannot be understood except in that histori-cally fixed context. There is no reason to assume that Locke ever attempted to create a philosophical system of his own or to found a school of philosophy with a distinctive set of characteristic doc-trines. There is considerable truth to both of these assertions. If we look at the genesis of Locke's major works, they are clearly prompted by issues highly specific to his time and place, and such questions about their origins are of obvious relevance to their comprehension. To take them entirely out of context is to run evident risks of mis-understanding. And it is undeniably true that Locke never took himself to be establishing a 'Lockean' school or teaching a special body of distinct 'Lockean' doctrines. So there is a challenge here that must be met by the author of any attempt to see Locke's work as a coherent whole.

The first point that needs to be made in response to this challenge is to insist that setting a philosophical classic in its historical context is in no sense incompatible with treating it as a work of philosophy. Historians of philosophy sometimes oppose a 'contextualist' approach to an 'analytical' one, but this is an entirely false antith-esis. Both in general and in the case of Locke in particular, the 'contextualist' and the 'analytical' approaches are complementary rather than antagonistic. If, for example, we treat Locke in the context provided by contemporaries such as Boyle and Newton, rather than that of successors such as Berkeley and Hume, we will find that we arrive at a picture of Locke that is simultaneously more historically accurate and more philosophically impressive.[2] We can thus grant the contextualist's point about the genesis of Locke's major works without abandoning the search for a guiding thread.

Even if Locke was not a system-builder, he was still a philosopher. His correspondence shows clearly that he was often asked to comment on the consistency of the views expressed in his various works. Can he, for example, deny that morality is an innate law written by God on each and every human heart (*Essay*, Book 1), and still claim that we have natural rights and duties discernible by Reason (*Second Treatise of Government*)? His opponents claimed that his empiricism undermines the moral law; friends such as William Molyneux and James Tyrrell urged him repeatedly to provide an account of the foundations of morality consistent with his rejection of innate principles. And is the *tabula rasa* thesis of the *Essay* consistent with the admission, in *Some Thoughts Concerning Education*, of seemingly inborn differences of temperament among children? Locke is not a system-builder, but he cared about the truth, and a man who cares about truth cannot be indifferent to consistency. There is no Lockean system of philosophy, but there is a distinctively Lockean point of view, grounded in his opinions concerning human knowledge and its limits.

My suggestion is that we focus on the epistemology, and start with Locke's often-stated claim that *we humans have been given enough knowledge for our needs*. We can know enough of the natural world for human arts such as agriculture, manufacturing, navigation and medicine, even though we remain hopelessly ignorant of what might be called 'the nature of Nature', that is, the underlying metaphysics of the supposed real essences of things. And we can know enough of God's existence and of the God-given moral law to grasp our duties towards one another as human beings and as citizens, despite remaining massively ignorant of the nature of God and even of our own souls. This combination of a modest agnosticism about metaphysics with confidence in ordinary empirical and moral knowledge is Locke's most distinctive feature among early modern philosophers. Many of his contemporaries would have denied that we can know our moral duties without an intensive training in their particular religion, or that we can gain an adequate grasp of the natural world without settling deep issues of matter theory such as the truth or falsity of atomism. Here Locke's thinking begins to sound strikingly modern: there are many living philosophers who ask precisely Locke's question, 'How can I build the widest possible consensus?', bringing in people from different backgrounds and traditions and getting them to sign up to some proposition of great practical importance despite their very different (and still unreconciled) starting points. This central Lockean distinction, between what we need to know for our practical concerns on the one hand, and what we don't need to know (and should learn to dispute peacefully and amicably) on the other hand, will inform the whole book.

Given this overall approach, we can expect problems of two kinds to arise for Locke. From the sceptical side, we can expect challenges to the positive knowledge-claims that he does make. He thinks, for example, that the existence of God can be demonstrated by Reason. But since he also says that the moral law is God-given, his demonstration of the existence of God had better be sound! If morality is independent of religion, sceptical doubts about the so-called 'proofs' of the existence of God are harmless intellectual games; if morality depends on religion for its foundations, a great deal more is clearly at stake. From the dogmatists' side, we can expect challenges to Locke's repeated claims that we don't need to know the metaphysics. He tells us, for example, in his famous account of personal identity, that my assurance of my own personal survival (and hence of the possibility of rewards and punishments after death) doesn't depend on any particular philosophical theory about the soul. But if he is wrong about this, it might turn out that the knowledge he tells us we *don't* possess (knowledge of the nature of the soul) is essential to the ordinary believer's assurance of an afterlife. We can thus expect Locke's position to be vulnerable to attacks from both sides – and this is exactly what we find.

A Word about Empiricism

Historians of early modern philosophy of a previous generation used to tell a story of two opposed schools or traditions, pitting 'The Continental Rationalists' (Descartes, Spinoza and Leibniz) against 'The British Empiricists' (Locke, Berkeley and Hume), with Kant's critical philosophy providing a final synthesis of the two schools at the end of the eighteenth century. The rationalists, we were told, thought that reason was supreme, and neglected experience; the empiricists trusted experience and had their doubts and reservations about reason. The story had a pleasing symmetry, and of course appealed to the prejudices of Anglo-Saxon audiences, who liked to think of themselves as plain no-nonsense folk, modestly following the teachings of experience and justifiably suspicious of too much high-flown speculation. This story still provides the narrative structure for many an undergraduate textbook or introductory course on early modern philosophy.

The problem with the story is that it is completely unhistorical, in two distinct but equally important senses.[3] In the first place (1), there is no reason to think that the historical figures in question thought of themselves as belonging to these two opposed camps. Locke might think of Descartes as rather too bold in his claims to grasp the respective essences of material and spiritual substances, but he nevertheless regards Descartes as a fellow 'modern' and an ally against the Aristotelianism of the schools. Berkeley constructs a metaphysical system that can be shown to have significant debts to Descartes and his disciple Nicolas Malebranche. When Hume writes to Michael Ramsay,[4] listing the books he should read before attempting Hume's own *Treatise*, he cites Descartes and Malebranche, Berkeley and Bayle, but *not* Locke! The 'two schools' story is an artefact of later historiography, not something that would have been recognized by the early modern philosophers themselves. And (2), any suggestion that 'the rationalists' appealed exclusively to reason and never to experience, while 'the empiricists' appealed exclusively to experience and never to reason is promptly refuted by the most cursory reading of the relevant texts. It would be very easy to document any number of appeals to experience in Descartes, Spinoza and Leibniz, and some crucial argumentative appeals to supposedly self-evident rational principles in Locke and Berkeley.

Should we, then, simply abandon the traditional terms 'Rationalist' and Empiricist' altogether? That might be an over-reaction. I intend to follow John Cottingham in treating 'rationalism' and 'empiricism' as *cluster-concepts*.[5] The obvious analogy here is with medicine. Doctors generally find it difficult to come up with neat lists of necessary and sufficient conditions for the presence of diseases, and often resort to formulae such as 'patients with disease D will tend to manifest some of the following symptoms S1. . . . n'. In similar manner, says Cottingham, historians of early modern philosophy should treat the terms 'rationalist' and 'empiricist'. A philosopher might be properly called a rationalist, we are told, if he exhibits a sufficient number of the following 'symptoms':

1. Distrust of the senses as a source of knowledge.
2. Reliance on reason as a source of informative knowledge about the world (not just about our concepts or our language).
3. Belief in innate ideas and innate principles.

4. Belief in an intelligible order of nature that the human mind can in principle grasp and somehow 'mirror'.[6]
5. Belief that causal relations are necessary (causal rationalism).
6. Appeals to and reliance on a mathematical or demonstrative model for human knowledge.

If we apply this test to Locke, we find that he shows only very weak symptoms of rationalism. By at least four of Cottingham's criteria, Locke emerges as a definite negative. He thinks that the senses do furnish us with knowledge appropriate to our nature and needs; he flatly denies the existence of innate ideas and innate principles; he rejects the presumptuous thought that we can or should try to think God's thoughts or see our world from a God's eye point of view; and he tells us in a number of places that natural sciences such as physics and chemistry cannot be done in a demonstrative manner. With regard to his reliance on reason, the evidence is more equivocal, but it is clear that he places significantly less weight on reason and more on experience than, for example, Descartes and Leibniz. And with regard to causal rationalism, the evidence is again equivocal, but Locke is clear that even if there are 'necessary connections' in nature, as he suspects, they will not generally be recognized and known *as necessary* by us. So if we look for these six symptoms characteristic of rationalism, we get four clear 'nos' and two equivocal 'maybes'. If we applied the same test to Spinoza or Leibniz, we would get a string of 'yeses'.

Many contemporary historians of early modern philosophy find themselves in broad agreement with Cottingham in regarding the old terms 'rationalism' and 'empiricism' as still capable of doing useful explanatory work, despite the serious reservations we have noted. Instead of artificially dividing up the philosophers of the seventeenth and eighteenth centuries into two opposed schools, they now ask, of any given philosopher, how much – or how little – he thinks reason can achieve a priori, working independently of experience from supposedly self-evident first principles. A philosopher who confidently appeals to innate ideas and innate principles, and who thinks that, working from such materials, reason can provide us with a wealth of a priori knowledge, will properly be characterized as a rationalist. A philosopher who rejects innate ideas and innate principles, and who appeals to experience far more than to reason in his account of human knowledge, will properly be characterized as an empiricist. This is how I propose to use the term 'empiricist' throughout the rest of this book. I shall use the traditional terms 'empiricism' and 'empiricist' in discussing Locke's philosophy, but the terms must be understood with two clearly stated provisos: (a) that we are not seeking to situate Locke in a distinct school or tradition, and (b) that an empiricist philosopher can and does at times appeal to reason and to supposedly self-evident rational principles. The difference here may be one of degree rather than of kind.

1

Life, Contexts and Concerns

1. Locke's Life

John Locke was born at Wrington in Somerset, a village a few miles south of Bristol, on 29 August 1632.[1] He was the eldest child of John Locke senior, a lawyer and clerk to the local Justices of the Peace, and his wife Agnes, both of good Puritan stock. During the Civil War, John Locke senior fought with the Parliamentary army, serving briefly as a captain under the command of Colonel Popham, MP for Bath. In 1647, at the end of the Civil War, Popham's patronage enabled John Locke junior to gain a place at the prestigious Westminster School, then under its respected but feared headmaster, Richard Busby. In his later reflections in *Some Thoughts Concerning Education*, Locke would be highly critical both of the curriculum then taught and of the severity of the discipline in the schools of his day, but there can be no doubt that he emerged from Westminster an accomplished Latin scholar, as evidenced by his winning a scholarship to Christ Church, Oxford, in 1652.

Christ Church would be Locke's main place of residence for the next fifteen years of his life, through the formative years between the ages of twenty and thirty-five. He graduated BA in 1656 and MA in 1658, and experienced no difficulties in accepting the Restoration of the monarchy in 1660. He received the necessary certificate of orthodoxy from the formidable new Dean, John Fell, later Bishop of Oxford, who had the task of purging the university of perceived foes to the restored order in Church and state. Locke's political views at this early period were significantly more conservative than those he later published in the *Two Treatises* and the *Letter concerning Toleration*; even so, he may have found it necessary from time to time to keep his opinions to himself in Royalist and High Anglican Oxford. The young Locke lectured on Greek, rhetoric and moral philosophy, and served as tutor to the sons of wealthier gentlemen who could pay for such individual tuition.[2] In order to keep his studentship at Christ Church, Locke was expected to take Holy Orders, but he was released from this obligation by a royal dispensation from King Charles II in 1666. There is no reason to suppose that Locke would have had any qualms of conscience about taking the requisite oaths – he remained until his dying day a communicating and loyal member of the Church of England – but a career within the Church seems never to have appealed to him.

It was during his years at Oxford that Locke developed an intense interest in natural philosophy. He read the works of Descartes and was impressed by the Cartesian search for clear and distinct ideas and for intelligible (i.e., mechanical) principles in the emerging disciplines of the natural sciences. Although he read Descartes with care and attention, he found himself sceptical of Descartes' over-reliance on reason, and drawn more strongly towards the Baconian tradition, with its emphasis on the importance of observation and experiment in the study of nature. At Oxford, the young Locke met John Wilkins, William Petty, Christopher Wren, Robert Hooke and Robert Boyle, all destined after the Restoration to become major figures in the newly formed Royal Society. Locke became a Fellow of the Royal Society in 1668, but his attendance was intermittent, and he made only modest contributions (e.g., some meteorological measurements) to its proceedings. A deeper and more lasting interest was in medicine, in which Harvey's famous discovery of the circulation of the blood was promising great advances. Like many of his contemporaries, Locke was intrigued by the relation between the circulation of the blood and respiration, but the supposed medical benefits of this pioneering work in physiology were slow to follow. Later, in London, he met the celebrated physician Thomas Sydenham, who argued forcefully that the practice of medicine should be based on careful clinical observations rather than on speculative physiological theories. Sydenham's strongly empiricist attitude to medicine is often reflected in Locke's own writings. Whether he regarded this anti-theoretical attitude as merely provisional ('we don't *yet* have the physiological knowledge we would need to base medical practice on physiological theory') or as permanent ('we can *never* hope or aspire to have the knowledge of physiology that we would need') is a subtle point to which we shall return.

An event that made a deep impression on the young Locke was a visit in 1665–6, as secretary to the ambassador Sir Walter Vane, to the German city of Cleves, in a province governed by the Elector of Brandenburg. After the horrors of the Thirty Years War, Cleves was one of a handful of German cities that had established a policy of religious toleration. Lutherans, Calvinists and Catholics attended their respective places of worship on Sundays, and did so, to all appearances, quite peacefully and amicably. Locke wrote with some astonishment to Robert Boyle that 'they quietly permit one another to choose their own way to heaven, for I cannot observe any quarrels or animosities amongst them upon the account of religion' (C I, 227–31). But if religious toleration is actual, it must be possible. Any philosophical arguments to prove that religious uniformity is necessary to social and political cohesion are therefore mistaken. Locke thus returned from Cleves convinced that there could be no good political arguments for enforcing religious uniformity. There might be other reasons for thinking that uniformity of religion is desirable within a state, but the claim of the social conservatives – Anglican in England, Catholic in France, Calvinist in Scotland and Holland – that religious diversity inevitably generates social strife was refuted by the evidence from Cleves.

The year 1666 was a fateful one in Locke's life, since it marks his first meeting with Anthony Ashley Cooper (1621–83), Lord Ashley, future Earl of Shaftesbury. At this period of his life, Ashley was still a loyal member of Charles II's government, serving as Chancellor of the Exchequer and later as Lord Chancellor, and defending even unpopular government policies in Parliament. In 1673, however, he was ousted from office, and began to build a power base as effective leader of the 'Whig' opposition to the policies of the king. Shaftesbury was fiercely anti-Catholic, and one key objective of the Whig Party was the exclusion from the succession of Charles's openly Catholic younger brother James, who would later reign briefly as King James II from 1685 until 1688. Locke joined Ashley's household in 1667, shifting his main place of residence from Oxford to London. The thirty-five-year-old Locke thus found himself moving first in government circles, and then right at the heart of the main opposition party. For a young intellectual to seek a royal or noble patron was nothing new or surprising in the seventeenth century: Thomas Hobbes, for example, had served the Cavendish family, and Leibniz was to serve the royal house of Hanover. The young scholar might serve as secretary, physician, tutor to the children of the household, librarian, and even as diplomat or marriage-broker. If he was wise, he would make himself generally useful in a wide variety of ways to his noble patron. But Locke's precise role in the Shaftesbury household remains unclear to this day. In a famous letter written from exile in Holland in 1684, Locke protests to Thomas Herbert, Earl of Pembroke, that he had entered the Shaftesbury household as a physician (he had certainly been involved in a surgical operation that saved the Earl's life), and that he had never written any political libels or been involved in any plotting against the King (C II, 661–6). He must have known that his enemies would never believe him or forgive him for his association with Shaftesbury.

For most of his adult life, Locke suffered from chronic chest complaints, almost certainly asthma and bronchitis, and his breathing difficulties were greatly exacerbated by the coal-burning fires of the winter season in London. In 1675, his poor health obliged him to quit England for an extended stay in France, first in Montpellier in the sunny south (1675–7), then mostly in Paris (1678–9). His letters reveal clearly that he was initially uncertain and hesitant in the French language, but gradually achieved a tolerable level of fluency and proficiency. He read the *Recherche de la Vérité* of Nicolas Malebranche, translated the *Essais de Morale* of Pierre Nicole into English, developed a sophisticated taste in French cuisine and made a number of lasting friends, including the polymath Nicolas Toinard and the physician, traveller and disciple of Pierre Gassendi, François Bernier. His four years in France also made him keenly aware of the growing persecution facing the French Protestants at the hands of the government of Louis XIV. The final revocation of the Edict of Nantes was to take place only in 1685, but it did not come out of the blue – Louis and his ministers were determined to enforce religious conformity, and French Protestants faced the terrifying prospect of having to provide board and lodging for squadrons of rowdy and ill-disciplined troops, or seeing their children forcefully removed to be re-educated as Catholics. Faced with such draconian measures, the exodus of the Huguenots was already beginning.

Locke returned in 1679 to an England in the midst of the Exclusion Crisis, in which Shaftesbury and the Whigs tried to force the exclusion of James, Duke of York, from his place as Charles's natural successor. (Charles had several illegitimate children by his various mistresses, but no legitimate heir by his wife Catherine of Braganza.) With the aid of the bishops in the House of Lords, Charles managed to get one Exclusion Bill voted down. The King later used the royal prerogative to dissolve Parliament, attempting to rule without it. He and his supporters, the court party or 'Tories', launched a fierce counter-attack against the Whig leaders, notably of course Shaftesbury, who was charged with treason and committed to the Tower in 1681. Acquitted by a solidly Whig jury, Shaftesbury knew that he could not escape re-arrest for long, and fled to Holland in 1682, dying there in 1683. Whether Locke was actively involved in the Whig politics of the Exclusion Crisis is hard to establish from the available evidence. He was spied upon at Oxford, but nothing substantial was ever proved against him at the time, and little positive evidence has emerged since. He may simply have been careful to cover his tracks and destroy any incriminating evidence, or he may have been telling the truth when he later insisted that he had always wanted to be simply a private gentleman and scholar, and emphatically not a political activist.[3] In any event, his close relation to Shaftesbury was bound to make him suspect in the eyes of the king's party, and the ever-cautious Locke left England for Holland in 1683, citing reasons of health. He was to be resident in Holland until after the so-called 'Glorious Revolution' ousted James II and established the Dutch Prince William of Orange and his wife Mary (James's daughter) on the throne, returning to England only in 1689.

Locke's enforced exile in Holland was intellectually the most productive period of his life. Deprived by royal decree of his Christ Church studentship in 1684, he had only his savings and the modest income from his rents in Somerset to sustain him, but he seems to have remained sufficiently well off to maintain his status as a gentleman. And he had many friends with whom he could discuss matters of mutual interest: travellers' tales, medicine, theology, education, politics and the affairs of Europe. With no formal duties to occupy him, he was able to turn his notes on various subjects into substantial and carefully crafted volumes. By the time of his return, he had the *Epistola de Tolerantia*, the *Essay Concerning Human Understanding*, and the *Two Treatises of Government* all ready for publication, although only the *Essay* would appear under his own name. These three works, all based on reworking of earlier draft materials, and all published in the year 1689, form the heart of Locke's philosophy. From 1689 until his death, a large proportion of his intellectual labours went into extending the *Essay* in its later editions, and defending the *Epistola* – still under the veil of anonymity – against the attacks of critics. (An English translation of the *Epistola*,

A Letter Concerning Toleration, had been published in London towards the end of 1689.) Locke was serious about preserving his anonymity as author of the *Epistola* and the *Two Treatises*, admitting it only at his death. When his close friend Philipp van Limborch let slip to a third party that Locke was indeed the author of the *Epistola*, Locke responded with real anger that 'you do not know what trouble you have got me into' (C IV, 62). Perhaps the ever-cautious Locke was on this occasion being over-cautious, as it is difficult now to discern precisely what 'trouble' he anticipated.

After the extraordinary Convention of both Houses of Parliament of January 1689 had agreed to confer the Crown jointly on William and Mary,[4] Locke found himself – for the first time in many years – moving once more in government circles. He even travelled from Rotterdam to London on the same ship that carried the new Queen, arriving on 12 February. Refusing the offer of an ambassadorial role on the twin grounds of ill health and a limited capacity to handle his liquor, Locke nevertheless hinted to his new patron Lord Mordaunt that he hoped to be of use to the new government in some capacity or other (C III, 573–6). Mordaunt was quickly appointed first Lord of the Treasury, and Locke accepted a government post as commissioner for excise appeals. He would later become a member of the Board of Trade, and advise the government on such difficult and delicate issues as coinage and interest rates. With the income from his rents, his government salary and some shrewd investments, he became for the first time in his life a wealthy man.

Although his government duties required his presence in London, Locke still found the air of that city inimical to his health, particularly during the winter months. As a place of retreat within reasonably easy reach of the capital, he hit on Oates in Essex, home of Sir Francis Masham and his wife Damaris. Damaris was the daughter of the Cambridge Platonist Ralph Cudworth, and a serious philosopher in her own right, able to engage with Locke on more or less equal terms in matters of philosophy and theology.[5] Their correspondence begins in 1682, and their relationship might have become more intimate if Locke had not fled to Holland in 1683. In 1685, Damaris married Sir Francis Masham, a widower with many children from his first marriage. Initially merely a house-guest, in 1691 Locke moved to Oates on a permanent and rent-paying basis, travelling to London only when his private or public business demanded it. For the first time in many years, he could gather together his books and papers, feel under no threat from the government, and live as a private gentleman and scholar in the manner that he had always wanted. His presence and intellectual companionship enabled Damaris to escape some of the enforced tedium of domesticity, and he became tutor to her son Francis Cudworth Masham, to whom he would later leave a substantial legacy in his will.

The final decade of Locke's life witnessed the emergence of two new works. *Some Thoughts Concerning Education* (1693) had its origin in a series of letters that Locke wrote from Holland to his friend Edward Clarke of Chipley (later MP for Taunton), concerning the education of his son. Although Locke never married and had no children of his own, he had a lot of experience in the field of education, having taught at Oxford and advised several gentlemen on the best course of studies for their sons. Much of this work seems commonplace today, but in its time it was extremely radical, arguing against much that was taken for granted in the pedagogy of the day. Corporal punishment, for example, is rejected as largely useless and only to be used in the case of flat disobedience to the tutor's commands. The child is always to be treated as a rational being, and its natural curiosity and interest in its world is to be directed into its studies. Latin grammar and composition may have their place, but languages are better taught by conversation than by books full of arcane grammatical rules. And the child's interest and delight in the natural world can readily be turned to the tutor's advantage, making subjects such as geography and botany a pleasure rather than a chore. The other major work from the final decade, *The Reasonableness of Christianity, as Delivered in the Scriptures*, appeared anonymously in 1695, and argues for the radical thesis that the simple belief that 'Jesus Christ is the promised Messiah' is sufficient to make a person a Christian. If an opponent insists that one must believe in the Trinity and the Incarnation, Locke asks whether there is evidence in the Gospels and the Acts that the Apostles believed such things. They were, after all, simple and unlearned men, innocent of metaphysics, and unlikely to have puzzled their understandings over the consubstantiality of the Son with the Father, or the precise ontological status of the Holy Ghost. And shall we, Locke dryly asks, set ourselves up as better Christians than Christ's own Apostles? If Christians could just agree on precisely what unites them as Christians, they might then learn to debate the more controversial parts of the Creed in a spirit of Christian brotherhood. Such was Locke's hope, but he cannot have been remotely surprised when the *Reasonableness* attracted hostile criticism.

Locke's final years are marked by a gradual withdrawal from public life. Visits to London became rarer, and he used his ill health as an excuse for resignation from his various committees. He oversaw the publication of a series of new editions of the *Essay*, and was pleased to see it translated into French (by the exiled Huguenot Pierre Coste) in 1700, and into Latin (by Ezekiel Burridge) in 1701. Since few scholars on the continent read English, these translations were essential means for transmitting his magnum opus to a wide readership and thus securing his continental reputation. Locke also found himself having to defend his works – both acknowledged and anonymous – against their critics. He defended the *Essay* (under his own name) against the criticisms of Edward Stillingfleet, Bishop of Worcester, who thought that Locke's views concerning substance threatened the Christian belief in the Trinity. And he defended the *Letter Concerning Toleration* against Jonas Proast and the *Reasonableness of Christianity* against John Edwards, writing in both cases under a veil of anonymity that began to wear very thin – the *Correspondence* is full of letters from people who had a shrewd idea of which works Locke had and had not written. He also continued, with his hostess Damaris Masham, to read the Bible and search for its deeper meanings, working at his death on a *Paraphrase and Notes on the Epistles of Saint Paul*. He died at Oates on 28 October 1704, shortly after listening to Damaris read to him from the Psalms.

2. The Contexts for the Major Works

Locke, we are told by some historians, did not set out to be a systematic philosopher. Each of his main works belongs in a specific historical context, and cannot be properly understood except as a response to the concerns of the moment. But is it not the mark of the genuine philosopher that he or she seeks to enunciate universal principles? And surely such principles, once formulated, can be reapplied to an endlessly expanding range of new problems? Any suggestion that Locke was only thinking narrowly about the problems of his day would belittle his significance for later generations of philosophers. We can grant the truth of the historical claim that each of Locke's works is prompted by a specific context or a specific set of events in his life, without drawing the conclusion that his principles can only be applied to the problems and situations that called them forth. We can read the philosophers of the past both as men of their time and as figures with something to say to us about our concerns. But let us, at least for the moment, grant the 'contextual' historian his or her point, and look briefly at what we can learn – from Locke's notebooks and letters – of the genesis of his main works.

The *Essay Concerning Human Understanding* owes its origin, according to Locke's own *Epistle to the Reader*, to a meeting of 'five or six friends' in his London rooms in Ashley's house.[6] Their original topic, we learn from Locke's friend James Tyrrell,[7] was 'the principles of morality and revealed religion', but the friends soon found themselves puzzled and at a loss, unable to resolve the difficulties they fell into. Locke's response was to take a step back:

> it came into my Thoughts, that we took a wrong course; and that, before we set our selves upon Enquiries of that Nature, it was necessary to examine our own Abilities, and see, what Objects our Understandings were, or were not fitted to deal with. This I proposed to the Company, who all readily assented; and thereupon it was agreed, that this should be our first Enquiry. (EHU, Epistle to the Reader, N 7)

Locke was thus prompted to attempt an account – conducted by the 'historical, plain method' characteristic of the natural historian – of our human intellectual faculties, their powers and their limitations. He initially thought that the subject could be dealt with 'in one sheet of paper', but the first version, Draft A (1671) already occupies thirty-five pages of a commonplace book, and the work was ultimately to expand into the four substantial books now familiar to readers. We have another draft (B), also dated 1671, and a variety of notes from the 1670s, but it was only during his Dutch exile that Locke found the time and leisure to collect his thoughts and compose the *Essay* more or less as we know it. In the same letter to the Earl of Pembroke of November 1684 in which he rebuts the charge of writing libellous political pamphlets, Locke explains that he has been writing 'upon that old theme *de Intellectu humano* (on which your Lordship knows I have been a good while a hammering)' (C II, 665). He sent an 'Epitome' of the *Essay* to Pembroke in May 1685, a modified version of which would later appear, in French translation, in Jean Le Clerc's *Bibliothèque Universelle et Historique* for 1688. Returning to England in 1689, Locke signed a contract to publish the *Essay* with Thomas Basset on 24 May. Significant additions were made to the second edition (1694) and the fourth (1700), the last to appear during Locke's lifetime. The

Essay always remained a work in progress, with its author wondering whether or not to include his critique of Malebranche, or the substantial piece 'Of the Conduct of the Understanding', both of which would eventually appear only among his posthumously published works.

What should we learn from this little excursion into the history and origins of the *Essay*? How does it affect our reading of the work when we learn from Tyrrell that Locke was prompted to think about the human understanding by reflections on morality and revealed religion? We might think to downplay the significance of that other oft-quoted passage from the *Epistle to the Reader* in which Locke sets himself up as an 'underlabourer' to great *scientists* such as Boyle, Huygens, Sydenham and 'the incomparable Mr Newton'. But that would not follow. Locke might have been prompted to think about epistemology by questions about religious knowledge, and been led on to further reflections about the natural sciences. A work can easily get away from its author's control, and start to expand into territories not originally envisaged. Locke might have looked to the natural sciences for epistemological lessons concerning what we can and cannot know, and then sought to reapply such lessons in the more fiercely contested context of religious debate. But Tyrrell mentions not just revealed religion but also morality, and what is most striking in Locke's body of published work is the absence of any in-depth discussion of the foundations of morals. This criticism is not ahistorical or anachronistic; nor does it rest on any misunderstanding of Locke's own projects and concerns. In his thirties, Locke had written a series of unpublished *Essays on the Laws of Nature*[8] for his Oxford students, and the topic remained of central importance to him throughout his life. Friendly correspondents such as Tyrrell and William Molyneux were forever urging him to publish his views on moral philosophy, and he was forever responding with hints and evasions. The glaring gap in Locke's work – and the gap that arguably does prevent it from forming a complete system of philosophy – is the missing treatise on ethics.

For the *Epistola de Tolerantia*, two distinct immediate contexts need to be borne in mind. The *Epistola* was written in 1685, and published anonymously at Gouda in Holland in 1689, written in Latin for a continental audience. An English translation by William Popple appeared in London in the same year, shortly after Locke's return to his native shores. The immediate context of the published work is the Revocation in 1685 by Louis XIV of the Edict of Nantes, which had guaranteed freedom of religion for French Protestants.

After the Revocation, the trickle of Huguenot refugees into England, Holland and Switzerland swelled into a flood. But the issues with which the *Epistola* deals were also the threats faced by Locke's friend Limborch and the Remonstrants in Holland, and by other religious minorities elsewhere. The argument of the published *Epistola* draws extensively on an unpublished earlier *Essay on Toleration* (1667), written for Ashley shortly after Locke's return from his visit to Cleves. The civil magistrate, Locke argues in both works, should not attempt to enforce religious uniformity by penalties, and should seek to suppress religious organizations only when they endanger the peace and security of civil society. In England, the great majority of the Protestant dissenters posed no threat to the security of the state and should therefore be tolerated; Roman Catholics, by contrast, are subjects of a foreign lord, and as such are suspect not on theological but on political grounds. Although Locke's argument is extended and deepened between the 1667 *Essay* and the 1689 *Epistola*, the essentials of his case remain the same. Belief cannot be coerced, so force will only produce hypocrisy. Coercion is in any case un-Christian and even anti-Christian. If would-be persecutors insist that they are promoting truth and suppressing heresy, will not every persecutor of every sect say the same? Whether they draw their supposed authority from Rome, or Wittenberg or Geneva makes no difference.

How much light do these two distinct contexts (England in 1667; France in 1685) shed on the arguments of the *Epistola*? If Locke were a mere hack journalist or pamphleteer, we might expect his views to alter in accordance with the politics of the moment. Toleration for Protestant dissenters but not for Catholics might be just an attempt to find some argument or other to back up his patron Ashley's prejudices. In fact, the arguments of the earlier and later works are very close, and the key principle that the proper job of the civil authorities is only to promote peace and prosperity is deployed with equal force and clarity in both. Did the dissenters, in the England of Charles II, pose any threat to the security of the kingdom? Were the Huguenots any threat to Louis XIV? If not, toleration is equally required in both cases. As for British Catholics, their allegiance to a foreign ruler makes them in Locke's eyes rightly suspect.[9] The *Epistola* may have been prompted by a very specific historical context, but its lessons are universal, and apply equally in our own age. Faced with an alleged threat from 'political Islam', politicians in the Western world need to distinguish clearly between those Muslims who advocate violence and those who do not. Only the former are to be prosecuted by the civil authorities, and then always on political and never on religious grounds. When Western political leaders insist that the West is not 'at war with Islam', it is Locke's principles that they should always have in mind.

Another work with a double context is the *Two Treatises of Government*. Published as it was in 1689, immediately after the so-called 'Glorious Revolution' of 1688–9 had confirmed William and Mary on the throne, it was inevitably cited by the Whig politicians of the day as supporting the justice of their cause. But the work was in fact drafted in the very different context of the Exclusion Crisis of 1679–81, when the Whig Party, led by Shaftesbury, was trying to exclude the Catholic James, Duke of York, from succession to the throne. Charles successfully blocked the Whigs' moves, and decided from 1681 to rule without Parliament, aided by money from Louis XIV. The Whigs feared that Charles and his brother would rule Britain on the model of absolutist France, and even try to reconvert the country to Roman Catholicism: 'popery' and 'tyranny' were seen as inseparable sides of the same coin. In this context, the publication in 1680 of the *Patriarcha* of the long-dead Royalist Robert Filmer (*c*.1588–1653) was bound to provoke a reaction. Published with an elaborate portrait of Charles II as its frontispiece, it defended the absolute prerogative of the King over his subjects. Filmer's twin doctrines of divine right and passive obedience were lauded by conservative clerics up and down the land, and prompted responses not just from Locke but from his friend Tyrrell and from Algernon Sidney. So the *Two Treatises* belong by right to a context fraught with peril (Sidney was put to death for treason in 1683), not one of eventual triumph. Locke's attack on Filmer in the *First Treatise* is a thinly disguised attack on those powerful courtiers and clerics who were defending royal absolutism. Locke has no particular interest in Filmer as such, but clearly feels the need to refute currently fashionable but false and dangerous political principles before going on to establish true ones.

How does our reading of the *Two Treatises* alter when we read them in a context provided by the Exclusion Crisis rather than the Glorious Revolution? In the first place, the attack on Filmer and the justification of resistance look much more radical and dangerous doctrines to be advocating in 1680 than in 1690. The *Treatises* remained unpublished, of course, during the reigns of Charles II and James II, but even so, the usually cautious Locke was taking a risk in daring to discuss the rights of the people against their kings. The context also helps to explain why Locke insisted on a strict veil of anonymity, only acknowledging authorship of the *Treatises* at his death. These were perilous and uncertain times, and a return to power of the Jacobites – with French support – could not be ruled out. But as regards the actual doctrines taught in the *Two Treatises*, knowledge of the context doesn't add greatly to our understanding of Locke's arguments. The context helps to explain why Locke feels the *First Treatise* is needed at all, but the substance of his critique of Filmer is timeless. Bad principles of government are bad principles, period. And the insistence of the *Second Treatise* on the need for the consent of the governed is equally timeless. In the context of the Exclusion Crisis the implied message is that 'the people will not consent to rule by the Catholic James, or to any attempt to rule Britain on the model of absolutist France'. In the context of the Glorious Revolution, the message is 'the people did not consent to James's rule, but do consent to rule by William and Mary'. Exactly who counts as 'the people', and how they are to make their consent known, is an obvious problem to which we must return.

The *Reasonableness of Christianity, as Delivered in the Scriptures*, published anonymously in 1695, belongs to the twin context of political and theological debate. The theological context is more straightforward to document. The 1690s saw a vigorous debate about the Christian doctrines of the Incarnation and the Trinity, with defenders of the orthodox Athanasian formula (three persons = one substance) ranged against Arians and Socinians. The defenders of the Trinity thought that their opponents hardly counted as Christians at all; doubters countered that the Athanasian formula was unscriptural and effectively unintelligible. To demand that a man believe something he cannot even understand, they argued, is to make him parrot nonsense and swear that he believes it. In the *Reasonableness*, Locke goes back to Scripture itself to determine what belief makes a man a Christian. That belief, he argues, is simply that Jesus Christ is the Messiah promised by God. Christians should of course search the Scriptures earnestly for further illumination on difficult and divisive subjects, but it is this simple shared belief that makes them all Christians in the first place. If this doctrinal minimalism were to be embraced, Athanasians, Arians and Socinians could cease calling one another names and agree to debate their theological difficulties in a sprit of Christian charity. It would also help the defenders of a revealed religion such as Christianity to defend it against the accusation of the deists that their doctrines are contrary to reason. To believe that there is a God is for Locke a matter of demonstration; to believe that Jesus Christ was sent by

God may reasonably be believed on the basis of the testimony of the Apostles. If these minimal commitments are all it takes to make a man a Christian, the 'reasonableness' of Christianity is much easier to defend against sceptics and deists.

The immediate political context is provided by one last attempt to formulate a bill for the 'comprehension' of the Protestant dissenters within the Church of England. If the Anglican clergy could be persuaded to adopt some version of doctrinal minimalism, the dissenters could be reabsorbed into the national Church on the basis of a sharp distinction between shared essentials and disputed non-essentials, about which churchmen could agree to disagree. While the main efforts of the Establishment for comprehension of the dissenters belong to the previous generation, another Comprehension Bill was brought before Parliament shortly after the Glorious Revolution, and was eventually set aside in favour of a Toleration Bill. The Anglicans, Locke writes to Limborch, are unsympathetic to both proposals, but 'whether this is conducive to their own advantage or to that of the state is for their consideration' (C III, 584). Locke would probably have favoured a very broad-based national Church, embracing almost all Protestant Christians, which would have necessitated the reduction of doctrinal essentials to a bare minimum. Given that the Anglican leaders were never likely to accept that, toleration of all religious views that pose no threat to the peace and security of the realm becomes the second-best but achievable goal.

3. Locke's Correspondence

Locke's correspondence, available to modern readers in eight substantial volumes, thanks to E. S. De Beer and the Clarendon Press, is a treasure trove of information both about his life and concerns and about the events and issues of his day.[10] Although obviously a crucial resource for scholars, these volumes contain rather less than we might have hoped for in at least three important respects. The main disappointment for the modern reader is likely to be the scarcity of letters from Locke's formative years. Volume One takes us to the year 1679, that is, well into Locke's middle age, and contains very few letters from the crucial formative years of the 1650s and 1660s. There is also the regrettable fact that many of Locke's own letters have been lost, so we are often forced to infer their contents from the preserved replies of his correspondents. And finally there is Locke's rather dry and matter-of-fact manner, which seems such an integral part of his mature character. Very rarely do we find any expression of strong emotion, or any deep pangs of anxiety about his present situation or future course. Perhaps the most poignant surviving letters are those from the winter of 1659–60, when the twenty-seven-year-old Locke describes himself to a friend as 'one of the mad men too of this great Bedlam England' (C I, 124), and writes to his father that he is thinking of taking up arms, if only he could be certain 'from whome I ought to receive them and for whome I ought to imploy them' (C I, 136–7). The whole country seems on the brink of another catastrophic civil war, and the young Oxford don views the prospect with manifest horror. But such obvious expressions of strong feelings are rare even in the early letters, and disappear altogether from the later ones. The mature Locke, although clearly capable of strong emotions, and of forming deep and lasting friendships, was not a man to wear his heart on his sleeve.

The letters are written in English, Latin and French, to a wide range of correspondents in Britain, France, Holland and occasionally much further afield. Locke had a lifelong interest in both physical and human geography, and was an avid consumer of travel literature. He took a keen and informed interest in the European colonies in America, and was forever asking various correspondents about the beliefs and customs of the peoples of India and the Far East. (The atheism of the highly civilized Thai people was an important part of the anti-innatist argument of Book One of the *Essay*.) Physical geography was of course crucial for agriculture and commerce, not to mention medicine: if the famous 'Jesuits' bark' can cure malaria, how many other similar cures may be awaiting our discovery as we explore more of the natural world? Medicine was another central topic of the correspondence: although he never formally practised, he was known as 'Doctor Locke' to many of his correspondents, who often sought his advice on questions of diet, regimen and treatment. Many of his correspondents were practising physicians, and they constituted, through their regular exchange of letters and pharmaceutical recipes, a sort of informal college of medicine. Locke's own views on the subject, influenced no doubt by Sydenham, were a sort of mildly sceptical empiricism. In a number of letters he expresses his doubts about the utility of attempting to base medical practice on physiological theory, and his sense that it would be better to proceed, as Sydenham had done, on the basis of Baconian natural histories of diseases.

Another prominent theme in Locke's correspondence is that of pedagogy. We have already seen that *Some Thoughts Concerning Education* owed its origin to a series of letters that Locke wrote from Holland to his friend Edward Clarke, concerning the right course of studies for his son. Locke's advice was always being sought on this subject, and he is forever recommending tutors, or books, or suitable programmes of study for the sons (much more rarely for the daughters) of his friends. Locke had a great deal of confidence both in his own expertise in this area, and in the power of education to shape the characters of children for good or ill. By the standards of his day, his advice generally seems moderate and sensible. But like many another would-be educational reformer, he found that his recommendations didn't always turn out well: Edward Clarke's son turned out to be no great scholar, and we know that the Third Earl of Shaftesbury (the grandson of Locke's patron) later blamed Locke for the perceived faults in his education.

Religion, both natural and revealed, is another ever-present subject in the correspondence. Locke took a sharp interest in the various proofs of the existence of God, and is clearly keen that this be a matter of demonstrative knowledge rather than mere probability. But there is far more revealed religion than natural religion in the letters. Locke corresponds with Damaris Cudworth about 'enthusiasm' in religion, with his French friend Nicolas Toinard about the Gospels, with Isaac Newton about the scriptural grounds for belief in the Trinity, and with Samuel Bold about the defence of *The Reasonableness of Christianity*. In his later years he also formed – rather strangely – more or less close relations with the most prominent deists, men such as John Toland, Matthew Tindal and especially Anthony Collins, to whom the elderly Locke writes with an unusual warmth of affection, describing him in a letter of 1703 as 'a Philosopher and a Christian' (C VII, 776). (Collins would later be attacked by Berkeley, in his *Alciphron*, as the prince of the atheists.) Locke considered himself, of course, to be a defender of revealed religion against the deists, but his insistence on the role of reason in judging the credentials of any claim to revelation, his defence of liberty of conscience, and his support for only a minimal Christian Creed might seem to place him closer to the deists on some issues than he himself would have liked.

Books furnish another of the recurrent themes of the correspondence. Locke is forever asking his various correspondents if they can get hold of a copy of some volume or other of travellers' tales, or theology, or natural history, or medicine. By the end of his threescore years and ten he had built up what was, by the standards of the day, a substantial private library.[11] By means of his correspondents in France and Holland (then as now a major centre of the publishing trade), he could acquire, even after his return to England in 1689, new books published on the continent. Through his friendship with Jean le Clerc, editor of the *Bibliotheque Universelle*, he was able both to keep up to date with news and gossip from the literary world, and also to find a natural publisher for the *Abrégé* of the *Essay*. Buying books, lending and borrowing books, commenting on books, seeking out books for friends, advising on suitable books for children and students – all these are activities that Locke clearly enjoyed, thus feeling himself a full participating member of the famous 'Republic of Letters'.

What subjects are conspicuous by their absence from the correspondence? Although there are of course lots of references to the political events of the day, there is remarkably *little* explicit discussion of political theory.[12] We have some letters exchanged with his Oxford friend James Tyrrell, but very little besides. It is possible, of course, that this simply reflects caution on the part of Locke and his correspondents. Careless talk, in the 1670s and 1680s, could cost lives, and any letter might easily be intercepted and read by government spies. So we should not infer that Locke wasn't thinking about political legitimacy and the social contract, and perhaps discussing such subjects in private, even if they rarely find their way into his letters. But it is striking that an author now regarded as one of the great political theorists should say so little about the subject in eight weighty volumes of correspondence. And there is remarkably little serious academic philosophy, apart from a dense and closely argued debate with Limborch about free will. Few of Locke's correspondents could maintain a philosophical correspondence with him on anything like equal terms, and he spurned efforts from Leibniz, by way of intermediates, to establish lines of communication concerning the great topics of the *Essay*.

The portrait that does emerge very clearly from the correspondence is the picture that Locke himself clearly wished to convey. He consistently depicts himself as an unassuming gentleman scholar of retired but bookish character, seeking always to stand at one remove from the hurly-burly of the world. Although he is drawn into the political fray first by his involvement with Shaftesbury, and then in his various roles as government advisor after 1689, he always insists that he prefers the private life. Give him his books, a small circle of friends, a decent competence to live on, and the freedom and leisure to think and to write, and he will be quite content to live out his days without seeking to impose his views on others. He has not the slightest ambition to become a philosopher-king. He does, however, still have the Puritan's keen sense of duty, and tries to apply it in a manner suited to his station in life. Although preferring the status of the gentleman scholar, he still feels the need to be of use to his fellow men, whether by helping to spread 'useful' empirical knowledge (e.g., in botany and medicine), or by advocating doctrines such as toleration that are conducive to civil peace and harmony, or by correcting various popular prejudices that threaten such peace. We think today of Locke as an academic philosopher, author of such canonical works as the *Essay* and the *Two Treatises*, but he would have viewed this characterization as a strange and misleading caricature.

4. Religion, Politics and Epistemology: Questions of Authority and Allegiance

Questions of authority and allegiance dominated seventeenth-century British philosophy in a manner and to an extent that is hard for the modern reader to appreciate. The idea that academic philosophy could be debated in an ivory tower, remote and detached from the incessant power struggles in Church and state, would have seemed preposterous to Locke's contemporaries. A seemingly abstract claim in metaphysics or epistemology would be certain to come under intense scrutiny from a host of quarrelling clerics, keen to tease out its implications for Christian belief and practice. If Locke expresses a doubt, for example, as to whether philosophy can prove the immateriality and natural immortality of the human soul, this might be a mere expression of epistemological humility and of his sense of the proper bounds of faith and reason. But, equally, it might be seen as a crucial concession to materialism and mortalism, and even as a threat to the authority of the Christian Church itself! If a philosopher reads Cicero and the Stoics, and attempts to spell out the moral 'Law of Nature' in terms comprehensible in principle to any rational adult, this might be seen either as a preparation for the precepts of the Gospel or as a potential threat to Christian morality. If the law of nature is sufficiently clear, why do we need the Gospel to teach us morality? Does Christianity teach new duties,

or merely back up already recognized natural duties with supernatural sanctions? What if the precepts of the Bible sometimes
appear to contradict the law of nature? And if the injunction to keep
one's promises and honour one's contracts is an essential precept
of the law of nature, what implications will this have for political
society?

In political philosophy, of course, the great debate of the century
was between the defenders of the divine right of kings on the one
side, and the advocates of social contract theories of various kinds
on the other. Neither theory was exactly problem-free. If the King
rules by an absolute prerogative, and subjects are bound to passive
obedience, then the King can take the lives, liberties and goods of
his subjects at will – whatever is theirs is his for the taking. They
can of course appeal, but only to magistrates whose role is to inter-
pret the King's own laws. The King is answerable to God but not
to man. The condition of his subjects, according to the opponents
of royal absolutism, is indistinguishable from slavery. But if the
state rests on a social contract, how can its authority be binding on
the great majority (women, children, the poor) who have never been
asked to sign that supposed contract? How is its authority transmitted from generation to generation? Who is to decide if the executive
branch of Government (the King and his ministers) has exceeded
its authority? Isn't the idea of the state as resting on a social contract
simply a recipe for endless political instability – a slippery slope
into chaos and anarchy?

In theology, the great issue was the contested legacy of the Reformation. If the criterion of truth, in matters of religion, is the voice
of the individual conscience – enlightened of course by the intensive
reading of Scripture – how can the Christian Church be maintained
as a single cohesive body? Given the subjective nature of its criterion, is it not inevitable that Protestant Christianity will disintegrate
into a cacophony of squabbling sects?[13] If it is impossible to coerce
the individual conscience and immoral to attempt it, will not each
and every Protestant Christian end up with his or her own personal
religion? This was the argument raised against the Reformers by
the defenders of Rome, and the problem that seventeenth-century
Anglicans had to resolve. The defenders of a single established
Church backed up by the force and authority of the state faced a
difficult choice. They could advocate a very broad national Church,
based on a few shared essentials, and permitting plenty of latitude
for individual differences. This would minimize – and hopefully
eliminate altogether – the need for coercion. Or they could defend

coercion, perhaps by indirect means (censorship, compulsory attendance at Sunday schools), arguing that the relatively mild sanctions
generally imposed (fines, exclusion from public offices) might be
justified by their results, and were clearly distinct from the tortures
and burnings of the Roman Catholic Inquisition. The former route
leads to Latitudinarianism; the latter to 'High-Church' Anglicanism. But, again, both groups face obvious problems. For the Latitudinarians, the obvious worry concerns the breadth of latitude to be
permitted. Can someone be a member of the Church of England if
they reject Christ's divinity, or the doctrines of Original Sin and
Atonement? As for the High Churchmen, they must explain why
they are permitted the use of coercion but other churches are not.
'Because we are right and they are wrong about the essential doctrines of the Christian religion' is always going to look question-
begging as a response.

Questions of authority and allegiance thus lie at the heart of the
great seventeenth-century debates in Church and state. The issues
become still more complex and intricate when politics and theology
become entangled, as they generally did. After Henry VIII, the
English monarch was also head of the Church of England. Many
Anglican clerics under Charles II preached the twin doctrines of
divine right and passive obedience. But what if the rightful heir to
the throne – and to titular authority over the English Church – is
an unbeliever or a Roman Catholic? The former possibility remained
unactualized; the latter became all too real for Anglicans when
James II succeeded his brother in 1685. And what if the liberty of
conscience championed by many Protestant preachers threatens the
very fabric of the social order? The soldiers of the parliamentary
army in the Civil War believed that they were obeying the dictates
of their conscience and doing God's work. Some of these men
wanted to do much more than defeat and depose the King; to them,
the whole fabric of society needed restoration, including even
claims to property. Civil order may require the public authorities to
put such radicals in jail, labelling them 'fanatics' and 'enthusiasts'.
But do we know who is and who is not in possession of a genuine
revelation? Do we have any criterion by which to distinguish the
real thing from the products of an overheated imagination?

For whom, the twenty-seven-year old-Locke asks in his ago-
nized letter to his father, should I take up arms? Whom should I
obey, and whose authority must I acknowledge? Is the public order
simply a matter of expediency? In that case we must take it upon
ourselves to determine how peace and security are to be achieved.

Or is it a matter of trying to determine the will of God? Has God given us a definite indication of a divine preference for absolute monarchy, or limited monarchy, or priestly rule? Or is the will of God simply that we humans live in peace and brotherhood, leaving us to our own resources to work out how those ends are to be achieved? Such questions of authority and allegiance lead almost inevitably into questions about knowledge. Do we know that there is a God who is our Creator, and who exercises His providential care over us? If so, do we have any way or ways, by means of reason, revelation, or both, to know His will? As for our duties to our fellow-men and fellow-citizens, has God inscribed these on each and every human heart at its creation? Or can we learn the universally binding precepts of the natural law by reflection on the nature of Nature and on shared human experience? Or is there no moral law but that of rational self-interest? The question of the twenty-seven-year-old Locke is the question that would preoccupy him for the rest of his life: do I know enough to determine where my duty lies?

Questions of authority and allegiance inevitably lead Locke into questions of epistemology. The 'Epistle to the Reader' that serves as a preface to the *Essay* makes the transition perfectly clear. After the discussions of the 'five or six friends' had led them only into puzzlement and perplexity, Locke concluded that it was time to step back from their disputes about morality and religion, and to address a more fundamental question:

> it came into my Thoughts that we took a wrong course; and that, before we set ourselves upon Enquiries of that Nature, it was necessary to examine our own Abilities and see what objects our Understandings were, or were not, fitted to deal with. This I proposed to the Company, who all readily assented; and thereupon it was agreed that this should be our first Enquiry. (EHU, Epistle to the Reader, N 7)

At the heart of the *Essay* lies a sharp distinction between the things we need to know and the things we do not need to know, and a corresponding claim to the effect that God has granted us knowledge of the things we need to know, while withholding knowledge of many things that we do not need to know. We need to know that we are creatures of a wise and powerful God, and under His providential care. We also need to have a sufficiently clear grasp of the law of nature to discern our duties to our fellow-men and fellow-citizens. We do not need to know the essences of material and immaterial substances; nor the precise details of the contrivance of parts that constitute the various species of animals, vegetables and minerals that make up the material world. Experience informs us of the existence of such a world, and we can frame more or less plausible hypotheses about its constitution, but such conjectures never amount to knowledge. A keen sense of our own cognitive limitations is the beginning of wisdom, a lesson taught by human and divine authority alike. The frontispiece of the earlier editions of the *Essay* had a single quotation, from *On the Nature of the Gods* by Cicero, one of Locke's favourite Latin authors:

> How fine it is to be willing to admit in respect of what you do not know, that you do not know, instead of causing disgust with that chatter of yours which must leave you dissatisfied too![14]

In the fourth edition of 1700, the epistemic humility recommended by Cicero and regarded by Locke as the summit of human wisdom is reinforced by the higher authority of Scripture:

> As thou knowest not what is the Way of the Spirit, nor how the Bones do grow in the Womb of her that is with Child: Even so thou knowest not the Works of God, who maketh all things.[15]

The project of the *Essay* is to examine, by a 'historical, plain method', the nature, powers and limitations of the human understanding:

> to inquire into the Original, Certainty, and Extent of humane Knowledge; together with the Grounds and Degrees of Belief, Opinion, and Assent; I shall not at present meddle with the Physical Consideration of the Mind; or trouble my self to examine wherein its Essence consists, or by what Motions of our Spirits or Alterations of our Bodies we come to have any Sensation by our Organs, or any *Ideas* in our Understandings; and whether those *Ideas* do in their Formation, any or all of them, depend on Matter or no. These are Speculations which, however curious and entertaining, I shall decline, as lying out of my Way in the design I am now upon. (EHU I, i , 2, N 43)

We can study the powers of our own minds by observation, without tackling the difficult and endlessly contested metaphysics of the mind–body problem. Locke doesn't tell us here that he suspects that such metaphysical knowledge is beyond us – that might be a conclusion of our investigations, but should not be assumed at the outset. The metaphysics of the mind–body problem is thus set aside as a matter of 'curious and entertaining' speculation, a subject to which we might return once we have mapped and determined our own intellectual powers. The project of the *Essay* has been launched, and it is to the working out of this project that we must now turn our attention.

2

The Theory of Ideas

1. The 'New Way of Ideas'

The term 'idea' is so familiar to users of the English language since the seventeenth century that it is hard to think of it as a technical term coined by philosophers. You might say, after hearing an unintelligible lecture on a totally obscure subject (e.g., the Christian doctrine of the Trinity) that you have no idea at all of what the lecturer was talking about. You might say that of course you know what a helicopter is (perhaps you have flown in one), but that you have only a hazy idea of how it works. You are, let us suppose, not an aeronautical engineer by training. Or you might say, perhaps in the context of a heated discussion in the pub, that a certain government policy is not consistent with your idea of democracy. Situations of all three of these types are common, and serve to introduce both the term 'idea' and some commonplace truisms about ideas. Ideas, it seems, can be either present or absent (the Trinity), either clear and distinct or obscure and confused (the helicopter), and either agreed or contested (democracy).

What is not a matter of doubt or controversy is that ideas, in our modern uses of the term, are subjective things, existing only in the minds of thinking beings and varying greatly in all three respects from one mind to another. A Christian theologian who has made an in-depth study of the early Councils of the Christian Church will probably deny that the Athanasian doctrine of the Trinity is inherently unintelligible, but might admit that the idea of the Trinity remains unclear and perhaps still contested. In the case of the workings of the helicopter, you could choose to make your idea clearer and more distinct by a suitable course of study. You would need to understand, at least, how it stays up, how it moves forward and how it is steered. In the political example, one man may emphasize something merely formal, such as universal adult suffrage, while his opponent focuses on something more substantive, such as the range and level of the citizens' participation in the political process. For the former, the disputed measure counts as democratic because carried out by a properly elected government; for the latter, it counts as undemocratic because insufficiently informed by public debate. In all these cases, each person forms their judgements on some subject X in accordance with their idea of X, but ideas of X can and do vary greatly from one thinker to the next.

This modern use of the term 'idea' dates from the seventeenth century, and can be traced back to the so-called 'father of modern philosophy', René Descartes (1596–1650). In ancient Greece, the term was used for the Platonic Forms, which were decidedly not conceived as subjective or mind-dependent in any way. When Socrates and his disciples are disputing about the Idea of Beauty, or of Justice, they are discussing the very essence or being of Beauty or Justice themselves, not how any particular persons think of or represent them. These Platonic Ideas are real in their own right, and in intellectual activity we humans can – at least in principle – sometimes grasp them. In Aristotle's modification of Platonism, the Forms are no longer confined to a special intelligible realm beyond the senses; they are present 'in' the concrete beings of our experience. But still they are conceived as perfectly objective, and as 'informing' the mind of the knower in both sensory and intellectual activity. When I observe a horse my mind takes on the sensible form of the horse (without its matter, of course); sufficient experience of horses and reflection on their nature and characteristics may enable me to grasp its intelligible form, the distinctive what-it-is-to-be-a-horse that distinguishes horses from other animals. In an important sense, the knowing mind *becomes* for the Aristotelian the object of its experience: this identity of knowing mind and known object both grounds the objectivity of our knowledge and cuts the ground from beneath various forms of sceptical doubt. Objective knowledge is the norm, and subjective factors are admitted only as idiosyncratic differences producing a certain level of background 'noise'.

The 'new way of ideas' of the seventeenth century emerges from the rejection of this Aristotelian picture of the relationship between the mind and its objects. Where the Aristotelian sees the object itself as being directly present to the knowing mind, at least as regards its form (which is, after all, what the object really *is*), the new philosophers of the seventeenth century think of the object as acting directly upon the sense organs and thus indirectly upon the mind of the experiencing subject to produce a mental representation of that object – an idea in its modern sense. Instead of having direct cognition of the horse itself, the experiencer now has direct awareness only of this idea and hence – indirectly and at one remove – of the horse. Each experiencer will have a somewhat different idea of the horse, and will of course make judgements based on their own ideas. In this account, the subjectivity of ideas is a given and a starting point for enquiry; objectivity is far from guaranteed and is something we need to strive for, perhaps by means of appeals either to a shared human nature or to intersubjective agreements of various kinds. Each of us will judge the world in accordance with our representations of it, but the very nature of such a representational theory positively invites sceptical doubts.

2. Three Key Ambiguities

The term 'idea' is used by many seventeenth-century philosophers, including Locke, in a manner that indicates a lack of awareness of the lurking ambiguities that threaten the unwary theorist. When reading the *Essay*, close attention to the argumentative context and a modicum of charity usually enable the reader to discern which sense of 'idea' Locke is deploying, but every reader must experience moments of frustration when the ambiguities threaten their grasp of the argument. The three most important ambiguities are the following:

(A) Idea as object versus idea as act.
(B) Idea as sensation versus idea as concept.
(C) Idea as occurrence versus idea as disposition.

(A) Idea as object versus idea as act

Locke defines the term 'idea', in the introduction to the *Essay*, as 'whatsoever is the object of the understanding when a man thinks', and adds that the term expresses 'whatever is meant by phantasm, notion, species, or whatever the mind can be employed about in thinking' (EHU I, i, 8, N 47). This definition has naturally led generations of readers to suppose that Locke was postulating a distinct realm of objects of thought and experience to serve as 'direct' or 'immediate' objects for the mind, which is then only aware of external objects 'indirectly' or 'mediately', by means of their ideas.

This standard interpretation of Locke's position is vulnerable to a related pair of objections, one philosophical and the other textual. The obvious philosophical problem is that this sort of 'indirect' or 'representative' realism seems to lead straight to so-called 'veil-of-perception' scepticism, in which the mind is forever cut off from the world by its own ideas. On this theory, critics such as Berkeley would allege, the supposed external world of mind-independent objects becomes a mere unknown and unknowable X, forever beyond our knowledge. It is as if I could see any number of pictures of a given woman, but could never see the woman herself. But if this were the case, how could I ever judge the fidelity of any given representation? The related textual objection is that Locke criticizes just such a position in his *Examination of Père Malebranche's Opinion of Seeing all Things in God*. According to Malebranche, ideas should be identified with the archetypes or blueprints in the mind of God, according to which He created (and still creates) all things. This gives Malebranche an account of how the human mind can represent its world by making our perceptions merely a form of limited participation in the infinite intellect of God.[1] Locke is unimpressed by Malebranche's arguments for this thesis of the 'Vision in God', and immediately spots the vulnerability of this position to an obvious sceptical objection. On Malebranche's view, he asks, does a man ever see the Sun?

> No, but on occasion of the presence of the sun to his eyes, he has seen the idea of the sun in God, which God has exhibited to him; but the sun, because it cannot be united to his soul, he cannot see. How then does he know there is a sun which he never saw? And since God does all things by the most compendious ways, what need is there that God should make a sun that we might see its idea in him when he pleased to exhibit it, when this might as well be done without any real sun at all? (PW 221, 254)

Now, if Locke was keenly aware of this objection to Malebranche's version of the theory of ideas, he must – on pain of outright inconsistency – have felt that his own version of the theory was immune to any such objection. According to one of the greatest

Locke scholars of the modern age, John Yolton, Locke followed Malebranche's critic Antoine Arnauld in simply identifying ideas with perceptions, that is, with mental acts rather than mental objects. In his famous critique of Malebranche, *On True and False Ideas*, Arnauld argued for ideas as mental acts or perceptions, and against any distinct realm of 'representative entities distinct from perceptions'.[2] According to Arnauld, ideas are not distinct entities in their own right: rather, each idea has a double aspect. In itself, it is simply a mode or state of the perceiving mind. But the modes or modifications of a mind are *intrinsically representative*, so each and every mode of a mind can be seen as having a characteristic and distinctive representative content. On this interpretation, the theory of ideas is perfectly compatible with direct realism in the theory of perception. When I am seeing a horse it is *the horse itself* that is the direct object of my perception; the idea is identified with the act of perception itself rather than with any supposed intermediate entity.

Locke owned a copy of *True and False Ideas*, although he does not seem to have followed the fierce ensuing controversy between Arnauld and Malebranche in any depth or detail.[3] According to John Yolton,[4] we should read Locke's critique of Malebranche in the light of Arnauld's *True and False Ideas*, and assume that Locke followed Arnauld in his conception of ideas. If Yolton is right, we face no problem in explaining why Locke thinks that Malebranche's version of the theory of ideas falls into scepticism while his version does not – Malebranche's theory requires a distinct realm of intermediate entities, whereas the Arnauld-Locke theory does not. But there are plenty of passages in the *Essay* that suggest that Locke thinks of ideas as objects rather than simply as acts. As we have already seen, ideas are introduced as 'whatsoever is the object of the understanding when a man thinks'; there is no suggestion here that ideas should be identified with mental acts. And, as Michael Ayers points out, there are other passages in the *Essay* that seem to demand the more robust notion of 'idea' as some kind of intermediate entity. In Book Four, for example, Locke writes that:

> since the things the mind contemplates are none of them, besides itself, present to the understanding, it is necessary that something else, as a sign or representation of the thing it considers, should be present to it: and these are *Ideas*. (EHU IV, xxi, 4, N 720–1)[5]

On the Yolton reading, this passage would reduce to the tautology that, in order to think about some object X, I need to have an idea (= perception) of X, but Locke clearly intends the thought to be informative rather than trivial. He also seems clearly to endorse the Malebranchian thesis, attacked by Arnauld, that tables and chairs, trees and horses cannot be literally 'present' to the mind, which thesis motivates the postulation of a realm of intermediate entities. I thus find myself in agreement with Ayers's judgement that Yolton's reading, which assimilates Locke's position to Arnauld's, requires us to read large chunks of the *Essay* against the grain of the text.

But if we reject the Yolton reading, are we not obliged to accuse Locke of outright inconsistency in accusing Malebranche of falling foul of veil-of-perception scepticism, while simultaneously advancing a theory of his own that is manifestly vulnerable to exactly the same objection? The answer to this question turns, I suspect, on the precise reason for Locke's rejection of Malebranche's theory. A crucial feature of Malebranche's theory is that external objects play no causal role at all in the generation of our sensory ideas: it is always God who causes sensory ideas to arise in human minds, with the external object serving at most as a sort of prompt or reminder. (Since God needs no prompt or reminder, the external object is really redundant.) But on Locke's theory, God has given to bodies real causal powers to act on our sense organs, and has ordained that agitations of our sense organs serve in turn as causes of our sensory ideas. The crucial difference that might justify Locke's claim that Malebranche's theory falls into veil-of-perception scepticism, while his own does not, is the all-important question of what causal role, if any, the external objects play in the generation of our sensory ideas. Malebranche's theory has God acting on the human soul directly; Locke's theory is one of delegated powers.[6] This may explain why Locke thinks his version of the theory of ideas is immune from the objection that he and others had levelled against Malebranche.

(B) Idea as sensation versus idea as concept

This is the distinction that would later be marked by Hume with his terminology of impressions and ideas. The experience of walking in the English woodland in the spring and actually seeing the blooming daffodils is clearly quite different from that of merely reading Wordsworth's famous poem. In the former case, Hume will say, you have the *impression* of yellow; in the latter, you have only the *idea*, which is a faint copy of the corresponding impression. All simple ideas, the empiricists will claim, are copied from their impressions; complex ideas like those of a golden mountain, a centaur, or a unicorn, may be formed in the imagination by recombination. A similar distinction arises for sensations such as pain: there is of course a world of difference between undergoing torture yourself and enjoying a thriller or a horror story involving at some point the use of torture by the villain. The victim has the impression of pain; the enthusiastic reader has only the corresponding idea, which is only a faint copy derived from previous experiences of actual pain. Without the idea, there could be no understanding of the storyline; without some previous personal experience of pain, there could be, on empiricist principles, no such idea. For those of us fortunate enough never to have experienced the agonies of the rack or the thumbscrew, the power of the imagination to augment its ideas may be brought into play. 'Remember', I might say to a child, 'that time when you caught your finger in the door. Well, the pain of the thumbscrew is like that, only much worse.'

It is to be regretted that Locke uses the one term 'idea', throughout the *Essay*, to refer both to impressions and to ideas, in Hume's sense. When he writes about 'the idea of yellow', or 'the idea of pain', he might be referring either to the sensations or to the corresponding concepts. This potential source of ambiguity, although it appears damaging, is in fact relatively harmless. The context usually enables us to understand 'idea of yellow' either as impression or as idea, in Hume's sense. And since Locke's primary concern, throughout the work, is with the understanding, and with how it comes to be stocked with the ideas it finds in its possession, we must assume that the focus of his interest is on what Hume would call 'ideas' and we might call 'concepts'. Ideas in the sense of sensations (Hume's impressions) play a crucial causal role, for Locke as for any other empiricist, in explaining how each human mind comes to be stocked with ideas in the sense of concepts, but it is concepts that are the subject matter of the *Essay*. Locke is far more interested in questions of meaning and understanding than he is in the physiology and psychology of the senses.

(C) Idea as occurrence versus idea as disposition

'Having the idea of X' is clearly ambiguous between an occurrent sense, which involves thinking about X right now, and a dispositional sense, which involves having the power to bring X to mind. A competent adult speaker of a natural language understands thousands of words, the expression of which in speech or writing will excite their corresponding ideas, enabling the language-user to understand what has been said or written. But although I understand the words 'unicorn', 'virus', 'duck-billed platypus', and 'oak', I may go days or weeks or even months (at least in the case of 'unicorn') without ever, as we say, bringing such things to mind. Linguistic competence thus involves the possession by the mind of thousands of ideas in this dispositional sense, involving a power of recall. The argument against innatism in Book One of the *Essay* turns crucially, as we will see, on the claim that ideas in the dispositional sense are in a crucial sense parasitic upon ideas in the occurrent sense. I could not be said, Locke claims, to have the idea of an oak, or a unicorn, in the dispositional sense if I had never perceived or thought about an oak or a unicorn in the occurrent sense. The actual experience, he thinks, must come first; the power of recall is a secondary effect. In the case of oaks, I have both personal experience and a whole variety of films, TV and books; in the case of unicorns, I have only fictional sources to draw on, but the same point stands.

Drawing this distinction, and establishing a firm grasp of ideas in the dispositional sense, is clearly essential for any attempt to understand the human mind. It takes only a moment's reflection to see that 'having an idea of X' is very often used to mark the dispositional sense, the sense that picks out an ability rather than its actual exercise. The overwhelming majority of the ideas that furnish my mind must, at any given moment, exist in a sort of latent state, available for deployment as and when required. Once again, Locke isn't always careful to distinguish ideas as occurrences from ideas as dispositions; once again, his sense is usually sufficiently clear from the context. The most important context in which this distinction plays a critical role is in the attack on innate ideas and innate principles in Book One of the *Essay*, to which we must now turn our attention.

3. The Attack on Innate Principles

The fundamental claim of the whole *Essay* is made at the start of Book Two, where Locke sets out his empiricist thesis that the human mind starts out as 'white paper, void of all characters, without any ideas', and asserts that the vast stock of ideas in the mind of a mature adult have all, without exception, been furnished by experience (EHU II, i, 2, N 104). This famous statement of the *tabula rasa* thesis contradicts the views of many of Locke's contemporaries, who believed in innate ideas and innate principles. Book One of the *Essay* launches an all-out attack on this doctrine of innatism (sometimes also labelled 'nativism'). There has been considerable discussion in the literature regarding Locke's precise targets in the polemic of Book One, but we can identify (at least) Descartes and his disciples, Cambridge Platonists such as Henry More (1614–87) and Ralph Cudworth (1617–88), and a number of contemporary Anglican clergymen, who thought that metaphysics and morality required innate ideas imprinted by God on each and every human soul at its creation.[7]

The strategy of Locke's attack on innatism is a twin-track one. He seeks to persuade his readers both that innate ideas and principles are redundant (because we can explain our stock of ideas without them) and that they are non-existent (because we have no good reasons to believe in their existence). The redundancy claim is made right at the start of Book One, where Locke mentions the 'established opinion' that the mind of man comes into the world already stamped with certain 'innate principles', and adds that:

> It would be sufficient to convince unprejudiced readers of the falseness of this Supposition, if I could only show (as I hope I shall in the following Parts of this Discourse) how men, barely by the use of their natural Faculties, may attain to all the Knowledge they have, without the help of any innate Impressions, and may arrive at Certainty, without any such Original Notions or Principles. (EHU I, ii, 1, N 48)

In other words, if the arguments of Book Two persuade the reader that all our ideas *could* have originated in experience, this in itself will suffice – at least for the unprejudiced mind – to persuade us that they *did in fact* do so. Book One would then be redundant. The attack on innate ideas was absent from Draft A of the *Essay*, making its appearance only in Draft B; it was also omitted from John Wynne's abridgement of the *Essay* for students at Oxford. Locke clearly believed that the empiricist theory of ideas could stand on its own merits, and command assent from unprejudiced minds, without the anti-innatist polemic of Book One. The problem, of course, is that not all readers would be unprejudiced. Many of them had been firmly informed, perhaps from the pulpit, that the doctrine of innate ideas played a foundational role in metaphysics and morality. Such prejudiced readers might need to be persuaded both that the grounds for belief in innate ideas and principles were very weak, and that religion and morality needed no such supports. This, we must surmise, is why Locke thought that he owed his readers the direct attack on innatism that he launches in Book One.

Before we can proceed, we need to distinguish innate principles from innate ideas, and to say something about the dependence or independence of the two claims. Locke is clear that innate principles would be impossible without innate ideas (EHU I, ii, 23), for the obvious reason that a principle needs to be stated in terms, and that the terms need to become associated with ideas if they are to be understood. To be told that *ex nihilo nihil fit* is an axiom of metaphysics is useless to the student ignorant of Latin. A man cannot assent to a proposition unless and until he has understood it; he cannot understand it until he has grasped its constituent terms; he cannot grasp its constituent terms without having the corresponding ideas. So there could be no innate principles without innate ideas. The inference the other way round is less straightforward. The Cartesians claim that the innate idea of God ('Being with all perfections') is stamped on each and every human soul at its creation. This idea, they argue, contains that of necessary existence. But lots of people doubt or deny the existence of God. The Cartesians must claim that the presence of innate ideas in each and every human mind gives us all the *potential* to arrive at knowledge that is independent of experience, such as demonstrative knowledge that God exists. Some humans, however, are too intellectually lazy to meditate and to actualize the knowledge that is implicit in their innate ideas. Innate knowledge, it seems, requires innate ideas, but innate ideas provide only the potential for innate knowledge.

Locke distinguishes supposed innate principles into 'speculative' and 'practical', the former belonging to metaphysics and the latter to morality. Pride of place among the speculative principles, we are told, goes to axioms such as 'Whatsoever is, is', and 'It is impossible for the same thing to be and not to be.' Why do some metaphysicians think that such principles are innate? The argument offered for this claim starts with the premise that these axioms command universal assent among mankind, and then advances to the claim that innateness provides the most plausible explanation of that universal assent. Locke disputes both the truth of the premise and the validity of the inference. Innatism, he argues, entails universal assent, so if universal assent is refuted, so too is innatism. But universal assent does not entail innatism: a proposition such as 'red is not green' might command universal assent (at least among the sighted, that is, those competent to form a judgement about colours), but no one presumably thinks it must therefore be innate. We get our ideas of colours from experience, and presumably come to give spontaneous assent to 'red is not green' as soon as we are in possession of these two distinct sensory ideas.

Locke's denial that the principles 'whatsoever is, is', and 'it is impossible for the same thing to be and not to be' are innately known is very straightforward. He thinks that innateness entails universal assent, and that these propositions do not in fact command universal assent:

> For, first, 'tis evident that all *Children* and *Ideots*, have not the least Apprehension or Thought of them: and the want of that is enough to destroy that universal Assent which must needs be the necessary concomitant of all innate Truths: it seeming to me near a Contradiction, to say, that there are Truths imprinted on the Soul which it perceives or understands not; imprinting, if it signify anything, being nothing else, but the making certain Truths to be perceived. (EHU I, ii, 5, N 49)

This is clearly too fast. Anyone familiar with the frailties of human memory will retort that there are lots of truths imprinted on human minds that we do not (currently) perceive. To rack one's brains in the attempt to recall some important fact is a matter of everyday experience, and certainly not 'near a contradiction'. Locke goes on, however, to make his real meaning plain. In those everyday cases of memory failure, the fact in question *has been* clearly apprehended at some past moment, but what the innatists are claiming is that propositions can be known without *ever* being apprehended. It is this claim that Locke thinks 'near a contradiction':

> To say a Notion is imprinted on the Mind, and yet at the same time to say, that the mind is ignorant of it, and never yet took notice of it, is to make this Impression nothing. No Proposition can be said to be in the Mind, which it never yet knew, which it was never yet conscious of. (EHU I, ii, 5, N 50)

Children and idiots have never in their lives entertained or affirmed the thoughts that 'whatsoever is, is', or that 'it is impossible for the same thing to be and not to be', so it is false that these propositions were imprinted on their minds at their creation, so these propositions do not command universal assent, so they are not innate. But these were our most plausible candidates for innate speculative principles. If innateness entails universal assent, and universal assent is false, we have a simple three-line refutation of innatism.

Stated in such bald terms, this argument would scarcely have impressed the defenders of innatism. They would have replied, almost to a man, that Locke has just demolished a straw man, not a position any actual innatist ever held. Descartes, for example, in his reply to Hobbes' objections to his *Meditations*, had already dismissed such a crude version of innatism. In saying that the idea of God is innate, he explained, 'we do not mean that it is always there before us. That would mean that no idea was innate. We simply mean that we have within ourselves the faculty of summoning up the idea.'[8] (He will have to add, of course, that this 'faculty' or power of summoning up the idea is not itself the product of experience.) In his *Comments on a Certain Broadsheet*, he explains that when he describes an idea as innate, he is using the term 'innate' in:

> the same sense as that in which we say that generosity is 'innate' in certain families, or that certain diseases such as gout or stones are innate in others: it is not so much that the babies of such families suffer from these diseases in their mother's womb, but simply that they are born with a certain 'faculty' or tendency to contract them.[9]

A similar account of innate ideas can be found in the writings of the Cambridge Platonists Henry More and Ralph Cudworth. On their broadly dispositional account of what it is for an idea or a principle to be innate, Locke's objection from 'children and idiots' misses the point entirely. Children and idiots have not actualized their dispositions to have certain thoughts or endorse certain principles, but this is no evidence of their absence. Locke is perfectly aware of the fact that his first argument against innatism will fall foul of this 'straw man' objection, since most of the advocates of innateness defend only a dispositional version of the theory. He thinks, of course, that he has further arguments up his sleeve. The problem with the dispositional version of innatism, he thinks, is that it collapses into triviality. If the innatist claims that 'A has innate knowledge that p' amounts to no more than 'A can come to know that p', then anything whatsoever that we ever come to know will come out, by that definition, as innate. If the innatist is campaigning only for an innate capacity, this point can be granted, since nobody ever denied it. But in that case, Locke asks, why contend for the special status of certain innate maxims?

If the innatist claims that the capacity of the mind to come to know certain types of truth (e.g., those concerning numbers) is entirely innate and independent of experience, and that this distinguishes a special and privileged category of a priori knowledge from ordinary empirical knowledge, Locke can counter-attack on two fronts. He can deny that our knowledge of numbers is entirely independent of experience, and insist that mathematics is the product of abstraction from experience. And he can and does retort that on this version of innatism, the whole of mathematics (not just the axioms) will come out as innate. If all that is required for knowledge of p to be innate is that the mind has the in-built capacity to recognize its truth, then $\sqrt{289} = 17$ will come out as every bit as innate as $1 + 1 = 2$. (The innatists might, of course, just 'bite the bullet' on this point.[10]) The overall thrust of Locke's argument takes the form of trying to impale the innatist on the horns of a dilemma. If the innatist says that innate knowledge must be actualized, then innatism is easily refuted by experience. If the innatist allows innate knowledge to be merely potential, then Locke retorts that his thesis is trivial.

Another possible move for the innatist is to distinguish explicit from implicit knowledge, and to argue that our knowledge of axioms may only be implicit. Locke thinks that this is just another variant of the dispositional theory:

> If it be said, The Understanding hath an *implicit Knowledge* of these Principles, but not an explicit, before this first hearing (as they must, who will say, that they are in the Understanding before they are known), it will be hard to conceive what is meant by a Principle imprinted on the Understanding Implicitly, unless it be this, That the Mind is capable of understanding and assenting firmly to such Propositions. (EHU I, ii, 22, N 59–60)

Unfortunately, this is just too fast. A piece of implicit knowledge might manifest itself in behaviour, independently of and long before explicit assent to a proposition. Child psychologists need to take seriously the possibility, for example, that our minds are pre-programmed to think in terms of the categories of cause and substance. A toddler's face can betray the thought 'where has the ball gone?', when a familiar object, presumed to have perception-independent existence, passes out of its field of vision. And the incessant 'why?' questions of the five-year-old may manifest a firm commitment to some version of the principle of sufficient reason.

The most sophisticated of Locke's critics, Gottfried Wilhelm Leibniz, pressed just this line of thought in Book One of his *New Essays*, written as a point-by-point defence of innatism against Book One of Locke's *Essay*. He argues that the dispositional version of innatism is far from trivial. The truths of reason, Leibniz argues, have a 'special affinity' with our faculty of reason:

> So it is not a bare faculty, consisting in a mere possibility of under-standing these truths: it is rather a disposition, an aptitude, a prefor-mation, which determines our soul and brings it about that they are derivable from it. Just as there is a difference between the shapes which are arbitrarily given to a stone or piece of marble, and those which its veins already indicate or are disposed to indicate if the sculptor avails himself of them.[11]

Commentators generally agree that Locke's arguments fail to refute the sophisticated dispositional version of innatism, and modern evolutionary psychologists need to take seriously the hypothesis that our minds come innately pre-equipped to think certain thoughts or to endorse certain principles as self-evident. One problem they must address and Locke could ignore was the question of whether such innately pre-programmed beliefs could ever amount to innate *knowledge*. Our evolutionary history may have hard-wired into our brains certain beliefs that it is useful for humans to have, and to acquire quickly and easily in childhood. Nothing of course follows about whether these beliefs are true, or justified. Locke's contemporaries could ignore this problem because they assumed that any innately pre-programmed beliefs have been given to us by a truthful God; today's evolutionary psychologists cannot help themselves to the far-too-hasty assumption that the set of useful beliefs coincides with the set of true beliefs. Evolution might well have equipped us with assumptions, either about the natural world or about ourselves, that are useful but false.

If any idea might be thought innate, Locke argues, that of God might have the best title, and of course many philosophers have claimed that this idea is indeed innate – that is, after all, the central claim of Descartes' *Third Meditation*. But, Locke insists, the evidence of the world travellers is solidly against any such claim. If the idea were innate, then all men should agree in a single universal religion. But of course men's ideas of God (or the gods) are extremely diverse and heavily culture-dependent, and there are entire peoples – even advanced and civilized peoples such as the Thais and the Chinese

– who are outright atheists (EHU I, iv, 8, N 88). Here Locke's intensive reading in the travel literature of his day is deployed to buttress his argument against innatism. The dispositional innatist can reply of course that God has indeed stamped his trademark 'God made this' on each and every human soul at its creation, but that this original impression, although never effaced, can easily be covered over and obscured by what one might call local cultural graffiti. Locke might retort that this innatist hypothesis, although unrefuted by his arguments from the diversity and cultural variation of religious beliefs, has little plausibility and no positive evidence in its favour. It might be true, but we have no glimmering of a reason for thinking that it is true. In such a dispute, the burden of proof surely lies with the innatist.

When the argument shifts from supposedly innate speculative principles to supposedly innate practical principles, Locke's reliance on the evidence of human cultural diversity is still more striking. The structure of his argument against innate moral principles is fundamentally the same as that against innate speculative principles. Innatism entails universal assent; but universal assent is false; therefore innatism is false. And even if universal assent could be found for some moral axiom such as 'do as you would be done by', its universality could be explained in terms of universal features of human experience, so this would provide no proof of innateness. Once again, Locke denies both the major premise of the innatist's argument and the validity of his inference.

After providing a lengthy account of the sheer diversity of human customs and practices, drawn of course from the usual evidence of the travellers' tales, Locke concludes that:

> He that will carefully peruse the History of Mankind, and look abroad into the several Tribes of Men, and with indifferency survey their Actions, will be able to satisfy himself, that there is scarce that Principle of Morality to be named, or *Rule of Vertue* to be thought on (those only excepted, that are absolutely necessary to hold Society together, which commonly too are neglected betwixt distinct Societies), which is not, somewhere or other, *slighted* and condemned by the general Fashion of *whole Societies* of men, governed by practical Opinions, and Rules of living quite opposite to others. (EHU I, iii, 10, N 72)

He is not, Locke explains, merely noting the obvious fact that moral rules are everywhere violated – that would clearly provide no evidence against their universally binding force. The point is the stronger one, namely, that the culturally approved moral rules themselves vary widely from one society to another:

> I grant the Objection good where Men, though they transgress, yet disown not the Law; where fear of Shame, Censure, or Punishment carries the Mark of some awe it has upon them. But it is impossible to conceive that *a whole Nation* of Men should all *publickly reject* and renounce, what every one of them certainly and infallibly, knew to be a Law: For so they must, who have it naturally imprinted on their Minds. (EHU I, iii, 11, N 72)

Moral codes regarding such matters as sexual relations, parental duties, property rights and divine worship are all enormously variable, and humans brought up in a given culture inevitably feel bound to observe its particular norms. If the evidence of history and human geography tells us clearly that not just human customs but human moral codes have varied enormously from one society to another, we have powerful evidence against the existence of a single universal moral law 'inscribed' on each and every human heart.

Locke insists that he is not denying the existence of a moral 'Law of Nature', to which each and every human is subject. Here he could draw on some of his own earlier work. In his early *Essays on the Law of Nature*, written for his students at Oxford, he had argued in the first two essays that there is a 'Law of Nature', knowable by the 'light of Nature'. In Essay Three, he had argued that the moral 'Law of Nature' is not inscribed in the minds of men.[12] Here in Book One of the *Essay*, the same basic message is repeated:

> I would not be here mistaken, as if, because I deny an innate Law, I thought there were none but positive Laws. There is a great deal of difference between an innate Law and a Law of Nature; between something imprinted on our Minds in their very original, and something that we, being ignorant of, may attain to the knowledge of, by the use and due application of our natural Faculties. And I think they equally forsake the Truth, who running into the contrary extreams, either affirm an innate Law, or deny that there is a Law, knowable by the light of Nature, i.e. without the help of positive Revelation. (EHU I, iii, 13, N 75)

Locke was always irked by the accusation that by denying the existence of innate moral principles, he was therefore denying the existence of a moral law of nature.[13] The precise content of the law of nature was never entirely clear – Locke would often refer in his correspondence to Cicero's *On Duties* for the best available statement – but of its existence he was certain. The existence of widely divergent moral codes among different human societies is thus, for Locke, emphatically *not* evidence of the truth of any sort of moral relativism. It merely provides evidence that knowledge of the true moral law of nature requires experience and reflection, and thus finds its clearest expression in the views of the wisest members of any given society. If the principles of the moral law were innate, he argues, they should be most clearly manifest in children and savages. The fact that we must turn for our knowledge of the law of nature to the wisdom of age and experience, that is, to men such as Aristotle and Cicero, shows clearly for Locke that such knowledge is the product of mature reflection on experience. Aristotle had famously claimed, in his *Nicomachean Ethics*, that a man needs to reach the age of sixty before he can write with authority on ethics; Cicero was well advanced in years before composing *On Duties*. Locke clearly thinks that we have, even in a state of Nature (i.e., without divine revelation) some knowledge of our duties towards God, towards our fellow-citizens and towards mankind in general, but that such moral knowledge requires age, experience and much thought. This evidence, he thinks, counts firmly against the claims of the innatist.

4. The Empiricist Project

The project of Book Two of the *Essay*, and the heart of the entire work, is Locke's attempt to show how the human mind, which enters the world as a *tabula rasa*, comes to be furnished with the vast stock of ideas characteristic of an educated adult in a civilized state. All these ideas, however rich and however diverse, can be traced back, he argues, to experience, and to their ultimate roots in sensation and reflection:

> All those sublime Thoughts, which towre above the Clouds, and reach as high as Heaven it self, take their Rise and Footing here: In all that great Extent wherein the mind wanders, in those remote Speculations it may seem to be elevated with, it stirs not one jot beyond those *Ideas* which *Sense* or *Reflection* have offered for its Contemplation. (EHU II, i, 24, N 118)

Ideas of sensation are too familiar to need any further comment – almost all philosophers have supposed that our ideas of *red*, *hot* and *bitter* are simple ideas derived from their respective senses, whereas by contrast our ideas of an elephant, a symphony like Beethoven's *Eroica* and a dish like *coq au vin* are complex combinations of ideas derived from the senses. Ideas of reflection need a little more explanation. The mind, says Locke, thinks and feels and wills, and is aware of its own activities of thinking, feeling and willing. This awareness gives each mind a second and distinct source of ideas, in addition to the ideas we derive through our senses:

> This Source of *Ideas*, every Man has wholly in himself: and though it be not Sense, as having nothing to do with external Objects; yet it is very like it, and might properly enough be call'd internal Sense. But as I call the other *Sensation*, so I call this REFLECTION, the *Ideas* it affords being such only as the Mind gets by reflecting on its own Operations within itself. (EHU II, i, 4, N 105)

Ideas both of sensation and reflection admit a simple/complex distinction, giving us a fairly straightforward breakdown into four groups, as follows:

Simple ideas of sensation: red, hot, sweet, etc.
Complex ideas of sensation: elephant, oak tree, fortress.[14]
Simple ideas of reflection: thinking, willing, pleasure, pain.
Complex ideas of reflection: feeling sad at the loss of a loved one, the pleasant anticipation of successfully completing a job, experiencing anxiety about the state of one's soul.

Some simple ideas, Locke warns us, can come into the mind by means of sensation and reflection alike. Such are our ideas of pleasure, pain, power, existence and unity (EHU II, vii, 1, N 128). There are pleasures and pains both of the senses and of reflection, and thoughts about power, existence and unity do not seem equivocal whether we are talking about the power of the will or that of a moving body, whether of the existence of angels or of sea monsters, and whether we are counting spasms of pain or wounds to the body. The same set of ideas, Locke thinks, informs judgements of the kind 'C can bring about E', 'X exists' and 'there are exactly 17 Ys', whether our ideas of Cs, Es, Xs and Ys stem from sensation or reflection. But for this to be possible, the same set of ideas must be applicable without equivocation in both contexts indifferently. We humans probably derive our concepts of number by counting cats and dogs, sheep and cows; but we could in principle have acquired the same number-concepts from counting spasms of pain, exertions of the will or attacks of guilty conscience over broken resolutions.

The simple ideas of sense, Locke insists, are all 'real', meaning thereby that they are reliable natural signs or indicators of the powers in bodies to affect our sense organs in certain ways.[15] A term such as 'red' can be used to designate either the power in the object to produce a certain sensation in our minds, or the sensation produced. Locke admits that he doesn't always use such terms with perfect precision and consistency, but hopes that sympathetic and careful readers will discern his meaning. When we say that blood, roses and rubies are all red, we are saying that such bodies possess a common power (grounded no doubt in some unknown arrangement of their sub-microscopic parts) to affect our sense organs in a certain way. So long as there is a reliable correlation between the idea (sensation) and the power, we can say that a simple idea is 'real', meaning thereby not that something like the sensation exists in the object, but merely that we can properly use the sign as a reliable indication of some property or power of that object. When we pick the red apples from the green ones, thinking that they will be sweeter, we are, in effect, making use of a natural sign-language established by God for our benefit. Simple ideas of sensation, says Locke in Book Four,

> *are not fictions* of our Fancies, but the natural and regular productions of Things without us, really operating upon us; and so carry with them all the conformity which is intended; or which our state requires: For they represent to us Things under those appearances which they are fitted to produce in us: whereby we are enabled to distinguish the sorts of particular Substances, to discern the states they are in, and so take them for our Necessities and apply them to our Uses. Thus the *Idea* of whiteness or bitterness, as it is in the Mind, exactly answering that Power which is in any Body to produce it there, has all the real conformity it can, or ought to have, with Things without us. And this conformity between our simple *Ideas* and the existence of Things is sufficient for real Knowledge. (EHU IV, iv, 4, N 564)

Commentators disagree on the vexed question of whether Locke thinks of ideas in imagist terms. Is our idea of a horse, or of an oak tree, something akin to a mini-picture, albeit less bright and vivid than the actual perception? Or should we follow Descartes and draw a sharp distinction between ideas and images, and between the understanding and the imagination? Michael Ayers[16] presents the clearest case for the 'imagist' reading, arguing that Locke's view builds on those of precursors such as Hobbes and Gassendi, and exhibits a consistent hostility to the opposed view of Descartes. 'Hostility to Descartes' conception of the intellect', Ayers writes, 'pervades the *Essay*.'[17] Against Descartes, Locke denies that we have a clear and distinct idea of the *shape* of a chiliagon (a thousand-sided figure); we have only a clear and distinct idea of the *number* of its sides, because we can imagine counting them one by one. And Locke's denial, again against Descartes, that we can have a clear positive idea of infinity (EHU II, xvii, 13), is also most naturally read in imagist terms. If ideas are images, then 'we have no positive idea of infinity' receives a perfectly natural reading; if ideas are acts of a supposedly pure intellect distinct from the imagination, then Locke's claims might seem groundless and even question-begging. Others have challenged Ayers's reading, and argued that the *Essay* is much less clear and conclusive on this issue than Ayers thinks.[18] If Locke is an imagist, ideas of the memory are, as Hobbes says, the products of 'decaying sense', like fading pictures, while the imagination has the power to reinvoke and recombine such mini-pictures. To produce a general theory along these lines, we will of course have to think in terms of a much extended sense of 'image', taking in not just the senses other than vision but also reflection. In this extended sense, 'images' explain such familiar phenomena as replaying 'in one's mind's ear' a favourite tune after a concert, and even (for ideas of reflection) revisiting in memory the felt grief of parting from a loved one, or experiencing pangs of sympathy for the sufferings of the heroine in a novel. On this issue, I find myself inclined to side with Ayers, who seems not only to get Locke's intellectual affinities (in particular, his anti-Cartesianism) right, but also provides at least a sketch of how the imagist might deal with proposed counter-examples.

Since complex ideas can be formed by recombination in the imagination, no guarantee holds for their 'reality'. Here Locke distinguishes carefully between ideas of substances and those of mere 'modes'. Our ideas of substances, he writes, generally group together the ideas of combinations of properties that are found together in nature. Ideas such as those of *elephant, humming bird, lemon* and *diamond* are formed in this way, out of lists of manifest properties. One obvious problem that arises here concerns the basis of classification. Although groupings of properties are provided by nature, it may be up to us to choose which resemblances to take as grounds for classification. Both fish and whales have a certain body shape and swim in the sea; both whales and cows have warm blood and suckle their young. Should we sort the whales with the fish or with the cows? Such questions raise deep problems regarding the respective roles of nature and convention in our systems of classification, and Locke has interesting and important things to say on the subject, to which we must return. But of course not all of our supposed ideas of substance have grounds in nature at all. The imagination can put together the ideas of a man's head and a horse's body, producing the idea of a *centaur*, which has no counterpart in nature. So our substance-terms may or may not have a real grounding in nature. As for our ideas of modes, here, Locke thinks, we are free to combine ideas as we please, so long as we do so clearly and consistently. Some combinations of ideas, he writes, are of course suggested by experience (he gives the example of seeing two men wrestle and forming the idea of wrestling), but many of our ideas of mixed modes will be inventions of our own minds, combining ideas not previously found together in experience (EHU II, xxii, 9, N 291–2). Terms such as *government, democracy, sonata* and *ode* are terms of human invention, in which we may combine simpler ideas according to our own choices. Once languages are established, of course, the meanings of these terms will become fixed by convention, and the user of an established natural language will be under some obligation to use them in a manner consistent with established norms. What counts here is clarity (i.e., using such terms in accordance with clear and stable definitions) and consistency; the question of any conformity or otherwise with nature simply does not arise.

In their reception of the simple ideas of sensation and reflection, our minds, Locke thinks, are entirely passive. The imagination does, however, possess certain active powers. It can augment or diminish ideas given in sense and reflection, and it can combine and separate them, producing new combinations. If I am talking to a child who has never seen a tiger, I can say 'a tiger is like a cat, but much bigger, and with black and orange stripes'. If the child already has the ideas of cat, black, orange and stripe, then he or she can form at least a rough idea of a tiger. A similar account can be given for our ideas of angels, demons and even God. Descartes had argued, in his *Third Meditation*, that the idea of God is innate, stamped upon each and every human soul by its maker at its creation. We have already seen that Locke rejects this position in Book One of the *Essay*, arguing that it is incompatible with the anthropological evidence of the sheer diversity of human religions. How then will an empiricist account for our idea of God, given that He is not an object of direct experience? The answer turns on our ideas of reflection, and on the mind's power to augment its ideas. We know what it is to think and will, so we need only imagine a being with these powers of thinking and willing, but vastly more intelligent and powerful than we are (EHU II, xxiii, 33, N 314). We can even continue to call God 'infinite' in power and wisdom, so long as we understand this is in its negative sense of *unlimited*, rather than supposing that the term conveys a clearly grasped positive idea.

Another important power possessed by human minds – but not, Locke thinks, by those of animals – is that of abstraction. Abstraction can be explained either in terms of the selective attention a mind can choose to pay to one part or aspect of an idea, relegating other parts or aspects to the background, or as the mind's capacity to create a new and slimmed-down idea from a richer one by a process of subtraction. In chapter 11 of Book Two of the *Essay* (EHU II, xi, 9, N 159), Locke presents a 'subtraction' account of the process of abstraction, claiming that we form general ideas such as *man* or *animal* by leaving out the many respects in which our ideas of particular men, or particular animals, differ from one another. If I start with the idea of a particular man, such as Barack Obama, I will represent him as male, mixed-race, tall, middle-aged and so on. By subtracting each differentiating feature in turn, I can arrive at the abstract idea of humanity, an idea that stands indifferently for humans old and young, black and white, tall and short, male and female and so on. Unfortunately, there is a clear tension between thinking of ideas as images and this 'subtraction' account of abstraction. It seems relatively easy to imagine how a 'selective attention' account of abstraction could account for our ability to use the idea of Barack Obama as a representative of humanity in general, but the 'subtraction' account seems to be asking me to *imagine*, that is, picture in my mind's eye, a human neither old nor young, neither tall nor short, neither black nor white, neither male nor female, and so on, for all the characteristics by which humans are differentiated from one another. Opponents of abstract ideas, starting with George Berkeley,[19] have denied that they can frame any such idea.

One particularly unfortunate passage occurs in chapter 7 of Book Four, in which Locke is discussing the difficulty of framing abstract ideas, and the reason we find so few in young children and none at all in brute beasts:

For example, Does it not require some pains and skill to form the *general Idea* of a *Triangle* (which is yet none of the most abstract, comprehensive, and difficult), for it must be neither Oblique nor Rectangle, neither Equilateral, Equicrural, nor Scalenon; but all and none of these at once. In effect, it is something imperfect, that cannot exist; an *Idea* wherein some parts of several different and inconsistent *Ideas* are put together. (EHU IV, vii, 9, N 596)

Not surprisingly, critics such as Berkeley pounced on this passage and made it a butt for their ridicule. But Locke was here being sloppy in expressing his meaning, and carelessly running together features of the idea itself and those of its objects. On a 'subtraction' account of abstraction, the abstract idea of a triangle is *in itself* neither equilateral, nor isosceles, nor scalene, and it is precisely this lack of determinacy that makes it capable of *representing* triangles of all three kinds. The right objection for Berkeley to press, and the one that will appeal to anyone who holds an imagist conception of ideas, is that if the idea of a triangle is a mini-picture before the mind's eye, then that image cannot be an image of a triangle without being itself equilateral, isosceles or scalene. Locke, his critics will allege, must either abandon the conception of ideas as images or abandon the 'subtraction' account of abstraction in favour of the 'selective attention' account.

3

Human Knowledge and Its Limits

1. Locke's Definition of Knowledge

Locke's account of knowledge, and of the all-important distinctions between knowledge, probable opinion and faith, make up Book Four of the *Essay*. Although last in order, Book Four is the heart of the *Essay*, and the final realization of its original project, which was, lest we forget, 'to enquire into the Original, Certainty, and Extent of humane Knowledge; together with the Grounds and Degrees of Belief, Opinion, and Assent' (EHU I, i, 2, N 43). After the attack on innate principles in Book One, the positive account of how our minds come to be stocked with ideas in Book Two, and an important digression concerning language in Book Three, we finally return to the main subject that had prompted Locke to write the *Essay* in the first place. What is knowledge? How much knowledge do we humans actually have? How much further knowledge can we hope for from the advance of the natural sciences? And where we lack knowledge, can we have a sufficient degree of assurance of the truth of our beliefs to provide a basis for action? The doctor may not know that a dose of quinine will cure his feverish patient – he may have only a list of symptoms to inform his diagnosis, and a statistical generalization to the effect that these symptoms usually subside after a dose of quinine – but this may be enough evidence to justify a course of treatment. The Christian may not know that Jesus Christ was the promised Messiah, but may have a rational and well-grounded faith based on the testimony of the Apostles. In many walks of life, it is clear, we lack knowledge and must be guided by probable opinion or by faith.

Locke's account of the nature of knowledge can be found in chapter 1 of Book Four, which begins as follows:

> Since *the Mind*, in all its Thoughts and Reasonings, hath no other immediate Object but its own *Ideas*, which it alone does or can contemplate, it is evident that our Knowledge is only conversant about them. (EHU IV, i, 1, N 525)

This is an astonishing and deeply counterintuitive claim. If asked to list some of the things I know, I might reply that I know that swallows can fly but pigs cannot, that common salt dissolves in water but chalk does not, that I live in Bristol and have a bay tree in my back garden, that the first Moon Landing took place in 1969 and so on. On the face of it, these are facts of various kinds about the world, and emphatically *not* facts about my ideas. Of course, I need to have the corresponding ideas in order even to entertain these thoughts in the first place, so we must grant that possession of ideas is a necessary condition for such items of knowledge, but it surely does not follow from this modest concession to the theory of ideas that our knowledge is 'only conversant about' our ideas. The very function of ideas, one might think, is to make possible knowledge of their objects, their *ideata* in the jargon of scholastic Latin. Just as a portrait of Henry VIII gives me some knowledge of what Henry VIII looked like, so my ideas should give me some knowledge of the external world around me. That at least is the common-sense view. By asserting that our knowledge extends only to our ideas, Locke seems to be laying himself wide open to the accusation of his critics that the theory of ideas is a one-way track to an extreme form of subjective scepticism.

Locke, however, makes it clear that he means exactly what he says. The chapter continues as follows:

> *Knowledge* then seems to me to be nothing but *the perception of the connexion and agreement, or disagreement and repugnancy, of any of our Ideas*. In this alone it consists. Where this Perception is, there is Knowledge; and where it is not, there, though we may fancy, guess, or believe, yet we always come short of Knowledge. For when we know that *White is not Black*, what do we else but perceive that these two ideas do not agree? When we possess ourselves with the utmost security of the Demonstration, that *the three Angles of a Triangle are equal to two right ones*, what do we more but perceive, that equality to two right ones does necessarily agree to, and is inseparable from the three Angles of a Triangle? (EHU IV, i, 2, N 525)

The claim that knowledge only extends to relations between ideas might seem to commit Locke to the thesis that only analytic truths, in the modern jargon, can be known at all. To know that A is B, on this view, the idea of A must be analysable into some complex BCD, and then the truth of 'A is B' will be brought to light by analysis as 'BCD is B'. Here the predicate term B is already, as Kant would later put it, implicitly 'contained' in the subject term A, and analysis amounts to a sort of 'unpacking' of what was already present. This interpretation of Locke has been defended by Lex Newman,[1] but is rejected by most other commentators. Jonathan Lowe, for example, thinks that one of Locke's key examples, 'white is not black', is self-evident but not analytic.[2] Since black and white are simple ideas, he argues, no process of analysis can reveal *not-black* in the idea of *white* or *not-white* in the idea of *black*. On this view, some of the relations between ideas are simply evident to the perceiving mind without being analytically true; others (e.g., 'a circle is not a square') will be *both* self-evident *and* analytic, because of course a few simple definitions will enable us to make explicit the contradiction involved in asserting both 'X is circular' and 'X is square'.

Locke's talk of ideas standing in relations of 'agreement' and 'disagreement' with one another may seem too vague – and too obviously metaphorical – to be of much help to his readers. Fortunately, he goes on to say more about the sorts of agreement and disagreement that he has in mind:

> But to understand a little more distinctly, wherein this agreement or disagreement consists, I think we may reduce it all to these four sorts:
> 1. *Identity*, or *Diversity*.
> 2. *Relation*.
> 3. *Co-existence*, or *necessary connection*.
> 4. *Real Existence*. (EHU IV, i, 3, N 525)

(1) When an idea is present to the attentive mind, it immediately perceives each to be what it is, and to be distinct from all other ideas. This perception, says Locke, is the foundation of all our knowledge:

> This is so absolutely necessary that without it there could be no Knowledge, no Reasoning, no Imagination, no distinct Thoughts at all. By this the mind clearly and infallibly perceives each *Idea* to agree with it self and to be what it is; and all distinct *Ideas* to disagree, i.e. the one not to be the other: And this it does without any pains, labour, or deduction; but at first view, by its natural power of Perception and Distinction. (EHU IV, i, 4, N 526)

We judge immediately and infallibly that white is not black, and that a circle is not a square, without any need to rely on abstract rules of logic such as 'what is, is', and 'it is impossible for the same thing to be and not to be'. Nor do these abstract general rules, once formulated by the logicians, add one iota of additional clarity or certainty to the particular judgements that fall under them. The mind, says Locke, always perceives these relations of identity and diversity at first sight, and any seeming disputes on this score will turn out on inspection to be purely verbal, that is, disputes about words and not about the ideas themselves.

(2) The mind can compare and contrast its ideas in a wide variety of ways, generating a vast category of perceptions of these relations. Such judgements of relation may be applied to ideas of substances, simple modes, mixed modes and, of course, relations themselves. (I might judge that a sibling is a closer relation than a first cousin, for example – this is a relational judgement about relations.) This second category of agreements and disagreements between our ideas looks vast and extremely heterogeneous, but Locke is content to leave the topic without going into greater depth or detail. Judgements of this kind will of course come up for discussion at numerous points scattered through the *Essay*.

(3) Judgements of '*co-existence* or *non-co-existence*' belong particularly, Locke continues, to our ideas of substances. When I judge that dogs bark and cats miaow, or that swallows fly but pigs don't, I am making judgements of this kind. Indeed, our substance-terms can be thought of in terms of complexes of ideas that are always found together in experience:

> Thus when we pronounce, concerning *Gold*, that it is fixed, our Knowledge of this Truth amounts to no more but this, that fixedness, or a power to remain in the Fire unconsumed, is an *Idea* that always accompanies, and is joined with that particular sort of Yellowness, Weight, Fusibility, Malleableness, and Solubility in *aqua regia*, which make our complex *Idea* signified by the word *Gold*. (EHU IV, i, 6, N 527)

Experience testifies to the existence in nature of a reliably correlated cluster of properties: yellow colour, metallic lustre, specific gravity 19.3 (in modern terms), malleability, fusibility, and solubility in *aqua regia* (a mixture of nitric and hydrochloric acids). On the basis of this experience, we form the complex idea *gold* to stand for anything with these properties. Experience then informs us of the co-existence of fixity with the list of properties that we have put together to form the complex idea of gold. We can now choose either to incorporate fixity into the complex idea itself, or simply to note the co-existence as a well-confirmed fact of experience.

Locke says nothing here to explain why, when he introduces this third category of agreements and disagreements between ideas, he called them judgements of 'necessary connection' as well as merely of 'co-existence'. If gold is a well-established natural kind, we may be confident that the property of fixity will *always* co-occur with the others, but why should anyone think that this is a *necessary* connection? If there is a necessary connection at all in such a case, it does not lie in the ideas themselves: a metal that is yellow and shiny, with a specific gravity of 19.3, that is malleable and fusible and soluble in *aqua regia* but that dissipates like smoke in the fire, does not seem to be ruled out by any inspection of our ideas. If for some reason such a metal is impossible, that impossibility must be located not in our ideas but in the natures of things themselves, perhaps in some fine details of corpuscular microstructure. As we shall see in the next chapter, Locke believes that such judgements of necessary connection may well be true, but are not and almost certainly could never be *known* to be true by humans. We might judge – and judge truly – that property P1 is necessarily connected with property P2, but could never know that this was the case from inspection of the corresponding ideas in our minds.

(4) The fourth category, judgements of 'actual real existence agreeing to any idea', seems, at least at first sight, to fly in the face of Locke's official definition of knowledge as involving always a relation between ideas. Here, most critics contemporary and modern agree, Locke cannot seriously defend his official definition, but must admit a category of knowledge that involves a relation not between two ideas but between an idea and (the actual existence of) a thing. The best defence of Locke's consistency is provided by Lex Newman,[3] who points out that Locke himself is clear, in his reply to Bishop Stillingfleet on just this question, that he intends this type of knowledge to fall under the general definition. In reply to the bishop, he insists that it is the idea of actual existence that supplies the 'agreeing' second idea when I judge that some external object such as an oak tree exists:

> Now the two ideas, that in this case are perceived to agree, and do thereby produce knowledge, are the idea of actual sensation ... and the idea of actual existence of something without me that causes that sensation. (WJL IV, 360)

Knowledge of actual existence can thus be brought under the general definition, but the consistency is bought at a high cost. Every fanatic judges that things really are as their fantasies represent them, so this 'agreement' between the idea of X (e.g., that of a ghost or of a purple cow) and that of actual existence looks all too easy. Will it not follow, the critic can insist, that every religious fanatic, madman or drug-smoking visionary will possess knowledge of real existence, by Locke's account? Fortunately, Locke will address just this objection in chapter 4, where he turns his attention to what he calls 'the reality of our knowledge'. A clear advantage of Newman's reading is that it thus renders Locke consistent in chapter 1, and defers the discussion of the objection that the ideal theory is merely 'visionary' until chapter 4, where the charge is explicitly faced.

2. Intuitive, Demonstrative and Sensitive Knowledge

Chapter 2 of Book Four is entitled 'Of the Degrees of our Knowledge'. Here Locke introduces three types or species of knowledge, and ranks them according to their respective degrees of certainty. There are, he explains, different ways in which the agreement or disagreement between any two ideas may be perceived. If we reflect, he says,

> we shall find that sometimes the Mind perceives the Agreement or Disagreement of two *Ideas* immediately by themselves, without the intervention of any other: And this, I think, we may call *intuitive Knowledge*. For in this, the Mind is at no pains of proving or examining, but perceives the Truth, as the Eye does light, only by being directed toward it. Thus the Mind perceives that *White* is not *Black*, that a *Circle* is not a *Triangle*, that *Three* are more than *Two* and equal to *One* and *Two*. Such kind of Truths the Mind perceives at the first sight of the *Ideas* together, by bare *Intuition*, without the intervention of any other *Idea*; and this kind of Knowledge is the clearest, and most certain, that humane Frailty is capable of. (EHU IV, ii, 1, N 530–1)

Intuitive knowledge, we are told, is both the clearest and most certain in its own right, and the foundation of all other knowledge. When a given idea is present to my mind, I cannot doubt that it is what it is, and is distinct from every other idea. Here no sceptical doubts can obtain a grip, and we have a certainty as firm as our condition allows.

The problem, of course, is that there are agreements and disagreements between ideas that are not immediately evident. An agreement or disagreement may be discoverable but not yet discovered. In such cases, says Locke, we seek appropriate intermediate or linking ideas. If intuition reveals that A = B and B = C, I can safely conclude that A = C, and regard this as an established item of demonstrative knowledge. This, says Locke, is what we mean by *reasoning*, and it is of course the heart of the mathematical sciences. If I can't just 'see' (i.e., intuit) that the angles of a triangle add to two right angles, I must search for some other angles to which I can compare them. In the famous Euclidean proof, these are of course the angles of a straight line, which we already know to be equal to two right angles.

Demonstrative knowledge can attain a high degree of certainty, but its certainty can never exceed, but must always fall more or less short of, that of intuition. This is for two straightforward reasons. In the first place, demonstration rests on intuition: without the two intuitions that A = B and B = C, the demonstration that A = C would be worthless. Each step of the proof must be intuited before the proof can be grasped and accepted as such. In addition, the sequential or step-wise nature of demonstration requires the involvement of the notoriously fallible faculty of memory. If I need to remember the output of step 6 of my proof before proceeding to step 7, and so on for a long and complex sequence of operations, it is no wonder that errors can creep in and doubts can reasonably be raised. A man who doubted that three is more than two, and equal to two plus one, would be dismissed as a madman; a man who wonders whether a given theorem in Newton's *Principia* has been validly demonstrated may be raising a serious objection.

Is the distinction between intuitive and demonstrative knowledge in the *Essay* meant to be an absolute one, or might Locke be happy to grant a degree of subject-relativity? Might a given proposition be intuitive for one mind and only demonstrative for another? There are reasons for thinking that Locke might have been happy to grant at least a measure of subject-relativity here. In Descartes' *Rules for the Direction of the Mind*, on which this part of Book Four of the *Essay* appears to be modelled,[4] the problems inherent in a sequential method are addressed in Rule Seven. If I want to know the relative magnitudes of A and E, says Descartes, on the basis of knowledge of the relations between A and B, B and C, C and D, and D and E, then I need to recall all these relations simultaneously to be confident of my result:

> So I shall run through them several times in a continuous movement of the imagination, simultaneously intuiting one relation and passing on to the next, until I have learnt to pass from the first to the last so swiftly that memory is left with practically no role to play, and I seem to intuit the whole thing at once. In this way our memory is relieved, the sluggishness of our intelligence redressed, and its capacity in some way enlarged.[5]

Descartes doesn't quite say that the role of memory here is altogether eliminated, and that the whole proof is grasped by the mind as a single Gestalt, but this is certainly the phenomenological 'feel' reported by many mathematicians. If this is right, then a proposition that is demonstrative for a mathematical apprentice might be intuitive for the master – the intermediate ideas might serve as a sort of dispensable scaffolding, enabling the connection between A and E to be perceived for the first few times, after which the connection is seen as intuitive. I see no strong reason why Locke should resist at least a modicum of subject-relativity in this area. A mathematical savant may just 'see' that a given number is prime, although others need to prove this by the long and plodding road of elimination.

It is generally assumed, Locke notes, that only the mathematical sciences are capable of demonstrative certainty, but this is over-hasty:

> to have such an agreement or disagreement as may intuitively be perceived, being, as I imagine, not the privilege of the *Ideas* of *Number*, *Extension*, and *Figure* alone, it may possibly be the want of due method, and application in us; and not of sufficient evidence in things, that Demonstration has been thought to have so little to do in other parts of Knowledge, and been scarce so much as aim'd at by any but Mathematicians. (EHU IV, ii, 9, N 534)

With the aid of a few clear definitions (EHU IV, iii, 20, N 552), Locke will later go on to claim, morality might be as capable of demonstration as mathematics (EHU IV, iv, 7, N 565). All we would need is to make sure that we set up our key moral terms to stand for clear and distinct ideas, and use them consistently in accordance with their specified definitions, and morality might become a demonstrative science. This is a claim to which we will need to return in chapter 7.

In addition to intuition and demonstration, Locke is prepared to concede the existence of a third kind of knowledge:

> There is, indeed, another *Perception* of the Mind, employ'd about *the particular existence of finite Beings* without us; which going beyond bare probability and yet not reaching perfectly to either of the forgoing degrees of certainty, passes under the name of Knowledge. (EHU IV, ii, 14, N 537)

The mere presence before my mind of an idea (image or sensation) of an external object is for Locke a straightforward case of intuitive knowledge, and as such immune from sceptical doubt.

> But whether there be anything more than barely that *Idea* in our Minds, whether we can thence certainly inferr the existence of anything without us, which corresponds to that *Idea*, is that, whereof some Men think there may be a question made: because men may have such *Ideas* in their Minds, when no such Thing exists, no such Object affects their Senses. (EHU IV, ii, 14, N 537)

Locke's first answer to this doubt is to appeal to the obvious and introspectible difference between actually seeing the Sun in the daytime and merely thinking about it at night, that is, to the distinction that Hume would later mark by distinguishing ideas (= concepts) from impressions (= sensations). To this, the obvious sceptical retort is to refer to dream images, which strike the mind with the force of impressions, but have no external object. Maybe, urges the sceptic, all our experiences of the so-called 'external world' are mere dream-images with no corresponding external reality. If, Locke replies, the sceptic maintains that what I call actually being in the fire is itself nothing but a dream, and that we can never know that such a thing as fire exists,

> I answer, That we certainly finding, that Pleasure or Pain follows upon the application of certain Objects to us, whose Existence we perceive, or dream that we perceive, by our Senses, this certainty is as great as our Happiness, or Misery, beyond which we have no concernment to know, or to be. So that, I think, we may add to the former two sorts of *Knowledge*, this also, of the existence of particular external Objects, by that perception and Consciousness we have of the actual entrance of *Ideas* from them, and allow these *three degrees*

of Knowledge, viz. *Intuitive, Demonstrative, and Sensitive*: in each of which, there are different degrees and ways of Evidence and Certainty. (EHU IV, ii, 14, N 537–8)

Probably aware of the inadequacy of this rather casual and dismissive response to the sceptic, Locke returns to this topic in his discussion of 'The Reality of our Knowledge', in chapter 4. Here he explicitly addresses the objection that his account of knowledge is merely visionary:

> If it be true, that all Knowledge lies only in the perception of the agreement and disagreement of our own *Ideas*, the Visions of an Enthusiast, and the Reasonings of a sober Man, will be equally certain. It is no matter how Things are: so a Man observe but the agreement of his own Imaginations and talk conformably, it is all Truth, all Certainty. Such Castles in the Air, will be as strong Holds of Truth, as the demonstrations of *Euclid*. That a Harpy is not a Centaur, is by this way as certain knowledge, and as much a Truth, as that a Square is not a Circle. (EHU IV, iv, 1, N 563)

If it is indeed the case, Locke replies, that our knowledge of ideas terminates in them and reaches no further, even in cases where 'there is something further intended', this objection will stand. The objection is a powerful one, and directed right at the heart of the theory of ideas:

> 'Tis evident, the Mind knows not Things immediately, but only by the intervention of the *Ideas* it has of them. *Our Knowledge*, therefore, is *real* only so far as there is a conformity between our *Ideas* and the reality of Things. But what shall be here the Criterion? How shall the Mind, when it perceives nothing but its own *Ideas*, know that they agree with Things themselves? (EHU IV, iv, 3, N 563)

This question, Locke continues, can be raised (a) for simple ideas, (b) for complex ideas of modes (e.g., mathematical and moral ideas) and (c) for complex ideas of substances. He proceeds to discuss each case in turn. In its reception of simple ideas (case a), the mind is merely passive: these ideas are

> the product of Things operating on the Mind in a natural way, and producing therein those Perceptions which by the Wisdom and Will of our Maker they are ordained and adapted to. From whence it follows that *simple* Ideas *are not fictions of our Fancies*, but the natural

and regular productions of Things without us, really operating upon us; and so carry with them all the conformity which is intended, or which our state requires: For they represent to us Things under those appearances which they are fitted to produce in us: whereby we are enabled to distinguish the sorts of particular Substances, to discern the states they are in, and so to take them for our Necessities and apply them to our Uses. Thus the *Idea* of Whiteness or Bitterness, as it is in the Mind, exactly answering that Power which is in any Body to produce it there, has all the real conformity it can, or ought to have, with things without us. And this conformity between our simple *Ideas*, and the existence of Things, is sufficient for real Knowledge. (EHU IV, iv, 4, N 563–4)

My idea (sensation) of yellow, Locke thinks, is the natural sign of a real yellow-making power in the external world, so when my senses give me the idea (sensation) of yellow, I can be rightly confident that there is something other than myself that has the power to produce this idea in my mind. Two obvious worries arise at this point. Locke speaks confidently of a *body* having the power in question, but this might seem question-begging. When a philosopher seeks to prove the existence of an external world, he might mean the common-sense world of bodies located in space, or he might mean something much weaker – just a realm of powers existing and operating independently of my will. It looks as if Locke's argument here gives him only the weaker conclusion, but in confidently talking of a *body* with the power to produce the ideas of whiteness and bitterness, he is assuming the stronger claim. One of Locke's most trenchant critics, the idealist Bishop Berkeley, would argue that only the will of a spirit can be a true cause, so the power to produce the sensation of yellow in a finite mind like mine must ultimately be located in the will of God. The other worry concerns the relation between the sign and what it signifies. It would be natural to assume that the relation is *one to one*, that is, that the yellow sensation serves reliably as an indication of a single property common to all yellow things. But perhaps the relation is *one to many*, and the things we call yellow form a diverse and heterogeneous group? Locke's allusion to 'the wisdom and will of our Maker' seems designed to address this worry and provide some reason for trusting that this is not the case. God's wisdom ensures that our simple ideas are well suited to our practical needs. We sort apples into red and green, and then find that the red ones are sweeter, a reliable correlation that we can all use in judging which apples to pick and eat, and that horticulturalists can use in deciding which types of apple to cultivate. We need to trust that God has not created us and set us in a world in which our simple ideas have no reliable correlations with the underlying natures of things.[6]

For complex ideas other than those of substances (case b), the problem of their 'fit' with reality simply does not arise:

> *All our complex* Ideas, *except those of Substances,* being *Archetypes* of the Mind's own making, not intended to be the Copies of any thing, nor referred to the existence of any thing, as to their Originals, *cannot want any conformity necessary to real Knowledge.* For that which is not designed to represent any thing but itself can never be capable of a wrong representation, nor mislead us from the true apprehension of any thing, by its dislikeness to it: and such, excepting those of Substances, are all our complex *Ideas.* (EHU IV, iv, 5, N 564)

Since our complex ideas of modes are products of the mind's own making, and are not intended to be copies of any mind-independent reality, the question of their correspondence or 'fit' with nature simply does not arise. What matters here are the twin virtues of clarity and consistency: we should use our terms in such a way that it is always evident whether a given idea is part of a certain complex idea or not, and we should take care to respect accepted usage. In mathematics and morality, we define our own terms, and demonstrative knowledge is possible when we reason carefully in accordance with the specified definitions.

As for our complex ideas of substances (case c), the possibility of a mismatch between ideas and reality must be taken seriously. Our ideas of substances consist of collections of simple ideas, but here the collection is supposed to be taken from the works of nature, so their composition

> may yet vary from them, by having more or different *Ideas* united in them, than are to be found united in the things themselves: From whence it comes to pass, that they may, and often do fail of being exactly conformable to Things themselves. (EHU IV, iv, 11, N 568)

In the case of our complex ideas of modes, Locke explains, the only criterion that counts is that of consistency, so we are at liberty to combine ideas as we please, so long as we do so without making any assumptions regarding whether or not the complex ideas thus framed have any grounding in reality. Our complex ideas of substances, however, are referred to 'archetypes without us', and afford us real knowledge only if they combine simple ideas that are actually found together in nature. Gold and crocodiles have real existence; the Philosophers' Stone and dragons are mere creatures of fiction. For a real substance such as gold, the powers to produce those simpler ideas that constitute its complex idea must regularly and reliably be found together in nature:

> Herein therefore is founded the *reality* of our Knowledge concerning *Substances*: that all our complex *Ideas* of them must be such, and such only, as are made up of such simple ones, as have been discovered to co-exist in Nature. And our *Ideas* being thus true, though not, perhaps, very exact Copies, are yet the Subjects of *real* (as far as we have any) *Knowledge* of them. Which (as has been already shewed) will not be found to reach very far: But so far as it does, it will still be *real Knowledge*. Whatever *Ideas* we have, the Agreement we find they have with others, will still be knowledge. (EHU IV, iv, 12, N 568–9)

The agreement Locke has in mind here is clearly that of co-existence. Let us suppose that 'gold' is a well-established natural kind term, based on thousands of years of human experience with the metal. Common usage of this term rests on *real knowledge* of the co-existence in nature of the set of properties we listed in the previous section. Even if we remain entirely ignorant of the 'real constitution' on which these manifest properties depend, and which 'really is the cause of the strict union of some of them with one another and the exclusion of others', we can still be justifiably confident, when we find a metal that is yellow, dense, shiny, malleable, fusible and soluble in *aqua regia*, that it will remain fixed in the fire. Locke thus fails to address the modern problem of scepticism about induction in its extreme or 'Humean' form.[7] If pressed on this difficulty, and asked whether we have any reason to assume that patterns of co-existence observed in the past will continue to hold in the future, he might have referred either to science or to theology, or more probably to some mixture of the two. The best scientists of the day, men like Boyle and Newton, held a 'corpuscular' theory of matter, according to which there will be a particular and stable arrangement of corpuscles which explains the co-occurrence of the manifest properties and guarantees – so long as the laws of nature remain fixed – that this co-occurrence will continue. As for our trust in the fixity of the laws of nature, this might be presented either as a precondition for scientific enquiry into nature, or as a rational faith in the ultimate trustworthiness of our Creator. Locke might well have endorsed the famous dictum of Albert Einstein, to the effect that 'the Lord is subtle but not malicious'. A God who created us in such a way that we naturally reason inductively from well-established generalizations of co-occurrence, but then created the universe in such a way that the laws changed inexplicably from time to time, would be truly malicious.

3. Human Knowledge and Ignorance

Chapter 3 of Book Four discusses the extent of human knowledge, marking the crucial distinction between those things we do know, those we can reasonably hope to come to know and those that must forever remain matters of faith or probability. Locke is clear that our knowledge, even of actual existence, is perfectly real:

> we have an intuitive Knowledge of our own *Existence*; a demonstrative Knowledge of the *Existence* of a God; of the *Existence* of any thing else, we have no other but a sensitive Knowledge, which extends not beyond the Objects present to our Senses. (EHU IV, iii, 21, N 552–3)

For the intuitive knowledge of our own existence, Locke doesn't refer us to the famous *cogito* argument of Descartes' *Second Meditation*, but his readers will inevitably have found themselves thinking of the meditator's discovery that the proposition 'I exist' is immune to all conceivable sceptical doubts – it can't even be entertained without being believed, while its negation 'I don't exist' is manifestly self-defeating. Here, Locke might say, the 'agreement' between the two ideas, that of *self* and that of *actual existence*, is perfectly intuitive. (How much self-knowledge is provided by the *cogito* argument is, of course, a distinct and much harder problem.) As for demonstrative knowledge of the existence of God, Locke will set out his own version of the cosmological argument in his chapter 10, a topic to which we shall return in our chapter 5. As for our knowledge of the external world provided by sensation, it extends only to the real existence of the powers needed to produce our sensory ideas, and of course to patterns of co-existence discoverable between those powers. Simple idea F is the natural sign of an F-making power; regular connection in sensory experience of simple ideas F and G indicates a reliable co-existence of the F-making power and the G-making power in Nature. We know many such reliable patterns of co-existence, and in the progress of natural knowledge can reasonably hope to discover many more.

It remains the case, however, that our knowledge is very limited. It follows from his definition of knowledge, Locke explains, that our knowledge can extend no further than our ideas. In fact it is much narrower than this. Intuition cannot reveal all the relations between the ideas that we possess. Having the ideas of a square and a circle, I can discern by intuition that a circle is not a square, but may never discern how to construct a square of the same area as a given circle. Intuition does not reveal this relation, and geometers have striven in vain to find the intermediate ideas that would make it a matter of demonstration. In the realm of mathematics, there are doubtless whole domains of demonstrable knowledge that are not yet demonstrated. As for sensitive knowledge, it reaches no further, says Locke, than 'the Existence of Things actually present to our Senses', and is thus narrower still in its scope (EHU IV, iii, 5, N 539). If he allows knowledge of regular co-existence, as he does, he will also have to admit memory here: clearly, I cannot know that the F-making power and the G-making power are reliably correlated in nature unless I trust at least my own memory. In most real cases, of course, I will also rely for this information on the testimony of others, which would not count as knowledge but only as probability in Locke's terms.

The extent of our knowledge, Locke warns, is as nothing compared to that of our ignorance. It will be useful to us, he says, to 'look a little into the dark side, and take a view of *our Ignorance*', which is 'infinitely larger than our Knowledge' (EHU IV, iii, 22, N 553). If we seek to understand the causes of our ignorance, we shall find that they reduce to the following three heads:

> First, Want of *Ideas*.
> *Secondly*, Want of a discoverable Connexion between the *Ideas* we have.
> *Thirdly*, Want of tracing, and examining our *Ideas*. (EHU IV, iii, 22, N 553)

We may lack simple ideas because we lack senses that other species of intelligent beings possess – there is not the slightest reason to suppose that there may not be beings with senses either of the same kind as ours but more perfect, or of a completely different kind altogether:

> But to say, or think that there are no such, because we conceive nothing of them, is no better an argument, than if a blind Man should be positive in it, that there was no such thing as Sight and Colours, because he had no manner of *Idea*, of any such thing nor could by

any means frame to himself any Notions about Seeing. (EHU IV, iii, 23, N 554)

Even in cases where we can have ideas, we may not have the precise and fully determinate ideas that we might hope for. We understand size, shape and motion tolerably well from our experience of the middle-sized bodies around us, so we at least understand what 'corpuscularian' natural philosophers like Robert Boyle are claiming when they say that the observable properties of bodies such as colour depend on the surface arrangements and motions of their invisibly small parts. But although this account is intelligible in principle, the details continue to elude us:

> *Bulk, Figure,* and *Motion* we have *Ideas* of. But though we are not without *Ideas* of these primary qualities of Bodies in general, yet not knowing what is the particular *Bulk, Figure,* and *Motion* of the greatest part of the Bodies of the Universe, we are ignorant of the several Powers, Efficacies, and Ways of Operation, whereby the Effects which we daily see, are produced. (EHU IV, iii, 24, N 555)

If our knowledge of bodies is thus limited, our knowledge of spirits is even more deficient. There may be, and probably are, Locke thinks, untold numbers of spiritual beings of various kinds,

> which are yet more remote from our Knowledge, whereof we have no cognizance, nor can frame to ourselves any distinct *Ideas* of their several ranks and sorts, we shall find this cause of Ignorance conceal from us, in an impenetrable obscurity, almost the whole intellectual World, a greater certainly, and more beautiful World, than the material. (EHU IV, iii, 27, N 557)

We know our own thoughts and feelings by the direct route of introspection; we can confidently infer similar thoughts and feelings in our fellow humans from 'their words and actions', and we can – Locke thinks – demonstrate the existence of a supreme thinking being, that is, God.

> But that there are degrees of Spiritual Beings between us and the great GOD, who is there that by his own speech and ability can come to know? Much less have we distinct *Ideas* of their different Natures, Conditions, States, Powers, and several Constitutions, wherein they agree or differ from one another, and from us. And therefore in what concerns their different Species and Properties, we are under an absolute ignorance. (EHU IV, iii, 27, N 558)

Even in those cases where we do possess ideas, we may not be able to discern any connection between those ideas. The new 'corpuscular' philosophers tell us that sensations such as colour, taste and smell are produced by the impact of insensibly small corpuscles on our sense organs. But we have not even a glimmering of an understanding of why one stream of corpuscles (or one type of agitation of the medium) should produce the sensation of *red* while another produces *blue*:

> These mechanical Affections of Bodies having no affinity at all with those *Ideas* they produce in us (there being no conceivable connexion between any impulse of any sort of Body, and any perception of a Colour, or Smell, which we find in our Minds), we can have no distinct knowledge of such Operations beyond our Experience and can reason no otherwise about them, than as effects produced by the appointment of an infinitely Wise Agent, which perfectly surpass our Comprehensions. (EHU IV, iii, 28, N 558–9)

Locke takes care to distinguish here between two distinct orders of ignorance. Even the greatest scientists of his age, men such as Boyle and Newton, would confess that they were largely ignorant of the detailed workings of nature such as the physics of light and colour. But this type of ignorance is in principle *curable*, and has of course been greatly reduced with later advances in physical science. By sharp contrast, there is the *incurable* ignorance of the mind–body union. We know that physical disturbances in our sense organs produce sensations in our minds, and that volitions in our minds produce motions of our limbs, but we have no conception of how this can be. Experience informs us that mind and body interact in certain regular ways, but this connection is 'not discoverable in the ideas themselves', which 'have no necessary dependence one on another'. If we shift from the seventeenth century to the twenty-first, and update the physics of light and colour, this problem remains unsolved. In Isaac Newton's famous prism experiment, he divides white light into the spectral colours. Physics teaches us that the light from one end of the spectrum, light of wavelength 7,000Å, tends to give us the sensation we call *red*, while light from the other end of the spectrum, light of wavelength 5,000Å, tends to give us that of *blue*, but the connection between a particular wavelength and the subjective feel or *quale* of redness is as obscure to us as it was to Locke. Modern philosophers of mind, following David Chalmers, call this the 'hard problem' of consciousness, and Locke's claim that it is in principle insoluble has not yet been refuted.[8]

A third source of ignorance is our failure to trace connections between ideas that are in principle perfectly discoverable. This ignorance is generally due to our 'want of finding out those intermediate *Ideas* which may show us what habitude of agreement or disagreement they have one with another' (EHU IV, iii, 30, N 560–1). Many people remain ignorant of mathematics simply for 'want of application' in comparing their ideas, and of course the extent of mathematical knowledge itself is continually expanding as ever more complex and remote relations of agreement and disagreement between our ideas of numbers and geometrical figures are discovered. But arithmetic and geometry are not the only disciplines in which demonstrative knowledge could be extended by proper intellectual discipline. Other subjects such as ethics might become capable of comparable rigour if men could just agree on clear definitions of the key terms, and then reason in strict accordance with these established definitions.

The overall upshot of chapter 3 is thus a picture of human knowledge as positively minute in extent compared to human ignorance. We may hope to extend our knowledge of patterns of co-existence in nature by the empirical methods of the natural sciences, but this will provide no deep insights into the reasons *why* these regularities hold. The corpuscularians tell us that such explanations can in principle be provided in terms of the arrangements and motions of the microscopic parts of bodies, but they provide us with no detailed knowledge of such microscopic mechanisms. And even if we somehow came to know such details about the sizes, shapes and motions of the invisibly small parts of bodies, we would gain no insight at all into the deep mystery of the mind–body problem. The intrinsic nature of a mind, and its relation to its associated body, remain utterly obscure to us, at least while we are in our present state.

4. Knowledge, Probability and Faith

Chapter 15 of Book Four discusses the nature of probability, while chapter 16 goes on to the important topic of the 'Degrees of Assent'. In the absence of knowledge, we will generally need to accept and act on propositions in which the 'agreement' or 'disagreement' of the ideas is not established by intuition, demonstration or sensation. Most of the propositions we accept and act upon will be such that 'we cannot have undoubted knowledge of their truth', but we can and should regulate our degrees of assent in accordance with the weight and strength of the evidence.[9] In a judgement of probability, Locke explains, we give our assent to some proposition on the basis of considerations that lend it more or less support, but fail to establish the connection between ideas needed for knowledge:

> And herein lies the *difference between Probability* and *Certainty, Faith* and *Knowledge*, that in all the parts of Knowledge, there is intuition; each intermediate *Idea*, each step has its visible and certain connexion; in belief not so. That which makes me believe, is something extraneous to the thing I believe; something not evidently joined on both sides to, and so not manifestly shewing the Agreement, or Disagreement of those *Ideas* that are under consideration. (EHU IV, xv, 3, N 655)

The grounds for such judgements of probability may, Locke explains, be found either in conformity to my own observation and experience, or in the testimony of others. Under the former heading, Locke will presumably include all those generalizations from experience that Aristotle had called 'for the most part' judgements. Locke has already claimed that we have *knowledge* of at least some cases of co-existence, so he might be prepared to assert that we *know* that common salt will dissolve in water, or that a strong dose of opium will put a man to sleep. He doesn't tell us how many cases we need to have observed, and how much variety we should seek to include, before knowledge can reasonably be claimed in such cases. On such matters, he will no doubt defer to the Baconian precepts of the *Novum Organum* and his friends in the fledgling Royal Society. His point is that for every case in which I can confidently affirm that 'All Fs are Gs', there will be a multitude of cases in which experience tells me only that 'Most Fs are Gs', or (even weaker), 'Most observed Fs have been Gs'. (Perhaps I have been observing an unrepresentative sample of Fs.) As a prescribing physician himself, Locke would rarely have been in a position to tell his patient 'this drug will relieve your symptoms'; the best he could claim would generally have been 'this drug has often been effective in similar cases'. Here the link between the idea of a given herb and that of a certain medicinal power is provided by experience not of uniform and universal co-existence (which would establish knowledge) but only of a 'for the most part' generalization. Large parts of our everyday lives, and of professions such as medicine and horticulture, will be based on such judgements.

Under the second heading, reliance on testimony, we must place most of our beliefs about history, geography, human affairs and, of course (for non-experts), even mathematics and the natural sciences. If a mathematician friend tells me that theorem T has just been proved, but doesn't give me the demonstration, I cannot, on Locke's account, come to know that T is true merely on the basis of this testimony. However expert my friend, and however trustworthy as a guide to his own subject, he sees the connection between the ideas and I do not. If a scientist friend (Newton, in Locke's case) tells me that experiments have established that white light is composed of all the spectral colours, I cannot come to know this merely on the basis of his testimony. For Locke, testimony can be and often is the ground of firm assurance, but cannot be a source of knowledge.[10] When we consider whether we ought to give our assent to some piece of human testimony, we ask the usual questions – familiar to lawyers and historians – about the trustworthiness of the witnesses. How many witnesses? Of what character? Are the witnesses consistent with one another? Do they have anything to gain from our credulity? Often, of course, and particularly in our assessment of claims about miracles and prodigies, we will have to balance considerations of this kind against considerations of the former kind, that is, conformity with the course of our own experience. To illustrate this point, Locke draws once again on his familiarity with the travel literature:

> And as it happened to a *Dutch* Ambassador, who entertaining the King of *Siam* with the particularities of *Holland*, which he was inquisitive after, amongst other things told him, that the Water in his Country would sometimes, in cold weather, be so hard, that Men walked upon it, and that it would bear an Elephant, if he were there. To which the King replied, *Hitherto I have believed the strange things you have told me, because I look upon you as a sober fair man, but now I am sure you lye.* (EHU IV, xv, 5, N 656–7)

Those of us who live in cold climates know that the King of Thailand was in error in this judgement, but was he being *irrational* in trusting what was, for him, the fixed and universal course of his experience (water never turns solid) rather than the testimony of an unknown stranger from distant lands? Short of an actual visit to Holland in winter, it is hard to see what might persuade the King. Of course, the next visitor from Northern lands might repeat the same story, which would mean that the Dutch ambassador could no longer be dismissed as a solitary liar or dreamer. At some point, the King may find himself thinking 'these Europeans surely can't *all* be liars or fantasists?' Alternatively, the Europeans might try to persuade the King by deploying an argument from analogy: just as oil congeals into fat, or molten metal sets in a mould as the temperature falls, so too fluid water solidifies into ice. This would bring the claim under a broader generalization, not about water as such but about the states of matter, and the observed role of heat and cold in bringing about changes of state. Considerations of this kind might weaken the King's conviction that the Europeans are all liars.

One common ground of judgements of probability that Locke is prepared to reject as irrational is mere conformity, that is, the tendency to pin our faith on the mere opinions of others rather than on their actual experience. This, he insists, is 'no true ground of probability', since human opinions are everywhere largely erroneous:

> And if the Opinions and Perswasions of others, whom we know and think well of, be a ground of Assent, Men have Reason to be Heathens in *Japan*, Mahometans in *Turkey*, Papists in *Spain*, Protestants in *England*, and Lutherans in *Sweden*. But of this wrong ground of Assent, I shall have occasion to speak more at large in another place. (EHU IV, xv, 6, N 657)

There may, of course, be all manner of prudential reasons for conformity, but there can be no good inference from 'Most of the people around me think that p' to 'I have a good reason to think that p', or to 'p is probably true'. Unless I know *why* they believe that p, their mere believing it is no reason for me to do so. History teaches us that errors of many kinds have been widely believed; what should count with me is the evidence, not the mere prevalence of the belief. The point is still more marked when we consider religious belief. If Fred goes to church on Sunday in England and Mustafa goes to the mosque on Friday in Turkey because this is simply local custom, their beliefs are equally groundless. If Christianity is true and Islam false (or vice versa), it is hard to see that Fred deserves reward and Mustafa punishment (or vice versa) for what seems simply a matter of geographical luck. A just God, the deists of Locke's day argued, could not dispense rewards and punishments on such arbitrary grounds.[11]

Chapter 16, on 'The Degrees of Assent', discusses how we do and how we ought to regulate our degrees of belief in those many cases in which knowledge is lacking but the affairs of life require action.

We frequently act, Locke admits, on the basis of already formed opinions, without feeling it forever necessary to revisit their grounds. This is in practice unavoidable, although it may of course be the occasion for 'great obstinacy in Errour and Mistake' (EHU IV, xvi, 3, N 658–9). The fault in such cases, Locke argues, lies in the original over-hasty judgement, not in sticking with a judgement already formed and lodged in the memory. If we were all more reluctant to leap to hasty conclusions, and more charitable towards what we take to be the errors of our fellow men, the world would be a better place:

> It would, methinks, become all Men to maintain *Peace*, and the common Offices of Humanity, *and Friendship, in the diversity of Opinions*, since we cannot reasonably expect, that any one should readily and obsequiously quit his own Opinion, and embrace ours with a blind resignation to an Authority which the Understanding of Man acknowledges not. (EHU IV, xvi, 4, N 659–60)

If you wish to change a man's mind, you must provide him with the evidence that – in your opinion, of course – refutes his view and confirms yours, and then leave him time and leisure to reflect and re-examine his position. But of course it is highly probable that each of us is guilty of the same prejudice and obstinacy that we condemn in others:

> For where is the Man, that has incontestable Evidence of the Truth of all that he holds, or of the Falsehood of all he condemns; or can say, that he has examined, to the bottom, all his own or other Men's Opinions? The necessity of believing, without Knowledge, nay, often upon very slight grounds, in this fleeting state of Action and Blindness we are in, should make us more busy and careful to inform our selves than constrain others. (EHU IV, xvi, 4, N 660)

After running through the degrees of assent we should give to different types of human testimony, Locke turns at the close of the chapter to a very different type of assent. There is a class of propositions, he informs us, that

> challenge the highest Degree of our Assent, upon bare Testimony, whether the thing proposed, agree or disagree with common Experience, and the ordinary course of Things, or no. The Reason whereof is, because the Testimony is of such an one, as cannot deceive, nor be deceived, and that is of God himself. This carries with it Assurance

beyond Doubt, Evidence beyond Exception. This is called by a pecu-
liar name, *Revelation*, and our Assent to it, *Faith*: which as absolutely
determines our Minds, and as perfectly excludes all wavering as our
Knowledge it self; and we may as well doubt of our own Being, as
we can, whether any Revelation from GOD be true. (EHU IV, xvi, 14,
N 667)

Granting for the moment the key presupposition that God can
neither deceive nor be deceived, we can confidently infer 'p is true'
from 'God has informed us through revelation that p'. The problem,
of course, lies in establishing the premise for this inference. There
are many competing claims to revealed knowledge, and some of
those claims are – to put it mildly – expressed in language that is
less than perfectly transparent. Just think of the Book of Revelations
from the Bible! So even if we grant that whatever God has revealed
to us must be true, and may properly be a ground for our firm
assent, two key difficulties remain:

> Only we must be sure, that it be a divine Revelation, and that we
> understand it right: else we shall expose our selves to all the Extrava-
> gancy of Enthusiasm and all the Error of wrong Principles, if we have
> faith and assurance in what is not divine Revelation. And therefore
> in those cases, our Assent can rationally be no higher than the Evi-
> dence of its being a Revelation, and that this is the meaning of the
> Expressions it is delivered in. (EHU IV, xvi, 14, N 667)

The customary opposition between faith on the one side, and
reason on the other, involves for Locke a serious misunderstanding
of their respective spheres and competences. If we are to give reasonable assent to the claim that a body of documents such as the
Christian Bible constitutes a divine revelation, we need evidence
(traditionally in the form of miracles and prophecies) that this is the
case. This evidence needs to pass the test of rational scrutiny. And
then, of course, we need the endless labour of the philologists if we
are to have a shred of confidence that we have correctly discerned
the original meanings of the sacred texts. Far from being separate
from reason, Locke concludes, it is in truth 'nothing else but an
Assent founded on the highest Reason' (EHU IV, xvi, 14, N 668).
But this is a topic to which we must return in chapter 5.

4

The Material World

1. Locke's Common-sense Realism

Locke has often been described as a philosopher of common sense. In many contexts, this description is seriously misleading, as Locke's views were often extremely radical and remote from ordinary opinions. When it comes to his defence of common-sense realism about the world of bodies, however, the description seems to be an apt one. We have already noticed the difficulty. Locke's account of our reception of the simple ideas of sensation as passive, and as indicating the existence of corresponding active powers in things, provides him with grounds for his claim that we possess *sensitive knowledge* of the external world. But to move from 'external' in the sense of *something* that operates independently of my will to 'external' in the sense of the familiar world of mind-independent bodies seems simply question-begging. Yet Locke seems to make just this move with unseemly haste.

In chapter 11 of Book Four Locke returns to the topic of 'Our Knowledge of the Existence of Other Things', that is, of the world of bodies. Although I may have no conception of *how* external things can produce in me the sensations of white and black that I experience when I write in black ink on white paper, I still have, he insists, full assurance *that* such external things exist:

> *The notice we have by our Senses of the existing of Things without* us, though it be not altogether so certain, as our intuitive Knowledge, or the Deductions of our Reason, employ'd about the clear abstract *Ideas*

of our own Minds; yet it is an assurance that *deserves the name of Knowledge*. If we persuade our selves, that our Faculties act and inform us right, concerning the existence of those Objects that affect them, it cannot pass for an ill-grounded confidence: For I think that no body can, in earnest, be so sceptical, as to be uncertain of the Existence of those Things which he sees and feels. (EHU IV, xi, 3, N 631)

Apart from the immediate assurance given by the senses themselves, four other considerations may be advanced to justify our confidence:

1. Anyone lacking particular organs of sense (eyes, ears, etc.) will never possess the corresponding sensory ideas. The sensory ideas thus come to us by means of those organs, but are not spontaneous products of the organs themselves – we do not see in the dark.
2. The mind's reception of the ideas of sensation is passive, working independently of – and often contrary to – the will. I can generally choose what topics I will think about, but have no such volitional control over my sensory experience.
3. Sensory ideas are often produced in us with pain, which indicates the disturbance produced in our own bodies by the operation of some external object on our sense organs.
4. The senses generally confirm one another – we frequently use the sense of touch to confirm or disconfirm the sense of vision, as in the famous example of Macbeth's dagger.

The problem, of course, is that such patterns of experience are perfectly consistent with Descartes' sceptical hypothesis of the malicious demon in *Meditation One*, or with Berkeley's idealism, in which a benign God replaces Descartes' malicious demon. Locke is aware of the possibility of such a response, and responds with ridicule rather than with further argument:

> But yet, if after all this, any one will be so sceptical, as to distrust his Senses, and to affirm, that all we see and hear, feel and taste, think and do, during our whole Being, is but the series and deluding experiences of a long Dream, whereof there is no reality; and therefore will question the Existence of all Things, or our Knowledge of anything: I must desire him to consider that, if all be a Dream, then he doth but dream, that he makes the Question; and so it is not much matter, that a waking Man should answer him. But yet, if he pleases,

he may dream that I make him this answer, that *the certainty of* things existing *in rerum Natura*, when we have *the testimony of our Senses* for it, is not only *as great* as our frame can attain to, but *as our Condition needs*. (EHU IV, xi, 8, N 634)

Our faculties are given us, Locke continues, for our preservation and 'accommodated to the use of life'; what matters is that our sensory ideas are reliable indicators of pleasure and pain:

For he that sees a Candle burning, and hath experimented the force of its Flame, by putting his Finger in it, will little doubt, that this is something existing without him, which does him harm, and puts him to great pain: which is assurance enough, when no Man requires greater certainty to govern his Actions by, than what is as certain as his Actions themselves. And if our Dreamer pleases to try, whether the glowing heat of a glass Furnace, be barely a wandring Imagination in a drowsy Man's fancy, by putting his Hand into it, he may perhaps be wakened into a certainty greater than he could wish, that it is something more than bare Imagination. (EHU IV, xi, 8, N 634–5)

The problem here is that an idealist like Berkeley will insist that he uses exactly the same empirical criteria (stability, coherence, pleasure and pain) to distinguish what we call 'the real world' from the phantasms of the imagination. For Berkeley, our ideas of vision are God's sign-language, indicating to us what tactile (and other) ideas we are going to experience if we perform certain actions.[1] So the glowing red of the fire is God's way of warning me of certain painful experiences that may be in store for me if I am not careful, and the red skin of a ripe apple is God's way of telling me that it will be sweet and nourishing. This theory tells us that some sensory ideas are natural signs of other sensory ideas; it involves no reference to any supposedly mind-independent things. When Locke says that the idealist distrusts his senses, Berkeley can deny the charge and insist that he respects all the plain man's inferences from ideas to other ideas (from the red colour to the pain in the case of the fire, or from the red colour to the sweet taste in the case of the apple). All that he denies, Berkeley will argue, is the philosophers' inference to a realm of things supposed (on no good grounds) to exist independently of all perceiving minds.

If asked to provide a principled defence of common-sense realism, two possible strategies might be available to Locke. He could claim that external-world realism is a natural belief, programmed into us by our Creator. If this is right, we can see the logical possibility of the thought that 'all the world's a dream', but will never in fact take it seriously. This line of thought is discussed – in sceptical vein – by David Hume (1711–76) in his *Treatise of Human Nature*,[2] and endorsed by Thomas Reid (1710–96) in his *Essays on the Intellectual Powers of Man*.[3] For Reid, it is one of the 'first principles of contingent truths' that 'those things do really exist which we distinctly perceive by our senses', and any attempt to doubt or deny such a first principle would be mere pretence and affectation. Some of Locke's language in this chapter suggests that he would be sympathetic to this line of response, notably, his expression of doubt as to whether he is dealing here with a real or a merely imagined opponent. The other possible reply for the common-sense realist would be to say that external world realism functions as the central assumption of a vast inference to best explanation (IBE), confirmed by its explanatory success in making sense of the consistency and coherence of our experience of the world. To mount such a defence of common-sense realism, one would of course need to show that it provides a better explanation of the consistency and coherence of the world of experience than the rival account given by Berkeley's idealism – without the backing of such a claim, the IBE would fail. Arguments of this kind have been given in the literature,[4] but are absent from Locke's text. He is clearly aware of the need to provide an IBE for his scientific realism, that is, his belief in the reality of sub-microscopic particles and mechanisms, but he seems to regard common-sense realism simply as a sort of default position and the opinion of all sensible thinkers.

2. Locke's Scientific Realism: The Corpuscular Philosophy

If Locke appears reluctant to present common-sense realism in the form of an IBE, the same cannot be said of his clear commitment to scientific realism, that is, to the reality of a domain of invisibly small sub-microscopic particles. The central tenet of the 'corpuscular' philosophy of scientists such as Robert Boyle is that the manifest properties and powers of observed bodies are explicable – at least in principle – in terms of the sizes, shapes, arrangements and motions of their invisibly small parts. The seventeenth-century 'corpuscularians' divided into two schools, led respectively by René Descartes (1596–1650) and Pierre Gassendi (1592–1655).

According to Descartes, the very essence of matter is three-dimensional extension. From this it follows, he argues in his *Principles of Philosophy*, that there can be no entirely empty space or vacuum, and that there can be no absolutely indivisible atoms – matter is infinitely divisible.[5] By contrast, Gassendi attempted to revive the matter-theory of Epicurean atomism, arguing against the Cartesians both for indivisible atoms and for the real existence of empty space or vacuum.[6] Since the debates between Cartesians and atomists about the essence of matter seemed interminable and perhaps irresolvable, some of the later corpuscularians sought to downplay their differences and concentrate instead on their shared explanatory programme for natural philosophy. Robert Boyle, for example, in his *Origin of Forms and Qualities According to the Corpuscular Philosophy* (1666), is careful not to take sides between the Cartesians and the Gassendists, warning his readers in his *Proemial Discourse* that he is writing 'rather for the Corpuscularians in General, than any part of them'.[7] Locke generally follows his friend Boyle in this regard, treating the corpuscular philosophy as a single explanatory programme for natural philosophy, while remaining largely silent about deeply contested issues such as the essence of matter. There are indications that he was closer to Gassendi than to Descartes on a number of controversial points,[8] but if pressed for his opinions on the deep issues of matter theory he would no doubt prefer to follow Boyle's studied neutrality.

What are the central claims of this unified 'corpuscularian' natural philosophy? The physical universe, we are told, divides into countless invisibly small corpuscles, which may be absolutely indivisible (atomism), or may merely remain undivided in the course of the usual operations of nature (Cartesianism). These corpuscles are differentiated from one another by their sizes, shapes, and local motions either through empty space (atomism) or through an extremely subtle aetherial fluid (Cartesianism). Because size, shape and local motion are often called the 'mechanical' affections of matter, this philosophy is sometimes also labelled the 'mechanical philosophy'. The corpuscles themselves are devoid of qualities such as hot and cold, colours, tastes, and smells, which are explained as subjective effects produced in the minds of observers as a result of the impact of streams of corpuscles on their sense organs. When a number of corpuscles come together to form a complex body, that complex body will have a determinate *texture* or arrangement of parts. It is on this texture that the observed properties and powers of the complex body depend. Just as the arrangement of its parts

explains why key K1 will open lock L1 but not L2, so the arrangement of the parts of gold will explain why it is soluble in *aqua regia*
(a mixture of nitric and hydrochloric acids) but not in *aqua fortis*
(nitric acid). In the case of the key, a skilled locksmith can observe
the arrangement of the parts of lock and key, and see that the parts
of K1 and L1 are congruent with one another. He could thus predict
in advance of observation that K1 will open L1 but not L2. In the
case of the gold and the *aqua regia*, we have no such detailed knowledge of the relevant textures. According to the corpuscular philosophy, the two cases are fundamentally analogous, but we may aspire
in vain to sufficient familiarity with the relevant textures to enable
us to understand the connection. For human chemists, the proposition that 'gold dissolves in *aqua regia*' may forever remain something we can know only by experience.

Why should we believe in the corpuscular philosophy? The question is explicitly addressed by Robert Boyle in his *Origin of Forms
and Qualities* (1666) and in his short essay *About the Excellency and
Grounds of the Mechanical Hypothesis* (1674).[9] In modern terms, it is
perfectly clear that Boyle's argument takes the form of an IBE. The
corpuscular or mechanical philosophy, Boyle argues, provides an
account of the workings of the natural world that is *economical* in
its principles (matter and motion), *intelligible* in its broad outlines,
and *comprehensive* in its scope. It is also, Boyle believes, increasingly
confirmed by its track record of explanatory success.[10] We can be
reasonably confident, Boyle thinks, that some corpuscular mechanism or other will explain any given natural phenomenon, although
we may remain in doubt regarding which of two or more rival
hypotheses is correct. Regarding the nature of heat, for example, the
Cartesians favoured a pure kinetic theory (heat just *is* corpuscular
agitation), whereas the Gassendists thought there were special 'cal-
orific' and 'frigorific' (cold-making) atoms.[11] Light was explained
by the Cartesians as a longitudinal pressure pulse through the aetherial medium, whereas atomists (and Newton) thought to explain
it in terms of a stream of light particles through empty space. Both
rival explanations are acceptably mechanical, that is, attribute to the
fundamental particles only sizes, shapes and local motions. We may
be reasonably confident, Boyle thinks, that some mechanical account
or other provides the true explanation of any given natural phenomenon; our degree of confidence in the truth of any particular
account will inevitably be much lower. If we wish to establish the
true causal mechanism, we will need to launch a series of experiments aimed at an eliminative induction, that is, at ruling out as

inconsistent with observation all hypotheses but one. We will generally find ourselves a long way short of this goal.[12]

When Locke discusses the corpuscular or mechanical philosophy in his *Essay*, he is not trying to provide independent philosophical argument in its support. He takes the truth of this philosophy – or at least its rational acceptability as the best current account of the nature of Nature – to have been established by Boyle and others. If we want to know the make-up of the natural world, he thinks, we philosophers must *ask the scientists*. The idea that philosophers sitting in their armchairs and reflecting on their ideas of substance, or essence, or matter, or space, should have some kind of special insight into the natural world seems preposterous to us today. Those of us who know some intellectual history may point to celebrated examples where the philosophers have said 'Nature must work thus and so', and the scientists have shown – by incontrovertible evidence – that nature does not work thus and so. Today's philosophers of science are very wary of laying down rules a priori for the natural sciences. But this attitude is post-Lockean, and in large part reflects Locke's influence, and in particular the modesty of Locke's conception of the role of the philosopher as underlabourer for the scientists. He spells out his vision of the relation of philosophy and the natural sciences in his *Epistle to the Reader* that serves as a preface to the *Essay*:

> The Commonwealth of Learning is not at this time without Master-Builders, whose mighty Designs, in advancing the Sciences, will leave lasting Monuments to the Admiration of Posterity; But every one must not hope to be a *Boyle*, or a *Sydenham*; and in an Age that produces such masters as the great *Huygenius*, and the incomparable Mr *Newton*, with some other of that Strain, 'tis Ambition enough to be employed as an Under-Labourer in clearing Ground a little, and removing some of the Rubbish, that lies in the way to Knowledge; . . . (EHU, Epistle to the Reader, N 9–10)

The under-labourer's role consists largely in ground-clearing, that is, in removing obstacles to the growth of the natural sciences. These obstacles mostly stem from previously accepted bodies of philosophy, notably the scholastic Aristotelianism still taught at the universities of Europe in Locke's time. The under-labourer must re-examine the empirical credentials of this established body of philosophy with a view either to its elimination as little more than groundless prejudice (e.g., the maxim that 'nature abhors a vacuum'), or its reformulation in acceptable corpuscularian terms (e.g., the reduction of the scholastics' forms to corpuscular textures). The under-labourer may also take it upon himself to explain to non-expert readers some of the implications of the new philosophy for our understanding of nature. The scholastics had taught that nature abhors a vacuum; the new philosophers tell us that this maxim is false, and that the pneumatic phenomena that had previously been explained in terms of nature's supposed horror of a vacuum are in fact simple mechanical consequences of atmospheric pressure. In place of an inexplicable *pull* by a mysterious agent called 'nature', we have a simple and readily intelligible *push* by the corpuscles of the atmospheric air. The scholastics talked of mysterious *substantial forms* and *real qualities*; the new philosophers explain that the forms and qualities of observable bodies are to be explained in a reductive manner in terms of the arrangements and motions of more fundamental particles.

3. Primary and Secondary Qualities

With this stage-setting firmly in place, we are now in a position to discuss Locke's famous distinction between primary and secondary qualities. This takes place in chapter 8 of Book Two of the *Essay*, modestly entitled 'Some further Considerations concerning our Simple Ideas' (EHU II, viii, N 132–43). Critics such as Pierre Bayle and George Berkeley have mistakenly thought that Locke was attempting to draw his distinction between primary and secondary qualities on the basis of reflection on their corresponding ideas, and have argued that the distinction cannot be drawn on that basis.[13] But this whole line of criticism betrays a serious misunderstanding of the nature of Locke's argument. The distinction between primary and secondary qualities is, for Locke, a fundamental feature of the mechanical or corpuscular philosophy, which is confirmed by its scientific successes.[14] Why should we believe that sizes, shapes and motions are physically real? Because the best available science tells us that they are, that is, our best models of the physical universe assume the reality of particles with sizes, shapes and motions. Why do we think that colours are merely subjective? Because we have a convincing account of our experience of these sensations that assumes only sizes, shapes and motions and needs no objective mind-independent colours. To explain our perceptions of things as possessing size and shape and motion, we find ourselves positing things (corpuscles) with sizes and shapes and motions; to explain our perceptions of things as red and yellow and blue, we need posit only corpuscles with sizes, shapes and motions. This is the philosophical ground of the primary/secondary-quality distinction, and it is immune to the objections of Bayle and Berkeley.

The chapter starts with the important distinction between the ideas themselves and their physical grounds in bodies. We need to respect this distinction, Locke warns, if we are not to make hasty and invalid leaps from features of our ideas to properties of objects:

> Thus the *Idea* of Heat and Cold, Light and Darkness, White and Black, Motion and Rest, are equally clear and *positive Ideas* in the Mind; though perhaps some of *the causes* which produce them, are barely *privations* in those Subjects, from whence our Senses derive those *Ideas*. (EHU II, viii, 2, N 132)

That darkness is a mere privation of light was a commonplace; whether cold is or is not a mere privation of heat (as the kinetic theory implies) was a matter of controversy addressed by Boyle in a short dialogue.[15] There is no particular reason, Locke warns, to think that a positive idea must always have a positive cause. Since sensation is produced in us

> only by different degrees and modes of Motion in our animal Spirits, variously agitated by external Objects, the abatement of any former motion, must as necessarily produce a new sensation as the variation or increase of it; and so introduce a new *Idea*, which depends only on a different motion of the animal Spirits in that Organ. (EHU II, viii, 4, N 133)

Cold strikes us in experience as a physically real and positive power, but if the comfortable existence of the human body depends on a certain level of agitation of its body parts, any cause that lowers that level of agitation below some threshold may be experienced as painful and even potentially life-threatening. On the basis of the theory of simple ideas as natural signs, we might expect the idea of cold to be a reliable indicator of this particular type of threat to our bodies. The sign serves its biological function equally well whether cold is a positive thing in its own right or merely a privation.

Locke is scrupulously careful, in the two sections immediately preceding his statement of the distinction between primary and secondary qualities, to prevent possible misunderstandings of his position. Sections 7 and 8 could hardly be clearer:

7. To discover the nature of our *Ideas* the better, and to discourse of them intelligibly, it will be convenient to distinguish them, as they are *Ideas* or Perceptions in our Minds; and as they are modifications of matter in the Bodies that cause such Perceptions in us: so that we *may not* think (as perhaps usually is done) that they are exactly the Images and *Resemblances* of something inherent in the subject; most of those of Sensation being in the Mind no more the likeness of something existing without us, than the Names that stand for them are the likeness of our *Ideas*, which yet upon hearing, they are apt to excite in us. (EHU II, viii, 7, N 134)

When I use a word such as *yellow*, I might be referring to a simple idea of sensation in my own mind, or to the yellow-producing power present in such things as sulphur, saffron and daffodils. What I must not do is think that this yellow-producing power need resemble the experiential quality of yellowness in any way. The relation between them, Locke explains, is the relation of a sign to what it signifies, and this is in general not a relation based on resemblance. There are of course such things as onomatopoeic words and pictographic scripts, but these are the exception rather than the rule.

8. Whatsoever the Mind perceives in it self, or is the immediate object of Perception, Thought, or Understanding, that I call *Idea*; and the Power to produce any *Idea* in our mind, I call *Quality* of the Subject wherein that power is. Thus a Snow-ball having the power to produce in us the *Ideas* of *White, Cold,* and *Round,* the Powers to produce those *Ideas* in us, as they are in the Snow-ball, I call *Qualities*; and as they are Sensations, or Perceptions, in our Understandings, I call them *Ideas*: which *Ideas*, if I speak of sometimes, as in the things themselves, I would be understood to mean those Qualities in the Objects which produce them in us. (EHU II, viii, 8, N 134)

Locke finds it difficult to avoid speaking of bodies as hot and cold, or red and blue, but he warns us explicitly to be on our guard against misunderstanding, and to read 'blood is red' as 'blood has the red-making power', or 'blood (normally) excites the sensation of red in human observers'. Ideas are in the mind; qualities are in bodies. Nothing could be clearer. He goes on to introduce three categories of 'qualities considered in bodies', making it perfectly clear that primary, secondary and tertiary qualities are all firmly located *in bodies*. I am labouring this point only because it has so often been misunderstood by critics since Berkeley, who have thought that Locke argues for the subjectivity or mind-dependence of secondary qualities. He does not. Among those qualities considered in bodies are, says Locke:

> First such as are utterly inseparable from the Body, in what state soever it be; such as all the alterations and changes it suffers, all the force can be used upon it, it constantly keeps; and such as Sense constantly finds in every particle of Matter, which has bulk enough to be perceived, and the Mind finds inseparable from every particle of Matter, though less than to make itself singly be perceived by our Senses. (EHU II, viii, 9, N 134–5)

Every body that we can observe has size, shape and mobility. We can of course alter the determinate sizes, shapes and motions of bodies, but we can never transform something with size, shape and mobility into something without those determinable properties. If we divide an observed body, we divide it into smaller observable bodies, each of which has size, shape and mobility. At some point in the process of division, we will divide an observable but very small body into invisibly small parts. Microscopes can extend the range of our sense of vision, and will confirm that each of these parts has size, shape and mobility. What if we continue to divide these microscopically small parts? At this point, for Locke, the rational criterion takes over from the empirical one: it is the mind or intellect that insists that a body can only be divided into other smaller bodies. We cannot conceive, he thinks, of a body being divided into anything other than smaller bodies, and we cannot conceive a particle of matter that does not have size and shape and the capacity for local motion.[16] Division, Locke insists, can never take away the 'original or primary qualities of body', which he lists here as solidity, extension, figure, motion or rest, and number.[17] Even the smallest corpuscles of matter – the atoms, if atoms exist – will have solidity (which for Locke, as for the atomists, is what distinguishes matter from empty space), and each will have its determinate size and shape and local motions vis-à-vis other atoms.

> Secondly, such Qualities which in truth are nothing in the Objects themselves, but Powers to produce various Sensations in us by their *primary Qualities*, i.e. by the Bulk, Figure, Texture, and Motion of their insensible parts, as Colours, Sounds, Tastes, etc. These I call *secondary Qualities*. (EHU II, viii, 10, N 135)

A careless reader might think that the word 'these' in this last sentence refers back to colours, sounds and tastes. But that would be inconsistent both with the grammar of the passage and with Locke's repeated insistence that ideas are in minds and qualities in objects. 'These' refers back to the *powers* in bodies to produce those sensations in us, and these powers or secondary qualities are perfectly objective. Colours, sounds and tastes are subjective or mind-dependent, but these are the ideas of secondary qualities, not secondary qualities.[18] When we call a body yellow or red we mean that it has the power to produce in our minds the corresponding idea. This power is, according to the corpuscularians, reducible to the texture of the complex body that possesses it. Single corpuscles will lack these powers for the simple reason that they are simple, that is, cannot possess complex arrangements of constituent parts.

How do external bodies act on our sense organs to produce the ideas of sensation? This, says Locke, is 'manifestly *by impulse*, the only way which we can conceive Bodies operate in' (EHU II, viii, 11, N 135–6). After the publication of Newton's *Principia*, which seemed to many of its critics to represent gravity as an action at a distance, Locke became less confident of any inference from inconceivability to unreality. God might, he warns, give powers to bodies that surpass our powers of comprehension. But the mechanical explanation of the workings of our bodily senses was not seriously in doubt in Locke's day. The mechanical theory of sound as a pressure pulse transmitted through the air was firmly established and, in optics, Huygens' wave-theory was opposed by Newton's corpuscular theory. What all such accounts share is their fundamentally mechanical nature. We perceive both the primary and the secondary qualities of bodies by means of the same underlying mechanisms:

> After the same manner, that the ideas of these original *Qualities* are produced in us, we may conceive, that the *Ideas* of *secondary Qualities* are also *produced*, viz. *by the operation of insensible particles on our Senses*. (EHU II, viii, 13, N 136)

Although the success of Newtonian physics led Locke to doubt whether matter *must* always act by impulse, he never seriously entertains the doubt that in the operations of the bodily senses it *does in fact* operate by impulse. For us to see, or hear, or smell a distant body requires the transmission from it to our sense organs either of a distinct stream of corpuscles or of a particular type of agitation of the intervening medium. From these considerations, Locke continues,

I think it easie to draw this Observation: that the *Ideas of primary Qualities* of bodies, are *Resemblances* of them, and their Patterns do really exist in the Bodies themselves; but the *Ideas, produced* in us by these *Secondary Qualities have no resemblance* to them at all. There is nothing like our *Ideas,* existing in the Bodies themselves. They are in the Bodies, we denominate from them, only a Power to produce those Sensations in us: And what is Sweet, Blue, or Warm in *Idea,* is but the certain Bulk, Figure, and Motion of the insensible Parts in the Bodies themselves, which we call so. (EHU II, viii, 15, N 137)

This passage has been misrepresented and misunderstood by critics since Berkeley. In the first place, we need to distinguish determinable qualities (having size, shape and local motion) from their determinate values (being a foot long, being square, moving due North with a velocity of 1 metre per second). Locke's resemblance thesis must apply to determinable qualities rather than to their determinate values. No moderately intelligent and thoughtful observer could suppose that there are no illusions of primary qualities, no cases in which we see a circle as an ellipse or a square as a rhombus. What Locke is saying is that our perceptions of things as having sizes and shapes is caused by those things having sizes and shapes. By contrast, our perceptions of things as having colours is caused by the interaction of their superficial parts with incident light, and the modifications of that incident light produced by the specific textures of those superficial parts. Whereas sizes and shapes appear in our best explanatory account of the nature of nature, colours do not. The resemblance thesis is a consequence of the mechanical philosophy, not a phenomenological thesis grounded in reflections on our ideas.

Locke goes on to discuss the subjectivity or mind-dependence of colours, tastes, smells, etc.:

The particular *Bulk, Number, Figure, and Motion of the parts of Fire, or Snow are really in them,* whether any one's Senses perceive them or no: and therefore they may be called *real Qualities,* because they really exist in those Bodies. But *Light, Heat, Whiteness, or Coldness, are no more really in them, than Sickness or Pain is in* Manna. (EHU II, viii, 17, N 137-8)

Passages such as this have been read as advocating the subjectivity of secondary qualities, but we have already seen that this is a misreading. Light and heat, whiteness and coldness are for Locke *ideas* of secondary qualities, so their mind-dependence is obvious and unproblematic. The corresponding powers in bodies are perfectly objective, and are grounded in determinate arrangements of parts (textures). There will of course be a relational aspect to any adequate account of these matters: a given texture will only ground a power to produce a certain idea in a being with appropriate (and functioning) sense organs. But these relations will themselves be every bit as objective as is the power of key K1 to open lock L1 but not L2, or of *aqua regia* but not *aqua fortis* to dissolve gold. Our experiences of heat and cold, colours, tastes and smells will be highly subjective, depending on the state and operations of our sense organs. And, of course, beings with different sense organs will have very different sets of sensory ideas. But the fact that the powers can only be captured in relational terms (a body with texture T1 has the power to produce a certain change in a body with texture T2) is perfectly consistent with a thoroughgoing commitment to objectivity.

The explanatory power of the mechanical philosophy is illustrated in sections 17–21, using a range of examples drawn largely from the works of Robert Boyle.[19] Locke ends the chapter with an apology to his readers for this 'little excursion into natural philosophy', but feels that it was necessary if readers are to understand the crucial distinction between those qualities that are present in bodies whether or not they are observed, and their effects on minds like ours. Once we understand this distinction, we are told, we can appreciate the subjectivity (mind-dependence) of colours, tastes, smells, etc., without this realization doing anything to shake our faith in the objectivity (mind-independence) both of the basic corpuscles themselves and of the textures (arrangements of parts) of the compound bodies formed from them. The powers grounded in these textures are equally objective, but of course relational in nature, because they will arise from relations of fit or congruity between the textures of different bodies, including of course our own.

4. Real and Nominal Essences

Book Three of the *Essay*, entitled simply 'Of Words', was the last to be written, and formed no part of the original project. Locke found himself drawn to discuss some issues in the philosophy of language in order to complete his account of the powers and limitations of the human mind. Much of our understanding of the world around us is expressed and conveyed in linguistic form, and it is important to grasp exactly what is being thus expressed and conveyed. We can't discuss meaning and understanding without saying something about language, and about how words come to have meanings. For the purposes of this chapter, the crucial terms are the names of substances, words like *tiger, crocodile, primrose, iron, gold, sulphur* and *water*. These names stand for complex ideas in the minds of those humans who use and understand them. But for substance-terms, unlike the names of modes, there are real patterns or regularities in nature, co-occurrences of the various powers that must be present in bodies of a certain kind if they are to produce their corresponding ideas in our minds. For the names of modes, it is a matter of convention which simple ideas we choose to combine to frame a new complex idea, to be marked out by a specific term such as *democracy*; for a substance-term like *gold* there are real patterns or regularities provided by experience. In political debate, there would be no point in trying to debate the real essence of democracy; what is required is simply clarity and consistency of usage. Politician A might say 'I will call a government democratic if it has features WXY'; politician B says 'I will call a government democratic if it has features XYZ.' Here there is no genuine matter of dispute between A and B: we might find A's complex idea more useful than B's, and thus prefer it on pragmatic grounds, or we might decide to use the term 'democratic' with subscripts, democratic(A) and democratic(B) to mark the distinct senses. But there would be no question regarding who is right and who is wrong. By contrast, once the term *gold* had come into human languages to stand for the complex idea of a particular type of metal, it was an empirical discovery that gold was soluble in *aqua regia*. Anyone who denied it would have been guilty of an error of fact.

What is going on when we classify natural things – animals, plants, minerals, metals, diseases – into sorts or kinds? Is our activity primarily driven by our own practical concerns or needs, in which case we will tend to class together things that strike us or affect us in the same way? The great eighteenth-century naturalist Buffon suggested at one point that we group together *animals dangerous to man*, so lions might be grouped together with scorpions and crocodiles. A botanist interested in herbal medicine might group together plants by their medicinal virtues, so the *cinchona* tree of Peru (the source of the famous 'Jesuits' bark') might be grouped with the familiar European St John's Wort. A mineralogist might group gemstones together on the basis of their market value. But such schemes of classification strike most of us as contrived and artificial, and as not adequately capturing the real kinships between things. From its beginnings in Plato and Aristotle, the human project of taxonomy or classification has sought to 'carve Nature at its joints', that is, to group together things that really belong together. Dangers and benefits to man, or prices in a human marketplace, seem too arbitrary and subjective to provide the basis for a truly natural classification. It is a natural and almost irresistible thought that God or nature has divided the objects of our world into *natural kinds*, and that for each natural kind there is a constitutive *real essence* (RE) that makes an object a member of that kind. For the corpuscularians, this RE will of course be a characteristic arrangement of corpuscles, on which the observed powers of bodies of that kind depend.[20]

Returning to the meanings of substance-words, we can ask whether a term such as *gold* or *lemon* picks out or refers to the REs constitutive of gold or lemons. If this were so, Locke thinks, we could not understand our own language. If I am to understand the term *gold*, he argues, the complex idea for which it stands must be composed of simpler ideas which I do understand, such as yellow, shiny, fusible, malleable, soluble in *aqua regia*, etc. This complex idea is called by Locke a nominal essence (NE), and the term is said to stand for this NE. He is suggesting – in strict accordance with his empiricist project – that we need to define each of our natural-kind words in terms of a characteristic set of observable properties. As the old empiricist maxim has it, 'If it walks like a duck and swims like a duck and quacks like a duck, then it's a duck.' Having distinguished NEs from REs in chapter 6 of Book Three, Locke insists that our ranking of things into sorts or kinds is always done by their NEs alone:

> The next thing to be considered is, by which of those Essences it is, that *Substances are determined into* Sorts, or *Species*; and that, it is evident, is *by the nominal Essence*. For 'tis that alone, that the name, which is the mark of the Sort, signifies. (EHU III, vi, 7, N 443)

We cannot sort things by their REs, Locke argues, for the simple reason that they are generally unknown to us:

> Nor indeed *can we* rank and *sort Things*, and consequently (which is the end of sorting) denominate them *by their real Essences*, because we know them not. Our Faculties carry us no farther towards the

knowledge and distinction of Substances, than a Collection of those sensible *Ideas*, which we observe in them; which however made with the greatest diligence and exactness, we are capable of, yet is more remote from the true internal Constitution, from which those Qualities flow, than ... a Countryman's *Idea* is from the inward contrivance of that famous Clock at *Strasbourg*, whereof he only sees the outward Figure and Motions. There is not so contemptible a Plant or Animal that does not confound the most inlarged Understanding. (EHU III, vi, 9, N 444)

We don't even grasp, Locke continues, what is the texture or arrangement of parts that explains why metals are malleable and rocks are not, still less the far more subtle and intricate 'fine contrivances' that make the 'inconceivable' real essences of plants and animals:

Therefore we in vain pretend to range Things into sorts and dispose them into certain Classes, under Names, by their *real Essences*, that are so far from our discovery and comprehension. A blind Man may as soon sort Things by their Colours. (EHU III, vi, 9, N 444–5)

Locke admits in chapter 10 that we do tend to tacitly assume that substance-terms stand for unknown REs, but this he labels an 'abuse of words', the source of much obscurity in our language (EHU III, x, 17–18, N 499–500). Even assuming that there are fully determinate and specific REs, they are products of God's craftsmanship, known doubtless to Him but not to us. Since classification is a human activity, it must proceed by human criteria, that is, in accordance with the complex ideas of observable properties we have combined together into specific NEs.[21] On the face of it, the argument appears unanswerable. On the basis of modern science, you might find yourself minded to retort, 'Yes, but now we do know the REs, and now at last can classify on that basis.' A physicist can tell us the electron configuration characteristic of gold; a biologist can tell us the entire DNA sequence of a tiger. But is all this high-powered science what is understood when the familiar terms 'gold' and 'tiger' are employed? This seems implausible, for two obvious reasons. One is that that the terms 'gold' and 'tiger' came into human languages long before the development of modern science, and are still used successfully by millions of people ignorant of any of that science. The other is that the science may change (our theories about electrons or DNA may alter), but the terms 'gold' and 'tiger' will continue to pick out gold and tigers. A latter-day Lockean could still provide a vigorous defence of his theory.[22]

The problem for Locke is that, as he himself grants, we do tend to assume both that our natural-kind terms pick out groups of bodies with determinate REs, and that those REs fix or determine the observed properties of things. If we just picked out *dense and yellow and shiny* as our NE of gold, we would have to say that some gold is soluble in *aqua fortis* and some gold is not. But what we in fact say is that gold (true gold) is insoluble in *aqua fortis*, and that there are other stuffs (e.g., 'fools' gold') that look like gold but are not gold. We assume a determinate (albeit unknown) RE, from which the observed properties flow, and thus infer from distinct observed properties to a distinct RE. If the empiricist maxim about ducks were true, an entirely alien organism quite unrelated to terrestrial ducks, or a sufficiently complex robot, could actually *be* a duck, but we generally do not believe this. We assume that what makes something a duck is some fact or facts about its DNA and perhaps its biological lineage (there are complexities here), and that extraterrestrial organisms and robots could resemble ducks in many ways but could not *be* ducks. The belief that natural-kind terms name NEs and not REs is in tension with a deep assumption underlying our inductive practices.[23]

But if we reject Locke's account of the meanings of the names of substances, we still need to rebut his key argument in support of his claim. How can we classify things by their REs if those REs are unknown to us? In modern philosophy of language, the best account is that of Saul Kripke in his famous *Naming and Necessity*.[24] What we do, says Kripke, is point to a sample of gold and say 'I shall call *this stuff* gold', where the demonstrative term '*this*' picks out the (unknown) RE, so that whatever has the same RE as our sample is also gold. Since we assume that RE determines observed properties (at least if we keep the environment fixed), any material that has different observable properties from those of our sample will not be gold. A material that appears to have all the same observable properties is likely but not absolutely certain to be gold – it is at least conceivable that there could be two distinct REs that give rise to the same observable properties. On this account, the demonstrative 'this' anchors a substance-term to a hidden RE, and the observable criteria that the empiricist lays such stress on are fallible indications of the presence of that same RE. The key difference is that, on the Kripkean theory, the Lockean nominal essence does not define the term. If it walks like a duck and swims like a duck and quacks like a duck, we have good inductive reasons for thinking that it probably is a duck, but we still might be wrong.

Is it unfair to contrast Locke's theory unfavourably with that of one of the great metaphysicians of our later age? Kripke, after all, had another three centuries of philosophy to draw on in developing his account. He could respond to Locke but not vice versa. But Locke himself had already noticed our tendency to assume that substance-terms pick out unknown REs, dismissing it as an abuse of language. And Locke's close contemporary Leibniz, in his *New Essays*, defends precisely the position that Locke rejects. The term 'gold', says Leibniz's spokesman Theophilus, signifies:

> not merely what the speaker knows of gold, e.g. something yellow and very heavy, but also what he does not know, which may be known about gold by someone else, namely: a body endowed with an inner constitution from which flow its colour and weight, and which also generates other properties which he acknowledges to be better known by the experts.[25]

Here Leibniz anticipates not only Kripke's claim that a substance-term like 'gold' picks out an RE rather than an NE, but also a point developed by Hilary Putnam about the 'linguistic division of labour' between experts and non-experts.[26] When I use a term such as 'gold', I use it with the assumption that there is a determinate corresponding RE that is known by the relevant experts, and I implicitly defer to their usage. The experts will, of course, use a significant body of physical and chemical theory. But this theory does not define the term 'gold'; if it did, every significant change of physical theory would involve massive reference-failure for the names of familiar materials like gold. The thought is that the term 'gold' picks out a determinate RE that we humans may gradually come to understand better in the course of the history of science.

One curious corollary of the Kripke-Putnam theory is worth noting. Since the link between the hidden RE and the manifest properties is environment-dependent, our use of properties such as colour to sort things into kinds may only work in a limited range of environments. Could a fruit that is blue and sweet and spherical *be* a lemon? A Lockean will consult his NE for 'lemon' and find that lemons are yellow and bitter and have pointed ends. A fruit that is blue and sweet and spherical just couldn't – by definition – *be* a lemon. But suppose the term 'lemon' stands for a Kripkean RE, perhaps for some highly specific facts about the DNA of lemon plants. When we humans first start to colonize alien planets, we take with us the seeds of some favourite species of terrestrial plants,

including lemons. Under the different environmental conditions
(light, gravity, soil chemistry) of the alien world, the lemon trees
flourish, but bear fruits that are blue and sweet and spherical. Are
these fruits *lemons*? Nothing has altered the plants' DNA; it is merely
that the expression of the genes is affected by the prevailing environmental conditions. The example is drawn from science fiction,
but the underlying thought was already familiar to Boyle and Locke.
Boyle wrote a short essay, *Of the Systematical or Cosmical Properties
of Things*,[27] emphasizing the mechanists' claim that the link between
intrinsic texture and manifest properties is heavily dependent on
subtle environmental conditions. The point is picked up by Locke
in chapter 6 of Book Four of the *Essay*. The mechanisms of the physical universe, he writes, are so complex and so interdependent that
we can never be confident that we have grasped them in their
entirety. Instead of saying that texture T* grounds observable property O*, we should always be careful to say that T* grounds O* in
environment E1, or perhaps in some range of environments E1-n:

> This is certain, Things, however absolute and entire they seem in
> themselves, are but Retainers to other parts of Nature, for that which
> they are most taken notice of by us. Their observable Qualities,
> Actions, and Powers, are owing to something without them; and
> there is not so complete and perfect a part, that we know, of Nature,
> that does not owe the Being it has, and the Excellencies of it, to its
> Neighbours; and we must not confine our thoughts within the surface
> of any body, but look a great deal farther, to comprehend perfectly
> those Qualities that are in it. (EHU IV, vi, 11, N 587)

We casually talk, even in these supposedly more enlightened
times, of a gene *for* blue eyes. But nothing about the gene guarantees
that any organism that possesses it will even develop eyes at all, far
less blue ones. What we mean, of course, is that organisms with this
gene will develop blue eyes in a range of environments taken as in
some sense 'normal'. Change the environment, and you change the
link between the gene and its expression in the form of some
observed characteristic. Boyle and Locke would not have been in
the least surprised.

5. Angelic and Human Chemistry

Natural philosophy, Locke warns us in a number of passages, is not
capable of being made a science. A great experimentalist like Robert

Boyle may, after a well-conducted series of experiments, be able to make well-informed guesses regarding the hidden properties of bodies, but this remains conjecture and not knowledge:

> This *way* of getting and *improving our Knowledge in Substances only by Experience* and History, which is all that the weakness of our Faculties in this State of *Mediocrity* which we are in in this World, can attain to, makes me suspect, that natural Philosophy is not capable of being made a Science. (EHU IV, xii, 10, N 645)

Since what Locke means by 'natural philosophy' is more or less the same as what we mean by 'the natural sciences', he seems – at least at first sight – to be making the paradoxical claim that physics and chemistry are not and can never aspire to be sciences. In fact, the only reason his claim sounds paradoxical to our ears is because of a shift in the meaning of the word 'science'. To a seventeenth-century philosopher, a science is a body of demonstrated knowledge. The model for a body of scientific knowledge is Euclid's *Elements of Geometry*, in which certain self-evident axioms are stated upfront, and all the theorems are rigorously deduced from those axioms, making them (almost) as 100 per cent certain as the axioms themselves. (There might remain some lingering doubt about the validity of the proofs.) No modern physicist or chemist thinks that we can do natural science in this way. If pressed, they will admit that their accounts of the electron configuration structure of the carbon atom, or the famous double-helix model of the structure of DNA, have the status of hypotheses, albeit ones that have stood up to rigorous testing and thus now command the assent of the relevant scientific communities. These models, however well confirmed by evidence, could always be refuted by new evidence.

The mechanical philosophy, for Locke, holds out the prospect of a genuine science of nature, but reserves such a science for beings superior to humans. If we could know the detailed sizes, shapes, motions and arrangements of the constituent corpuscles of bodies, he writes,

> we should know without Trial several of their Operations one upon another, as we do now the Properties of a Square, or a Triangle. Did we know the Mechanical affections of the Particles of *Rhubarb*, *Hemlock*, *Opium* and *a Man*, as a Watchmaker does those of a Watch, whereby it performs its Operations, and of a File which by rubbing on them will alter the Figure of any of the Wheels, we should be able to tell before Hand that *Rhubarb* will purge, *Hemlock* kill, and *Opium*

make a man sleep; as well as a Watch-maker can, that a little piece
of Paper laid on the Balance, will keep the Watch from going till it
be removed; or that some small part of it, being rubb'd by a File, the
Machin would quite lose its Motion, and the Watch go no more. The
dissolving of Silver in *aqua fortis,* and Gold in *aqua Regia,* and not *vice
versa,* would be then, perhaps, no more difficult to know, than it is to
a Smith to understand, why the turning of one Key will open a Lock,
and not the turning of another. (EHU IV, iii, 25, N 556)

Such knowledge of nature is possible in principle, and may actually be possessed by the angels,[28] but it is not possible for us. Human
doctors must establish by the slow route of experience that rhubarb
will purge, opium put a man to sleep and hemlock kill. There are
in fact two distinct types of ignorance here, and Locke isn't always
at his best in distinguishing them. There is our ignorance of the
detailed microstructures or textures that constitute the REs of
natural substances. Here, of course, modern science has gone far
beyond that of Boyle and Newton. For Locke, this modern science
(in *our* sense of the word) is still not *knowledge* in his strict sense,
because it is not intuitive or demonstrative or sensitive, and because
it still remains inherently fallible. But if he were pressed on this
point, he might concede that we humans could in principle gain
such a body of well-confirmed and mutually supporting hypotheses that they command the *rational assurance* of all unprejudiced
minds. There would still remain the deeper ignorance of the nature
or essence of material substance itself. Here Locke would say that
modern science cannot enlighten us. If I ask a modern physicist
what an electron is, he will tell me that it has a mass of $1/1836$ and
a charge of -1. If I ask him what mass and charge are, he will tell
me how massive and charged bodies behave, and perhaps teach me
Newton's and Coulomb's laws. But suppose I press my question,
and insist that I don't want to know what an electron will do under
certain circumstances (e.g., if moving through a magnetic field), but
what it is, in itself, in its *intrinsic nature*. At this point the physicist
might try to explain the properties of the electron in terms of some
supposedly smaller parts – which would merely push my question
one step back. More probably, the physicist might say that we know
the natural world only as a collection of powers – that this is all we
do or can know of it. And this is precisely Locke's point.

Locke frequently asserts our complete ignorance of the nature or
essence of matter. He clearly and explicitly rejects the Cartesian
thesis that the essence of matter is simply extension in

three dimensions, favouring instead the atomist thesis that matter is differentiated from empty space by the property of solidity (EHU II, iv, 1, N 122–3). But we should not infer from this that Locke was a committed or dogmatic atomist. His argument probes more deeply than this, and concludes with a principled agnosticism about the essence of material substance. We derive our idea of solidity, according to Locke, from our sense of touch, and should distinguish it from impenetrability. The latter he conceives as a mere power; the former is whatever provides the positive ground of that power. This idea of solidity is, he writes, 'the idea most intimately connected with and essential to body'. Although our senses reveal it to us only in bodies bulky enough to make an impression on us, our minds can and do go further:

> the Mind, having once got this *Idea* from such grosser sensible Bodies, traces it farther; and considers it, as well as Figure, in the minutest Particle of Matter, that can exist; and finds it inseparably inherent in Body, wherever or however modified. (EHU II, iv, 1, N 123)

If matter is differentiated from space by this feature of solidity, then the Cartesians are wrong to suppose that the very conception of vacuum or empty space is incoherent. If a body moves out of the space it occupied, and no other body moves in to fill that space, the space will be left empty. We can thus, Locke argues, at least conceive of a space without solidity. Whether there are actual empty spaces is of course a further question: Locke's point in this section is simply that actually empty space cannot be ruled out on conceptual grounds. There might be empirical reasons for thinking that the so-called 'Boylian vacuum' created by the air pump contains a subtle aetherial fluid – one might, for example, be committed to a wave theory of light, and argue that the transmission of waves requires a medium. Christiaan Huygens would endorse this argument; Isaac Newton would reject it; Locke was familiar with both these giants of science, and would not have thought it his business to adjudicate between them. The philosopher, after all, is only an under-labourer. But one cannot argue, with the Cartesians, that the Boylian vacuum is extended, therefore it is material. Matter is differentiated from mere space by the property of solidity. To this extent at least, Locke sides with the atomists against the Cartesians.

But if we seek to enquire further into the nature of solidity, our enquiries will quickly be frustrated:

> If any one asks me, *What this Solidity is,* I send him to his Senses to inform him: Let him put a Flint, or a Foot-ball between his Hands; and then endeavour to join them, and he will know... The simple *Ideas* we have are such, as experience teaches them us; but if beyond that, we endeavour, by Words, to make them clearer in the Mind, we shall succeed no better, than if we went about to clear up the Darkness of a blind Man's mind, by talking; and to discourse into him the *Ideas* of Light and Colours. (EHU II, iv, 6, N 126–7)

Locke distinguishes in words between the bare power he calls *impenetrability,* and its supposed positive ground, which he calls *solidity.* But in fact we know the positive ground *only* by its role in grounding the power, so to say that 'all bodies are solid' is just to say that 'all bodies have that feature F, whatever it may be, that grounds the power of impenetrability'. This gives us no real insight into the nature or essence of matter. The Cartesians must be wrong; the atomists might be right to posit a fundamental level of *solid* atoms with sizes, shapes, motions; but of course the bottom level of nature may turn out to be something yet more remote from our comprehension. This is a real possibility, deliberately left open in Book Four of the *Essay* (EHU IV, iii, 11, N 544). Ultimately, this is a question on which we philosophers must defer to the scientists.

5

God and Religion

1. Faith and Reason in Religion

The respective roles of faith and reason in religion have been a source of lively and often acrimonious debate through the ages, not just within Christianity but also within Judaism and Islam, and no doubt within other religious traditions as well as the Abrahamic religions of the West. For religious teachers and figures of authority, there are perils on both sides. Suppose we emphasize the role of reason, and claim that the existence of God and the immortality of the human soul can both be demonstrated by metaphysical argument. Religious belief could then be established on a firm rational basis. But what then is the role of the special revelations given to the prophets? Why do we need dreams, and visions, and angelic messengers, if the truths of religion can be established in the same way that the truths of geometry are established? Why should we need the Torah, or the Bible, or the Quran, and whole tribes of specialists poring over the sacred texts to extract every slight nuance of their meaning? On the other hand, suppose we minimize the role of reason in religion, and emphasize instead those of faith and authority. A revelation is claimed; a sacred text is delivered into the hands of a prophet; the duty of his followers is henceforth that of submission. Sceptics will immediately point out that we have been provided with no reason for believing that there is a God at all – still less a God who cares enough about us to provide a revelation of His will. And even if there is a God who might send us a revelation of His will, there are many rival claims to revelation. They cannot all be true, but could all be false. You either have no criterion at all, or a merely subjective one which is even worse – every fanatic would have as good a claim to be the founder of a new religion as Jesus or Mohammed.

Within the mainstream Churches of the West, a sort of 'golden mean' emerged regarding the role of reason within religion. Natural theology (which is a branch of philosophy) should prove the existence of God, and of a God who might reasonably be expected to care about us. This means that the natural theologian must refute not just the atheist but also the Epicurean (whose gods don't care about anything as trivial as human welfare or suffering) and the Spinozist (who flatly denies that God could care about or love humans). But after establishing the existence of a God who might have a Providential concern for humans, the natural theologian should hand over to the priest, who claims special (revealed) knowledge of God's plans and purposes, and in particular His commands for His human creatures. The natural theologian should also establish that the human soul can exist without its body, thus establishing at least the possibility of an afterlife. But then he must hand over to the priest, who can inform us in graphic detail of the sort of experiences in store for saints and sinners in Heaven and Hell. The basic idea is of a division of intellectual labour, in which natural theology provides the basic substructure and revealed theology adds the detailed superstructure.

In Descartes' letter to the theologians of the Sorbonne, which served as a preface to his *Meditations,* he emphasizes the need for 'demonstrative proofs' of the existence of God and the immortality of the soul. Believers will, of course, accept both doctrines as a matter of faith, but what shall we say to the unbelievers? Few people, he thinks, would lead lives of virtue unless persuaded of an afterlife with rewards for virtue and punishments for vice, so to convince the doubters we need proofs of God and of the afterlife. Mere faith cannot serve here:

> It is of course quite true that we must believe in the existence of God because it is a doctrine of Holy Scripture, and conversely, that we must believe Holy Scripture because it comes from God; for since faith is the gift of God, he who gives us grace to believe other things can also give us grace to believe that he exists. But this argument cannot be put to unbelievers because they would judge it to be circular.[1]

The existence of God both can and should be proved by natural reason, thus giving believers a reason for belief independent of the gift of grace – and leaving the atheist without any excuse for his unbelief. As regards the soul, Descartes continues, some philosophers have argued that, as far as unaided human reason can take us,

> there are persuasive grounds for holding that the soul dies along with the body and that the opposite view is based on faith alone. But in its eighth session the Lateran Council held under Leo X condemned those who take this position, and expressly enjoined Christian philosophers to refute their arguments and use all their powers to establish the truth; so I have not hesitated to attempt this task as well.[2]

The philosophers Descartes has in mind here are the Latin Averroists, who were condemned by the Lateran Council of 1513, and in particular Pietro Pomponazzi, whose *De Immortalitate Animae* (1516) defied the Council and argued that the immortality of the soul, although an article of Christian faith, was not demonstrable by human reason. As a Christian, says Pomponazzi, of course I assent to this doctrine; as an Aristotelian philosopher, I judge that the balance of the philosophical arguments is against it.[3] A number of considerations of various kinds might lead a philosopher to espouse the doctrine of mortalism, the thesis that the soul naturally dies with the body. One might start, as Pomponazzi did, with the Aristotelian doctrine that the soul is the form of the living body, and then deny that forms can have existence entirely independent of matter. One might study at medical school and probe the mysteries of psychosomatic medicine, arriving at the conclusion that the human mind – whatever it may be in metaphysical terms – is manifestly designed to exercise its functions by means of the organs of the human body.[4] Or one might adopt a tactic of the ancient sceptics and develop an explicit analogy between humans and the supposedly lower animals. If the souls of cats and dogs perish with their bodies, the sceptics ask, why not also the souls of men?

It was also possible to argue for mortalism on explicitly scriptural grounds, arguing that the doctrine of an afterlife with rewards and punishments is taught in the Bible not as a doctrine of natural theology but as something supernatural, believed entirely as a matter of faith. The poet Milton argued for mortalism, and he read his

Scriptures as closely as any man alive. The doctrine finds explicit
expression in Richard Overton's pamphlet *Man's Mortalitie* (1645),
which crops up in Locke's correspondence for 1661 (C I, 166–7). So
Locke would be fully aware of the issue at stake between the Cartesians on the one side, and a host of opponents on the other. Can
we establish by philosophical argument that the human rational
soul is, of its own nature, the sort of thing that can exist independently of the body, and can thus continue to exist when the body is
decaying in its grave? Or is the afterlife a doctrine that Christians
believe only as a matter of faith, resting on assurances given in the
Bible?

The other obvious problem in this area concerns the criteria for
something – a dream or vision, an utterance or a fragment of text
– to count as a genuine revelation, that is, as coming from the mouth
of God Himself. Given that there any number of hotheads and
fanatics out there, all claiming to have their own personal hotlines
to the Deity, third parties will inevitably find themselves in need of
a criterion to distinguish a bona fide revelation from the rantings of
madmen and the impostures of frauds. At this point the theologians
have generally pointed to two sets of criteria, labelled 'internal' and
'external'. The internal criteria are the purity of the life and doctrine
on display – are the life and words of this man *worthy* of God? This
obviously presupposes that we already have some notion of what
sort of life a true prophet should lead, and what sort of doctrines
he should preach. Worries about circularity might raise their ugly
heads once again. Are we so confident that God *wouldn't* use a
vicious man as an instrument for spreading His word? The external
criteria are the usual 'outward' signs of miracles and (fulfilled)
prophecies, which are meant to indicate to third parties that the
self-proclaimed prophet is speaking with supernatural assistance,
and hence with divine authority.

All this is familiar introductory philosophy of religion. That third
parties need a sign or criterion to accept a revelation as genuine was
not controversial in Locke's day. The original disciples had the evidence of their own eyes for plenty of miracles – notably of course
the Resurrection – while later Christians must place their trust in
the testimony of the disciples. What became a matter of controversy
was whether the supposed recipient of a revelation is equally in
need of a criterion. For the orthodox, the answer was 'no': revelation
was supposed to be inherently self-certificating, leaving its recipient
in no doubt of its origin. All recipients of a genuine revelation know
that they are so. (This of course does not entail that anyone sincerely

claiming revelation must automatically be right – it is important to be clear about the logic here.) It was Spinoza who challenged this orthodoxy, arguing in chapter 2 of his notorious *Tractatus Theolgico-Politicus* of 1670 that the Hebrew prophets needed external signs to be confident that their dreams and visions were sent by God. A vivid imagination, however intense the experiences it provides, can never guarantee objective truth.

The issue would become an important one for Locke in his dealings with the 'enthusiasts' of his own day, of whom he was highly critical. Anyone can claim a personal hotline to the Deity, and thus claim to speak with divine authority, but for every bona fide prophet there will be many frauds and no doubt also many self-deceivers, men who sincerely believe themselves to be God's messengers, but on grounds that perhaps not even they themselves should believe to be adequate.[5]

2. Locke on Faith and Reason

For Locke, reason plays two crucial roles within religion. First and foremost, it is the job of reason to provide a proof of the existence of God. As we have already seen, Locke thinks that the existence of God is *demonstrable*, not merely probable. To that end, he launches in chapter 10 of Book Four of the *Essay* a version of the 'cosmological' proof of God's existence. Unfortunately, as we shall see, Locke's version of the cosmological proof is hopelessly invalid. He might have shifted his ground either to a better version of the cosmological argument, or perhaps to the argument to design favoured by contemporaries such as Boyle and Newton. But the design argument is only probabilistic, and Locke wants demonstration. If the existence of God is demonstrable by human reason, then atheists must be either stupid or perverse. If the existence of God is merely probable on the evidence, space is left for atheism as a sincere and thoughtful position. There may be political reasons why Locke wants to close off this space: he will, after all, place atheists beyond the pale in the *Letter on Toleration*.

The other crucial role for reason within religion is to establish and apply the criteria for something to count as a genuine revelation. For a religion such as Christianity that rests its authority on a claim to revelation, we need to establish two things: that the Bible as we have it is a true revelation from God, and that we understand its teachings correctly. To establish the former thesis is a matter of the usual signs, both internal and external, but with the emphasis clearly on the latter. Far from being opposed to reason, a revealed religion such as Christianity must appeal to reason at this point to vindicate its claims. We need to establish that it is rational to believe the accounts of the first Christians, as they have been handed down to us, and that the miraculous events they report did indeed happen as reported. Without the guidance of reason in this matter, claims to knowledge based on revelation will fail to carry any weight. A sceptic can just say 'I grant that *if* it all happened like it says in the book, that would convince me, but I don't see any reason why I have to believe this.' As Locke puts it in chapter 18 of Book Four:

> Whatever GOD hath revealed is certainly true; no Doubt can be made of it. This is the proper Object of *Faith*: But whether it be a divine Revelation, or no, *Reason* must judge; which can never permit the Mind to reject a greater Evidence to embrace what is less evident, nor allow it to entertain Probability in opposition to Knowledge and Certainty. (EHU IV, xviii, 10, N 695)

If some proposition p is evident to me by the light of reason (e.g., a theorem of geometry, well-understood and grasped by means of its proof), then any purported revelation of a proposition q incompatible with p must be rejected:

> There can be no evidence that any traditional Revelation is of divine Original, in the Words we receive it and in the Sense we understand it, so clear, and so certain, as that of the Principles of Reason: And therefore *Nothing that is contrary to, and inconsistent with, the clear and self-evident Dictates of Reason, has a Right to be urged, or assented to, as a Matter of Faith, wherein Reason hath nothing to do.* (EHU IV, xviii, 10, N 695–6)

If a passage in the Bible – perhaps on the building of the Temple at Jerusalem – indicates a value for Π of 3, or of 22/7, I must not infer that the geometers' proof that Π is irrational is invalid, but that we have failed to understand the passage in question, or have translated it incorrectly. I am as confident as I can be that Π is irrational, and thus that there cannot be a revelation to the contrary. Issues become more entangled – and much more heated – when we shift from mathematics to metaphysics. Protestant theologians could confidently dismiss the Catholic dogma of transubstantiation, the supposedly miraculous transformation of the wafer and the wine into the body and blood of Christ. Since this is unintelligible, they can confidently argue, it cannot be required as an article of Christian belief. But the vast majority of Protestant theologians still believed in the doctrine of the Trinity, and in the Athanasian formula (three persons = one substance) that was said to be at the heart of Christian belief. If this too is unintelligible, some of the more radical Protestant theologians began to argue, it cannot be required of us that we believe it. We can parrot the words, but we cannot grasp the ideas those words are intended to convey. If so, we must look more closely at those passages of Scripture that are interpreted by orthodox theologians as shadowing forth the doctrine of the Trinity. The texts in question might have been twisted from their original purpose, or might be mere corruptions, as Newton argued in a manuscript text that passed through Locke's hands.[6] Locke's claim that revelation can never contradict reason, and that we should reject supposed revelations that purport to overthrow reason as impostures or misunderstandings, might have truly radical implications for a religion such as Christianity.

If revelation cannot contradict reason, what is its proper role? For Locke, it can supplement our knowledge on subjects where reason is silent. It is, for example, plausible to suppose that there may be intelligent beings superior to us, and possessed of powers and faculties we lack. Reasoning by analogy, Locke argues, can show that this is probable (EHU IV, xvi, 12, N 666), but could never establish it as known. The existence of angels and demons could, however, be made known to us by revelation, if God thinks it sufficiently important. If we are confident that the scriptural account of the roles and offices of angels is a genuine revelation, we can accept it as such, since it merely fills a manifest gap in our natural knowledge, and does not contradict anything we know by nature. And the details of Christ's Second Coming, and of the Resurrection of the Dead, and the Last Judgement, are clearly the sorts of things that could never be objects of natural knowledge but could only be known by the supernatural aid of revelation. There remains plenty of room, within a Lockean theology, for revelation to supplement reason and observation, thus supplying us with new knowledge that we could never have gained by our unaided powers. Although Locke was on friendly terms with the major deists of his age, he was never himself a deist. A revealed religion such as Christianity can, in his view, involve mysteries,[7] in the sense of propositions accepted on faith but not discoverable by reason alone. It cannot contain anything manifestly unintelligible or contrary to reason. What theologians should never do, Locke insists, is to cry up faith in opposition to reason and in defence of 'extravagant opinions and ceremonies'. Such a crying up of faith against reason is, Locke thinks, responsible for most of the absurdities of the prevailing systems of religion that continue to 'possess and divide Mankind', and to cause all manner of troubles (EHU IV, xviii, 11, N 696).

3. Locke's Cosmological Proof

Many people in Locke's day believed that the idea of God was an innate one, engraved, as it were, upon our souls by our Creator. This thought lies at the heart of Descartes' 'trademark' argument for the existence of God in the *Third Meditation*, and was also endorsed by many theologians with Platonist and Augustinian leanings.[8] For an empiricist like Locke, the idea of God must have proper credentials in experience.[9] We know what it is to think and to will, as we have these ideas from reflection on the contents of our own minds. The imagination has the power to augment its ideas. So we can conceive of an intelligent being much wiser and more powerful than human beings. On this basis we can come to have the idea of a supreme intelligence ruling over our world. This is how an empiricist has to account for our possession of an idea of God. But even if there is no innate idea of God, as Locke has already argued in Book One of the *Essay*, God has not left Himself without witness:

> THOUGH GOD has given us no innate *Ideas* of himself; though he has stamped no original Characters on our Minds, wherein we may read his Being: yet having furnished us with those Faculties, our Minds are endowed with, he hath not left himself without witness: since we have Sense, Perception, and Reason, and cannot want a clear proof of him, so long as we carry our selves about us. (EHU IV, x, 1, N 619)

The proof of the existence of God, Locke insists, is of a degree of evidence 'equal to mathematical certainty', although – like many mathematical proofs – it requires thought and careful attention. We start with a simple existential claim:

(P1) Something now exists.

Our greatest certainty on this score is the certainty of our own existence, which for Locke has the highest grade of intuitive certainty, beyond the reach of any genuine doubt.

(P2) Nothing can come from nothing.

This again is for Locke a matter of intuitive certainty, of a degree of evidence at least equal to that of any proposition in Euclid. But from P1 and P2 alone, Locke argues, we can infer the existence of an eternal being:

> If, therefore, we know there is some real Being, and that Non-entity cannot produce any real Being, it is an evident demonstration, that from Eternity there has been something; Since what was not from Eternity, had a Beginning; and what had a Beginning, must be produced by something else. (EHU IV, x, 3, N 620)

The problem with this, as any novice in logic can point out, is that 'from eternity there has been something' is ambiguous. It could be taken to assert that (A) *something or other* has existed at any moment of past time – there has never been absolute nothingness. Or it could be taken to assert that (B) some particular thing has existed from all eternity. It is the weak reading (A) that follows from Locke's premises, but he needs the strong reading (B) that does not follow. The fallacy is known by logicians as a quantifier-shift, and is usually illustrated by examples of the 'every nice girl loves a sailor' variety. Even if it were true that every nice girl does love a sailor, it plainly does not follow that some particular sailor (lucky man!) is loved by every nice girl. Locke's argument commits exactly the same fallacy, as critics such as Leibniz were not slow to point out.[10]

Locke goes on to try to show that the eternal being must be supremely powerful, but his argument here fares no better:

> Next, it is evident, that what had its Being and Beginning from another, must also have all that which is in, and belongs to its Being from another too. All the Powers it has, must be owing to, and received from the same Source. This eternal Source then of all being must also be the Source and Original of all Power: and so *this eternal Being must be also the most powerful*. (EHU IV, x, 4, N 620)

Even if we grant the premise that if A owes its existence to B, A thereby also derives its powers from B, nothing will follow about the existence of a single eternal and supremely powerful being. The ancient atomists could accept that some things (the atoms) have existed from all eternity, and that whenever atoms come together to form a compound body, the compound body owes its properties and powers to its constituent atoms.[11] Given the importance of texture or arrangement of parts in atomist accounts of qualities, it is crucial that the compound owes this debt to its constituent atoms taken collectively rather than individually. An atomist could thus accept that whenever a finite thing such as a cat comes-to-be, it owes its distinctive powers to the atoms from which it has come to be – those powers do not spring from nothing, but are reductively explicable in terms of the sizes, shapes, motions and arrangements of the atoms. The atomists were as keen on the maxim *ex nihilo nihil fit* as Locke himself.

Locke's next attempt looks a little more promising. We know from immediate experience, he insists, not just that something or other exists, but that at least one 'knowing, intelligent being' exists. From this we can launch an argument in the form of a dilemma:

> There was a time then, when there was no knowing Being, and when Knowledge began to be; or else there has been *a knowing Being from Eternity*. If it be said, there was a time when no Being had any Knowledge, when that eternal Being was devoid of Understanding. I reply, that then it was impossible there should ever have been any Knowledge. It being as impossible, that Things wholly void of Knowledge, and operating blindly, and without any Perception, should produce a knowing Being, as it is impossible, that a Triangle should make it self three Angles bigger than two right ones. For it is as repugnant to the *Idea* of senseless Matter, that it should put into it self Sense, Perception, and Knowledge, as it is repugnant to the *Idea* of a Triangle that it should put into it self greater Angles than two right ones. (EHU IV, x, 5, N 620–1)

Here Locke is staking his argument on a metaphysical thesis of the *irreducibility of the mental*, which he takes to be discoverable simply by inspection of our ideas. If this is right, then mind and intelligence couldn't simply have arisen in the course of the evolution of life on Earth, perhaps as an emergent consequence of some level of complexity of the organization of mindless atoms. The ordinary powers of compound bodies will be reducible to the arrangements of their parts, as Boyle and the corpuscularians have taught us. But the mind, Locke is telling us, is entirely different, and we can know it to be irreducible simply from the inspection of our ideas. This is a bold metaphysical claim, but it is backed up by no argument. A critic will reply with two obvious rejoinders. In the first place, the irreducibility thesis has been asserted without proof, and might simply be denied. But even if the irreducibility thesis is true, it doesn't greatly advance the cause of theism. If there is now at least one mind, and minds couldn't have arisen from anything mindless, it will follow that there have always been minds. It will not follow that there must be a single supreme or eternal mind. To argue from 'at all moments of past time, some mind or other has existed' to 'some particular mind has existed at all moments of past time' would be to commit another quantifier-shift fallacy.

Locke's version of the cosmological proof is hopelessly broken-backed and cannot be rescued. The flaws in his reasoning at this point are so obvious that it is puzzling that he didn't take the opportunity, during his successive revisions of the *Essay*, either to buttress his own argument or to abandon it in favour of another attempted proof of God's existence. If he wants a version of the cosmological argument, he might champion the argument *ex contingentia mundi*, from the contingency of all things in the observable world to the existence of a necessary being as their ground. This is the 'Third Way' of Aquinas, and versions of it can be found in the writings of Locke's contemporaries such as Leibniz and Samuel Clarke. The argument takes us into some deep waters, but it isn't manifestly fallacious, as Locke's 'proof' is. Alternatively, Locke might simply have resorted to the ever-popular argument to design favoured by friends such as Robert Boyle and Isaac Newton. So why doesn't Locke make either of these moves? Our answers here can only be speculative.

Locke may well have thought his version of the cosmological argument disarmingly modest in its requirements. It needs only the simple ideas of existence and of duration, both of which he thinks he can establish on proper empirical grounds, and then the compound idea of existence-at-a-time, which is simply a product of combination. And it needs only the assumption that nothing comes from nothing, which has as good a claim to self-evidence as any axiom of metaphysics. The argument *ex contingentia mundi* requires much richer resources, both in terms of concepts and premises. We need to grasp the twin concepts of *necessary existence* and *contingent existence*, which will inevitably lead us into the dark waters of modality. Locke may have wondered whether we have clear ideas corresponding to these terms – later empiricists such as David Hume would deny this.[12] And the argument *ex contingentia mundi* requires, as an essential argumentative step, the application of the principle of sufficient reason to the entire physical universe taken as a whole. Critics have objected to this step in the argument, stating that we can ask the reason for any given contingent thing, but that the question why this entire sequence of contingent things exists rather than some other possible sequence, or no universe at all, is somehow ill-formed or illegitimate. There are deep and controversial issues here. So we can see the attractions for Locke of his own disarmingly modest version of the cosmological argument. It's just a pity that it's so manifestly invalid.

As for the argument to design, we know that it was championed by many of Locke's contemporaries, including natural scientists of the calibre of Boyle and Newton. Locke gave a brief outline of this argument in his early and unpublished *Essays on the Law of Nature*,[13] and never abandoned his belief in its fundamental soundness. There are plenty of passages in the *Essay* that show his continued allegiance to the inference from the order and harmony of nature to the existence of a wise and benign presiding intelligence. In Book One, for example, after dismissing the claim that the idea of God is innate, Locke goes on to dispel fears that his rejection of innatism will foster atheism:

> For the visible marks of extraordinary Wisdom and Power, appear so plainly in all the Works of the Creation, that a rational Creature, who will but seriously reflect on them, cannot miss the discovery of a *Deity*. . . . (EHU I, iv, 9, N 89)

And towards the very end of the *Essay*, in chapter 20 of Book Four, on 'Wrong Assent, or Error', he endorses a probabilistic version of the design argument, which can be traced back as far as Cicero's *De Natura Deorum*:

> Whether it be probable, that a promiscuous jumble of printing Letters should often fall into a Method and Order, which should stamp on Paper a coherent Discourse; or that a blind fortuitous concourse of Atoms, not guided by an understanding Agent, should frequently constitute the Bodies of any Species of Animals: in these and the like Cases, I think, no Body that considers them, can be one jot at a stand which side to take, nor at all waver in his Assent. (EHU IV, xx, 15, N 716)

There can be no doubt that Locke was both fully aware of the design argument, and fundamentally sympathetic to its aims and methods.

It was the preferred argument both of his favourite Latin author Cicero and of friends such as Boyle and Newton; it was the argument of his own *Essays on the Laws of Nature*; there are several passages throughout the *Essay* that show clearly that he is still firmly committed to it. And, of course, the argument to design has the crucial virtue, for an empiricist, of having good empirical credentials. It is easy to cast it in the form of an inference to best explanation, from the order of the visible universe to the postulation of an intelligent cause. Alternatively, it can be presented in the guise of an analogical argument, arguing from the principle 'like effects have like causes'. Since the contrivance of parts we observe in artefacts such as machines is the result of intelligence, analogy suggests a similar intelligent cause for the still greater levels of contrivance discernible in the parts of animals and plants. Or we can follow Cicero and argue probabilistically against the Epicurean theory that plants and animals have come-to-be through the chance combinations of atoms. For an empiricist like Locke, the design argument must have had enormous appeal.

The other obvious advantage of the design argument is that it can – at least in principle – provide grounds for belief in a providential Deity, a God who has some care or concern for His human creatures. This is precisely the point at which natural theology is meant to provide a foundation for revealed religion. Believers in revealed religion need to assume not merely that there is a God but that this Being cares about us, wants us to live in a certain way, and is willing and able to provide some indication of His intentions. A metaphysical proof of the existence of an eternal Being, or a necessary Being, falls a long way short of this. Even the proof of an eternal Mind or Intelligence, which is what Locke thinks he can supply, would provide at best minimal grounds for the belief in providence. In Aristotle's philosophy, for example, there is an eternal intelligence (God), but the only worthy object for God's contemplations is His own perfections. But if we argue from the order of nature, we can argue that it has been designed to suit our needs, and thus infer benevolence as well as wisdom. There are obvious objections from natural evils of various kinds, but the prospects of proving a providential Deity by means of the design argument are surely better than those of any cosmological proof. And it is precisely a providential Deity that Locke wants to establish.

So why does Locke insist that the existence of God is a matter of demonstration rather than of sound judgement? And why does he provide us with such a hopeless attempt at a demonstration? We can guess at an answer to the first of these two questions; the second remains a puzzle. We know that he wanted a demonstration of God's existence, and we have suggested that this might be for reasons that are ultimately political, to justify the denial of toleration to atheists. If a cult grew up in our own society of Pythagorean cranks who believed that all numbers are rational, that is, can be expressed as ratios n/m, would we permit Pythagorean parents to withdraw their children from geometry classes lest they become infected with Euclidean heresy? Euclid's proof that the square root of 2 is irrational is one of the most beautiful of the mathematical proofs coming down to us from the ancient world, and produces 100 per cent conviction as soon as fully grasped. There can surely be no toleration for demonstrable error. But if the probabilistic version of the design argument is sound, the Epicurean atheist is even crazier than the man who thinks he can write Shakespearean sonnets by jumbling up a set of scrabble letters and tipping them out on to the board. There are opinions not demonstrably false but still beyond the pale of toleration. Should we tolerate flat-earthers, and allow flat-earther parents to withdraw their children from geography classes? Most of us will answer 'no', but we may then find ourselves unable to draw a clear line between opinions too crazy to be tolerated, and eccentric minority views that deserve to be regarded as having some claim to be treated seriously. If there were a clearly valid demonstration of the existence of God, difficult questions of this kind could be ducked and we could provide a clear justification for not permitting atheists to teach and defend their views.

As regards the second question, we must hold up our hands and admit that we have no good answer to offer. Locke was a very careful author, and made substantial revisions to large parts of the *Essay* in its later editions. But the 'demonstration' of the existence of God remained effectively unchanged, despite its manifest invalidity. We have explained why Locke might have preferred his simpler version of the cosmological argument to the metaphysically richer versions favoured by contemporaries such as Leibniz and Clarke. He wants an argument that relies only on the simple ideas of existence and duration, and on the simple principle that nothing comes from nothing. But he could and should have seen that his argument is little better than a howler. Even the greatest of philosophers can have an off day.

4. The Reasonableness of Christianity

What, Locke asked, makes a man a Christian? Is there a minimal set of sufficient conditions, fundamental to the faith, belief in which is enough to make a man a member of the Church? Or must one believe all the propositions of a long and detailed Creed, dissent from any one of which necessarily implies exclusion? On the former view, Christianity is a 'broad Church', admitting great variety of opinions on all points considered inessential. On the latter view, there is at most one true and 'narrow' Church, and anyone outside the true Church is a heretic of some kind. (It would be logically possible that there are no true Churches and no true Christians at all.) For a man who grew up during the English Civil War (in large part a war of religion), and who had close friends among the persecuted Protestants of France, the former option must have seemed vastly more attractive. Hence Locke finds himself involved in the search – common to many Protestant theologians of broadly liberal views – for the true fundamentals of the faith. If these can be fixed, then Christians can agree to disagree – in a scholarly and temperate manner – over the remaining points of doctrinal disagreement. Instead of fierce quarrels about who is in and who is out, Christians should agree to the broadest inclusion possible, and then have brotherly disputes about still contested points of theology. As a political programme, this is the dream of the advocates of *comprehension* within the Church. Locke liked the idea, but eventually came to see that comprehension was impracticable in England in political terms, and that a toleration Bill would have much better prospects for success.

Where should we search for the fundamentals of the faith? For a good Protestant like Locke, there can be only one answer to this question: we must search the Scriptures. In particular, Locke argues, we must search the four Gospels and the Acts of the Apostles to determine what the first Christians believed, and what was required for conversion and baptism.[14] This is the project of the *Reasonableness of Christianity*: to strip away layer upon layer of later Christian theology and go back to the primary sources.[15] What did Christ tell his disciples about himself and his mission; what did the Apostles require of their very first converts? The authority of Scripture is supreme: if the Scriptures tell us that a particular confession of faith F is sufficient to make a man a Christian, then any self-proclaimed human authority that claims F is not sufficient is un-Christian. Here Locke finds himself in the company of many Protestant theologians, although most of them would have been very unhappy at Locke's radical conclusions. It is not in the least surprising that the *Reason-ableness* and its *Vindications* were published under the veil of ano-nymity, and only acknowledged by Locke at his death.

The surprising conclusion Locke reaches as a result of his inves-tigations is that the simple belief that 'Jesus Christ is the promised Messiah' was enough to make a man a Christian. There are, of course, a number of background assumptions we would need to spell out to give sense to this belief, and these are of course precon-ditions for Christian belief. One needs to believe that there is a God, and a God who cares enough about humans to send us revelations of His will. One needs to believe that the Old Testament contains records of a number of revelations given to the prophets, including revelations of a promised Messiah. One needs to have some concep-tion of what the term 'Messiah' signifies in its original context. Locke is not, as his fierce critic John Edwards claimed, trying to establish a Christian Creed reduced to a single proposition.[16] That objection simply rests on a misunderstanding, as Locke pointed out at some length in his two published *Vindications* of the *Reasonable-ness*. He is not trying to write a new Christian Creed, a list of propo-sitions slimmed down from thirty-nine[17] to just a single one; he is asking what additional belief, on top of the background assump-tions already widely accepted among a community such as the Jews, suffices to mark a man out as a Christian.

The glaring omission from Locke's account is, of course, the metaphysics of the Trinity and the Incarnation. The earliest Chris-tians are not required to give their assent to Christ's divinity, or to the consubstantial nature of Father, Son and Holy Ghost. The dis-ciples, according to the Scriptures themselves, were unlearned men, innocent of deep and dark matters of Greek metaphysics. They would almost certainly have understood nothing of the later debates between Athanasians and Arians, and might well have been driven to distraction by the great battle over the famous iota. Is the Son *homoousios* (same substance) with the Father, as the orthodox have been taught since the great Council of Nicaea (AD 325), or is he merely *homoiousios* (of like substance)? But surely these men were Christians, even if innocent of – and perhaps even contemptuous of – metaphysical subtleties? If this is correct, it follows that belief in orthodox accounts of the Trinity and the Incarnation cannot be essential for membership of the Church of Christ. The Arians, who thought that the Son was the first of creatures, the highest of the angels, could still count as Christians by Locke's test. Even the notorious Socinians, who believed that Christ was just a man with a superhuman mission and authority, can count as Christians.[18] In response to the accusations of Edwards[19] and others, Locke continued to deny that he had been influenced by the writings of the Socinians, or that he was himself a secret Socinian. Arguing for a Church broad enough to include Arians and Socinians is not equivalent to arguing for the truth of either position. On a strict point of logic, this is clearly correct: one could be a firm believer in the Athanasian formula and still favour a broad and inclusive Church. The problem, of course, is that the divinity of Christ is central to much of what the orthodox take to be essential features of Christian faith and practice, so the defenders of orthodoxy are always going to say that Arians and Socinians aren't 'real' Christians.

Do we know Locke's own views? We know that, despite explicit protestations to the contrary, he was thoroughly familiar with anti-Trinitarian views in theology. We know that he was in close correspondence with committed anti-Trinitarians such as Isaac Newton. And we have the evidence both of his 'Second Reply' to Edward Stillingfleet, Bishop of Worcester, and of his letter of May 1695 to his friend Limborch. The bishop had levelled against Locke the accusation that the doctrines of the *Essay* favoured Socinianism, and suggested that Locke should clear himself of the charge by an explicit profession of faith in the doctrine of the Trinity, 'as it has been received' in the Christian Church. Locke replied, with his characteristic dry wit, that:

> My lord, my Bible is faulty again; for I do not remember that I ever read in it either of these propositions, in these precise words, 'there are three persons in one nature, or, there are two natures and one person'. When your lordship shall show me a Bible wherein they are so set down, I shall think them a good instance of propositions offered me out of Scripture; till then, whoever shall say that they are propositions in the Scripture, when there are no such words, so put together, to be found in holy writ, seems to me to make a new Scripture in words and propositions, that the Holy Ghost dictated not. (WJL IV, 343)

Strictly speaking, all Locke is saying here is that the Athanasian formula is not to be found in Holy Writ, not that he himself doubts or denies its truth. The letter to Limborch of 1695 arguably comes closer to an explicit profession of unbelief in the Trinity. 'I read with great joy', Locke writes to Limborch, '[Chapter 8 of Book 5 of your *Theologia Christiana*,] from which I perceived that one theologian was to be found for whom I am not a heretic' (C V, 371). Limborch had defended in his *Theologia* a position very close to the one being worked on – in secret – by Locke, that is, that the confession of faith that makes a man a Christian is simply that 'Jesus Christ is the Messiah', and thus that Arians and Socinians can be counted among Christians. Locke's letter does not amount to an explicit rejection of the Trinity, but comes close to it. After all, the opinions for which he would or would not be a heretic are his views about Christ, not his views about who is or is not a Christian. The most natural reading of Locke's letter is that he was seriously entertaining doubts about the scriptural basis for the belief in Christ's divinity, and was reassured to learn that such doubts would not make him a heretic in the eyes of at least one respected Protestant theologian. John Marshall sums up the evidence, and concludes that 'it is very likely that Locke held some form of Unitarian belief when writing the *Reasonableness*'.[20] This was the view of Locke's contemporaries, and of most modern scholars, but the evidence remains less than conclusive.

There are two clearly distinct argumentative contexts for the *Reasonableness*. We have been discussing the debate over fundamentals within the Church, and the difficulty of establishing criteria for inclusion within the company of the faithful. But there is of course another context suggested by the title. A crucial advantage of his 'broad Church' theology, Locke can argue, is that it allows Christians to defend the reasonableness of their faith against the deists. If the Christian religion requires belief in the Trinity and the Incarnation, the very intelligibility of these doctrines can be queried. Can a man be God? Can God be (somehow) both three and one? Christian theologians have, of course, spent countless hours of study and reflection, and written many vast and learned tomes, trying to shed light on these mysteries. One may reasonably doubt whether such labours have illuminated the mysteries or served only to darken them. The foes of Christianity will claim that we can't assent where we can't even understand: we can parrot the words but can attach no clear ideas to them. But if the Christian religion requires only our assent to 'Jesus Christ is the promised Messiah', and the role of the Messiah is then explained in terms of a special divine mission and authority, there is nothing here for reason to baulk at. This will be a proposition 'above reason' in the sense that it could never be discovered by reason alone, but in no way contrary to reason, or inconsistent with anything that reason discovers. The *Reasonableness* teaches a single broad Church with a simple and readily intelligible Creed, and the barest minimum of metaphysics. A crucial advantage of my type of theology, Locke is telling his readers, is that it enables Christians to defend the reasonableness of their religion against sceptics and deists.

5. God and the Law of Nature

The objection to his *Essay* that irked Locke the most, and that prompted some of his sharpest replies, was that his rejection of innate ideas and innate principles undermined morality. His Oxford-based friend James Tyrrell wrote to him in February 1690, warning him that:

> I find the divines much scandalized that so sweet and easy a part of their sermons: as that of the Law written in the heart is rendred false and uselesse: but you know the narrownesse of most of their principles. (C IV, 11)

In a later letter, written in June of the same year, Tyrrell reports the view of 'some thinking men' at the university that, by denying the existence of a moral law inscribed on to every human soul at its creation, Locke is effectively denying the very existence of a moral law of nature at all. You explicitly admit, Tyrrell writes to his friend, three standards against which men judge their actions. These are: (1) the law of God as known to Christians through revelation; (2) the laws of 'politick societys'; and (3) the law of fashion and local custom. But then, he continues, the pagans in a state of nature will have only local customs of praise and blame to judge their actions by:

> by which hypothesis, if Drunkennesse, and sodomy, and cruelty to Enemyes (for example) (which are not vices directly contrary to the peace of civil society) should be in any Countrey (as I thinke I can shew some examples of that kind: out of the Spanish and other relations of America) thought praise worthy; and that those that could drink most; or enjoy most boys and be most cruel (not only) should be counted the gallantest, and most virtuous, but be so indeed. (C IV, 101)

Tyrrell knows very well that his old friend is touchy and prickly, and not at his best in responding to criticism. He reports, he writes, not his own but 'other men's censures', and asks for help in replying to them on Locke's behalf. You do not, Tyrrell writes again, tell us where to find God's laws, if not in the Scriptures. Is there any evidence in nature – and thus accessible to all men without the aid of revelation – that we are subject to a moral law at all (C IV, 107–8)? Can it be demonstrated that there is an afterlife with rewards for virtue and punishments for vice, and thus proper sanctions to back up the force of the law? Christians believe this because it is taught them in Scripture, but the evidence from the ancient world is that pagan philosophers held all manner of opposing views on the subject. Locke's reply shows him at his most touchy. Instead of thanking an old friend for helping him clear up a possible misunderstanding, he responds in vitriolic terms:

> I see you or your friends are so far from understanding me yet rightly that I shall give you the trouble of a few lines to make my meaning clearer, if possible, then it is, though I am apt to thinke that to any unprejudiced Reader, who will consider there what I ought to say, and not what he will phansy I should say besides my purpose, it is as plain as any thing can well be – L1, C3, S13, where it was proper for me to speake my opinion of the Law of Nature, I affirme in as direct words as can ordinarily be made use of to Expresse ones thoughts that there is a Law of Nature knowable by the light of Nature. (C IV, 110)

There are, Locke explains, three types of laws against which men can judge their actions. These are the divine law, municipal or civil law, and the law of custom and reputation. The divine law can be made known to us either by revelation or by the natural light of reason. In the second and subsequent editions of the *Essay*, Locke tries to make this perfectly clear:

7. The *Laws* that Men generally refer their Actions to, to judge of their Rectitude, or Obliquity, seem to me to be these three. (1) The *Divine* Law. (2) The *Civil* Law. (3) The Law of *Opinion* or *Reputation*, if I may so call it. By the Relation they bear to the first of these, Men judge whether their Actions are Sins, or Duties; by the second, whether they are Criminal, or Innocent; and by the third, whether they be Vertues or Vices.

8. *First*, The *Divine* Law, whereby I mean, that Law which God has set to the actions of Men, whether promulgated to them by the light of Nature, or the voice of Revelation. That God has given a Rule whereby Men should govern themselves, I think there is no

body so brutish as to deny. He has a Right to do it, we are his
Creatures: he has Goodness and Wisdom to direct our Actions to
that which is best: and he has Power to enforce it by Rewards and
Punishments, of infinite weight and duration, in another Life: for
no body can take us out of his hands. (EHU II, xxviii, 7–8, N 352)

But if the divine law of Nature is not inscribed upon our souls
in their very creation, how are we to know it without the aid of
revelation? The question is addressed in Locke's early and unpublished *Essays on the Law of Nature*, written for his students at Oxford.
In a series of eight essays, clearly designed to serve as part of a
course of moral philosophy, the thirty-year-old Locke raises and
answers the following series of questions:

E1. Is there a rule of morals, or Law of Nature given to us? Yes.
E2. Can the Law of Nature be known by the Light of Nature? Yes.
E3. Is the Law of Nature inscribed in the minds of men? No.
E4. Can Reason attain to the knowledge of Natural Law through
    sense experience? Yes.
E5. Can the Law of Nature be known from the general consent of
    men? No.
E6. Are men bound by the Law of Nature? Yes.
E7. Is the binding force of the Law of Nature perpetual and
    universal? Yes.
E8. Is every man's own interest the basis of the Law of Nature? No.

After rejecting the 'inscription' theory of innate principles of
morality in Essay Three, Locke presents his own account of natural
law in Essay Four. We come to know our duties, he argues, by a
combination of reason and sense-perception working together. The
senses provide the materials for all our knowledge of the world;
reason allows us to probe more deeply and advance in ordered
steps from things known to things unknown, from effects to causes.
Experience teaches us that our world is 'constructed with wonderful art and regularity', and thus indicates the existence of 'a powerful and wise creator of all these things' (ELN 153). Starting with
materials provided by sense-perception, reason can thus teach us of
the existence of a deity presiding over our world. Although the idea
of God is not innate, 'all men everywhere are sufficiently prepared
by nature to discover God in His works, so long as they are not
indifferent to the use of the inborn faculties and do not refuse to
follow whither nature leads' (ELN 155). From the very make and
constitution of our minds and bodies, Locke argues, we can infer

God's intentions in our creation, and thus discover what sorts of lives we should lead.

The problem for a theory of this kind is one of motivation and sanctions. Does the perception of a moral duty automatically motivate a man to do it, or must the moral law be backed up by external sanctions? The difficulty is that the exercise of the moral virtues does not generally serve self-interest. Justice can cost a man money; temperance can lose him his friends; courage can cost him his life. If one believes in an afterlife with rewards for virtue and punishments for vice, this problem of motivation is easily solved. Moral virtue will just be enlightened self-interest, involving a crucial element of foresight and the ability to discount lesser present goods in the name of greater future ones. But the ancient philosophers, we know, struggled to prove the afterlife on the basis of natural reason alone. Plato advances arguments for the immortality of the soul in the *Phaedo*, but with the best will in the world they can hardly be taken as demonstrative. Aristotle is not entirely clear on the subject, but most scholars read *De Anima* as denying individual immortality. The Epicureans flatly reject immortality, arguing that the atoms of the human soul disperse like a fine vapour when the body dies. Locke boasts no greater insight into the nature or essence of the soul than the ancients possessed. Indeed, he is certain, on the basis of his own empiricist principles, that we have no insight into the substance of the soul.

It seems that Locke finds himself obliged to argue from the morality to the metaphysics rather than vice versa. If we know (A) that we are subjects of the moral law, and know also (B) that the moral law could have no authority over us unless backed up by proper sanctions, then such sanctions must exist. Somehow or other, our Creator must have arranged things that there are rewards for virtue and penalties for vice. These must somehow be built into the very fabric of our world, quite independently of people's beliefs concerning them. The problem with this line of argument is that either (A) or (B) could easily be denied. Without the aid of revelation, Tyrrell's Oxford friends thought, Locke's theory leaves us subject only to the civil law and to the law of reputation. For both of these there are proper sanctions of civil penalties and public disapproval of various kinds. But why should I feel bound to observe the promptings of my conscience if I know I can cheat and steal with impunity, and be regarded as a hero by my peer group? Consider a member of a modern gang in a city where the police have lost control of the streets. He can go on a looting spree with little or no fear of civil penalties. The more he steals, the higher his prestige among his peers. It seems that he can deny either the existence or the authority of the moral 'law of nature' without obvious absurdity.

Locke's problems in this area are made worse by his increasing commitment to hedonism in his moral psychology, a commitment clearly spelled out in chapter 20 of Book Two of the *Essay*:

> Things then are Good or Evil only in reference to Pleasure or Pain. That we call *Good* which is *apt to cause or increase Pleasure, or diminish Pain in us; or else to procure, or preserve us the possession of any other Good, or absence of any Evil*. And on the contrary, we name that *Evil* which is *apt to produce or increase any Pain, or diminish any Pleasure in us, or else to procure us any Evil, or deprive us of any Good*. By Pleasure or Pain, I must be understood to mean of Body or Mind, as they are commonly distinguished; though in truth they be only different Constitutions of the Mind, sometimes occasioned by disorder in the Body, sometimes by Thoughts of the Mind. (EHU II, xx, 2, N 229)

In fact, Locke thinks, it is the *felt* absence of some acknowledged good that spurs us into action. Without this feeling of *uneasiness*, we can rest content with the lack of many things judged to be worth having:

> The uneasiness a Man finds in himself upon the absence of anything whose present enjoyment carries the *Idea* of Delight with it, is what we call Desire; which is greater or less, as that uneasiness is more or less vehement. Where, by the bye, it may perhaps be of some use to remark, that the chief, if not only, spur to humane Industry and Action is uneasiness. For whatever good is propos'd, if its absence carries no displeasure nor pain with it; if a Man can be easie and content without it, there is no desire or endeavour after it. (EHU II, xx, 6, N 230–1)

The moral law needs to be backed up by appropriate sanctions. These can either be internal or external. For the sanctions to motivate us, they must excite uneasiness of some kind. For an external sanction, there is the obvious threat of punishment, and there is no problem in explaining how this can motivate us. Anyone might be uneasy if the torments of Hell are a real prospect for them. But natural philosophy struggles to find good arguments for the existence of an afterlife with rewards and punishments. If this is a bare speculative possibility, affirmed by some philosophers and denied by others, its motivational power is much diminished. We are forced to ask whether there are any immanent and this-worldly sanctions for wrongdoing. Some of the ancient Greeks thought so, but Locke's hedonism makes it difficult for him to follow them, unless there is a felt uneasiness in wrongdoing as such. And this seems, all too often, to be simply contrary to experience. If God has written a moral law of nature into our very constitution and faculties, and discoverable by reason and experience, it has to be confessed that its traces are often very faint.[21]

6

The Soul and the Afterlife

1. The Immortality of the Soul

We have already seen in the previous chapter that Catholic philosophers were ordered by the Lateran Council to prove not only the existence of God, but also the immortality of the human soul. Many Anglican philosophers, too, thought that this was part of the proper job of natural theology, although this was always a matter of some controversy.[1] Strictly speaking, the immortality of the soul cannot be demonstrated by Christian philosophers. If one believes in an omnipotent God, then of course one believes that He can annihilate at will any or all of His creatures, including human souls. But philosophy might nevertheless provide a proof that the human rational soul is *really distinct* from its body, and is thus the sort of thing that *can* exist without the human body, and that (God willing) it *will* continue to exist when the body is decomposing in its grave. This is what Descartes attempts to prove in his *Sixth Meditation*. His main argument is the argument from clear and distinct ideas. My idea of material substance (*res extensa*), he argues, is simply that of extension in three dimensions. My idea of mind or thinking substance (*res cogitans*) is that of a thinking and willing being. The clear and distinct idea of matter does not include thinking and willing; the clear and distinct idea of mind does not include extension. Mind can thus be conceived without matter and vice versa. But what can be conceived independently can exist separately. So matter can exist without mind and mind without matter.[2]

An obvious objection to the argument from clear and distinct ideas is that it seems to play fast and loose with the scope of the crucial negation. Descartes seems to be moving from 'my clear and distinct idea of matter does not represent it as thinking' to 'my clear and distinct idea of matter represents it as not thinking', and from 'my clear and distinct idea of mind does not represent it as extended' to 'my clear and distinct idea of mind represents it as not extended'. The validity of this move is discussed in the *Objections and Replies*, particularly the *Fourth Objections* and *Fourth Replies*, in which Descartes responds to his most perceptive critic, Antoine Arnauld. On the face of it, the move from 'My idea of F does not represent it as G' to 'my idea of F represents it as non-G' is obviously invalid, and could be met by a barrage of counter-examples. Descartes needs to claim that what does not hold for ideas in general does hold for the special category of clear and distinct ideas. The crucial step is made most explicitly by the greatest of the second-generation Cartesians, Nicolas Malebranche. A clear and distinct idea, he writes in one of his many replies to Arnauld, excludes whatever it does not include.[3] So the clear and distinct idea of matter excludes thought, and the clear and distinct idea of mind excludes extension.[4] If this premise is granted him, then Descartes' argument from clear and distinct ideas to substance dualism looks valid, and critics must shift their ground and query whether we in fact possess the clear and distinct ideas claimed.

But even if metaphysics could prove that the human soul is an immaterial substance distinct from the body, and capable of existing without it, this would not prove individual immortality. Suppose, as many thinkers in the ancient world believed, that each individual human soul quits its body at death, is then washed in the waters of Lethe (forgetfulness), and subsequently returns to a new human body to start a new human life. No trace of memory of its past life or lives is left to it. If this cyclical process continues without end, the soul may be immortal, but no *person* is immortal. The Christian promise of an afterlife is directed to each individual person. To be told, 'the soul now thinking and feeling in you will continue to think and feel, but in a distinct self or person' is not the same thing at all. *Your* thoughts and experiences could still come to an end. If you read Dante's *Inferno*, or *Purgatorio*, the souls of the departed are only too eager to tell the tales of their deeds while they were in the land of the living, and their vivid autobiographical memories of their sins allow them to see the justice of their punishments. Proving the existence of an immaterial substance that thinks and feels is not proving that the identity-conditions for this immaterial substance are also the identity-conditions for a person. Philosophers such as Plato, arguing for the existence of an immaterial soul, have tended to assume that a proof of the soul's immateriality would also carry with it a proof of personal survival after death. It is one of Locke's great achievements as a philosopher to show clearly that this is simply mistaken.

2. Can we Prove the Immateriality of the Soul?

The Cartesian argument for the immateriality of the soul rests on the argument for substance-dualism in the *Sixth Meditation*. According to Cartesian dualism, there are two entirely distinct types of being or substance, *res cogitans* (thinking substance) and *res extensa* (extended substance). For each type of substance, we can attain a clear and distinct idea of its essence, of the very *being* of that kind of entity. These clear and distinct ideas, for the Cartesian, do not come to us through experience but are part of the innate furniture of our minds, needing only the discipline of the *Meditations* to bring them into full awareness.

Locke will of course entirely reject this innatist account of our ideas of material and mental substance. In chapter 23 of Book Two of the *Essay* he offers his own empiricist account. Whether in sensation or reflection, he writes, experience presents us with co-occurrences of ideas that frequently occur together. A combination of size, shape, colour and taste makes up the complex idea of an apple; a combination of memories, thoughts, feelings and intentions makes up the complex idea of a mind. In sensation and reflection alike, ideas come to us in patterns or clusters. But then, says Locke,

> not imagining how these simple *Ideas* can subsist by themselves, we accustom our selves to suppose some *Substratum*, wherein they do subsist, and from which they do result, which therefore we call *Substance*. (EHU II, xxiii, 1, N 295)

Locke is not being entirely precise in his language here. Red and sweet, as we have explained, are not secondary qualities in the apple at all, but only the ideas of secondary qualities. What exists in the apple to cause us to see it as red and taste it as sweet are the corresponding red-making and sweet-making powers. His point is that our minds are reluctant to regard bodies as mere bundles of

powers, and posit or suppose some ground or substratum, something to tie the bundle together and perhaps in principle explain
their co-occurrence. We might, of course, go deeper into natural
philosophy and invoke a corpuscular account of our perceptions of
colours, sounds, smells and tastes. But if we do this, we shall only
postpone the acknowledgement of our ignorance. We end up with
an account in terms of corpuscles each of which has size, shape,
solidity and local motion. But what explains this bundling of properties at the corpuscular level? If we say that this is material substance, we shall, Locke thinks, be saying very little:

> So that if any one will examine himself concerning his *Notion* of *pure
> Substance in general*, he will find he has no other *Idea* of it at all, but
> only a Supposition of he knows not what support of such Qualities,
> which are capable of producing simple *Ideas* in us; which Qualities
> are commonly called Accidents. If any one should be asked, what is
> the subject wherein Colour or Weight inheres, he would have nothing
> to say, but the solid extended parts: And if he were demanded, what
> is it, that the Solidity and Extension adhere in, he would not be in a
> much better case, than the *Indian* before-mentioned; who, saying that
> the World was supported by a great Elephant, was asked, what the
> Elephant rested on; to which his answer was, a great Tortoise: But
> being again pressed to know what gave support to that broad-back'd
> Tortoise, replied, something, he knew not what. (EHU II, xxiii, 2, N
> 295–6)

Our idea of material substance, Locke concludes, is only an
'obscure and relative' one, conceived merely as a something-or-
other that serves a specified role. We are reluctant to believe that a
body is nothing but a bundle of powers, as this would leave too
many unanswered questions about the conditions of the bundling.
The corpuscular philosophy can in principle answer questions
about bundling at the level of observable bodies – it could in principle explain why gold is yellow and soluble in *aqua regia* in terms
of its texture. But the corpuscular philosophy presupposes recog-
nizably material particles, so metaphysical questions about the
nature or essence of matter are merely shifted to the next level
down. An atom, we might say, is a thing with properties FGH. But
what the term 'thing' signifies here remains entirely obscure. The
structure of our language seems to require us to talk of things with
bundles of powers rather than just bundles of powers *simpliciter*,
but it is not clear that thing-talk serves any explanatory role (EHU
II, xxiii, 3, N 296–7).

What holds for material substance holds equally for mental substance. Reflection provides us with the ideas of thinking and feeling and willing, not to mention pleasure and pain. But we find ourselves unable to conceive of a mind as simply a bundle of thoughts and feelings, memories and intentions, nice and nasty experiences. We find ourselves supposing a ground or substratum for all these thoughts and feelings to subsist in, and saying that a mind or spirit is a *thing* capable of thinking, just as a body is a *thing* capable of local motion. In both cases, our idea of the supposed *thing* or substance is merely an obscure and relative one: we can conceive of the role-filler only in terms of its specified role. It follows, Locke continues, that:

> *We have as clear a Notion of the Substance of Spirit, as we have of Body;* the one being supposed to be (without knowing what it is) the *Substratum* to those simple *Ideas* we have from without; and the other supposed (with a like ignorance of what it is) to be the *Substratum* to those Operations we experiment in our selves within. (EHU II, xxiii, 5, N 297–8)

Some philosophers have claimed that the idea of mind or spirit is more obscure or confused than that of body, but Locke denies this. The corpuscular philosophy is, he thinks, our best account of the nature of the material world. But the corpuscular philosophy requires particles that are extended but perfectly solid. If they are extended, they possess parts. These parts cling together throughout the entire course of nature. But the nature of the 'cement' that binds the parts and accounts for their cohesion is utterly obscure to us. The corpuscular philosophy also requires that the corpuscles have the power to communicate motion to one another by impulse, but the grounds of this power are utterly unknown. Experience tells us that bodies can move one another by impulse, just as it tells us that a mind can move its organic body by an act of will, but the grounds of these two powers are equally 'obscure and inconceivable'. Whether we are thinking about bodies or about minds, the same conclusion follows:

> For when the Mind would look beyond those original *Ideas* we have from Sensation or Reflection, and penetrate into their Causes, and manner of production, we find still it discovers nothing but its own short-sightedness. (EHU II, xxiii, 28, N 312)

The mind, we learn from experience, is something capable of thinking and feeling and willing, and also something capable of directing not only its own thoughts but also many of the motions of its associated body by acts of will. Do we know any more about the nature or essence of this 'something'? According to Descartes, *actual thinking* is the very essence or being of the mind – a mind can no more cease to think than a body can cease to have size and shape. Locke dismisses this claim with disarming modesty in one of his most famous passages. He is discussing, in chapter 1 of Part Two of the *Essay*, claims made by Platonists and others about whether the soul thinks prior to its embodiment:

> But whether the Soul be supposed to exist antecedent to, or coeval with, or some time after, the first Rudiments of Organisation, or the beginnings of Life in the Body, I leave to be disputed by those, who have better thought of that matter. I confess my self, to have one of those dull Souls, that doth not perceive it self always to contemplate *Ideas*, nor can conceive it any more necessary for the *Soul always to think*, than for the Body always to move; the perception of *Ideas* being (as I conceive) to the Soul what motion is to the Body: not its Essence, but one of its Operations. (EHU II, i, 10, N 108)

The disarming modesty of saying that he (Locke) will leave this question to others 'who have better thought of that matter' is of course disingenuous. Since experience is silent on this matter, there is nothing to dispute. Experience equally doesn't tell us that our minds continue to think during deep and dreamless sleep, but that all these sleep-thoughts are forgotten upon waking. The Cartesians claim that this is so, but they are arguing merely to defend their pet hypothesis against an obvious objection:

> 'Twill perhaps be said, that the *Soul thinks* even *in* the soundest *Sleep, but the Memory retains it not.* That the Soul in a sleeping Man should be this moment busy a-thinking, and the next moment in a waking Man, not remember, nor be able to recollect one jot of all those Thoughts, is very hard to be conceived, and would need some better Proof than bare Assertion to make it believed. (EHU II, i, 14, N 111)[5]

Of course if actual thinking is the essence of the soul, then it will follow that the soul, so long as it continues to exist, continues to think. Nothing can exist without its own essence, which, in the original Greek from which the term is derived, is the very being of a thing. But the assertion that actual thinking is the very essence of the soul has no basis in experience:

> I would be glad also to learn from these Men, who so confidently pronounce, that the humane Soul, or which is all one, that a Man always thinks, how they come to know it; nay, *how they come to know that they themselves think, when they themselves do not perceive it*. This, I am afraid, is to be sure, without proofs, and to know without perceiving: 'Tis, I suspect, a confused Notion, taken up to serve an Hypothesis; and none of those clear Truths, that either their own Evidence forces us to admit, or common Experience makes it impudence to deny. For the most that can be said of it, is, that 'tis possible the Soul may always think, but not always retain it in memory: And I say, it is as possible, that the Soul may not always think; and much more probable, that it should sometimes not think, than that it should often think, and that a long while together, and not be conscious to it self, the next moment after, that it had thought. (EHU II, i, 18, N 114–15)

Our idea of the substance of the soul is, for Locke, only an obscure and relative one, the notion of a something-or-other that has the powers of thinking, feeling, willing and moving its associated organic body. But if this is right, the Cartesian argument for substance dualism collapses. If our idea of matter is of a something-or-other X that provides a ground or substratum for extension and solidity and mobility, and our idea of mind is of a something-or-other Y, that provides a ground or substratum for thinking and willing, how could we tell whether X and Y were distinct or not? For Descartes' argument to go through, he needs the two ideas in question to be clear and distinct, and he needs the assumption made explicit by Malebranche that a clear and distinct idea excludes whatever it does not include. In place of Descartes' two clear and distinct ideas, each providing insight into the very essences of *res extensa* and *res cogitans* respectively, Locke offers us only obscure and merely relational ideas, picking out X and Y simply by their roles and giving zero insight into their essential natures. It looks as if the Cartesian argument for substance dualism is going to be a non-starter, and we will have no certain way of showing that whatever it is in us that thinks and feels is immaterial.

This conclusion is drawn in a famous passage in chapter 3 of Book Four of the *Essay*, on the extent – and the limitations – of human knowledge:

We have the *Ideas* of *Matter* and *Thinking*, but possibly shall never be able to know, whether any mere material Being thinks, or no; it being impossible for us, by the contemplation of our own *Ideas*, without revelation, to discover, whether Omnipotency has not given to some Systems of Matter fitly disposed, a power to perceive and think, or else joined and fixed to Matter, so disposed, a thinking immaterial Substance: it being, in respect of our Notions, not much more remote from our Comprehension to conceive that GOD can, if he pleases, superadd to Matter a Faculty of Thinking, than that he should super-add to it another Substance with a Faculty of Thinking; since we know not wherein Thinking consists, nor to what sort of Substances the Almighty has been pleased to give that Power, which cannot be in any created Being, but merely by the good pleasure and Bounty of the Creator. (EHU IV, iii, 6, N 540–1)

Philosophy, according to Locke, can prove the existence of a supreme and eternal thinking being (God), and can refute reductive material-ism, the thesis that thought and feeling and volition are reductively explicable in terms of the sizes, shapes, motions and arrangements of mindless material corpuscles. But these things accomplished, philosophers still face a baffling choice between two mysteries. Either God has mysteriously 'superadded' thought and feeling to a material thing (the human body) that is not, by its own nature, capable of it, or He has mysteriously linked each and every human body to an entirely distinct type of entity, namely, an immaterial soul. On the first hypothesis, that of an organic body plus 'super-added' powers, we have to attribute to some bodies faculties and powers that we cannot readily conceive to belong to them.[6] This seems to count against this hypothesis, until we realize that on the second hypothesis, substance dualism, we must attribute to bodies the power to produce ideas (sensations) in a substance of an entirely different kind, merely by means of motion. When a stream of cor-puscles strikes the back of my retina and causes me to see the colour red, the corpuscles act on my retina by means of their motions, but it is unintelligible to us how mere motion can effect changes in an immaterial substance. The two hypotheses end equally in some-thing utterly mysterious:

> For since we must allow he [God] has annexed Effects to Motion, which we can no way conceive Motion able to produce, what reason have we to conclude, that he should not order them as well to be produced in a Subject we cannot conceive capable of them, as well as in a Subject we cannot conceive the motion of Matter can any way operate upon? (EHU IV, iii, 6, N 541)

For Locke, the mind–body problem is the ultimate mystery, beyond the powers of philosophy to resolve. In this, he is echoed by a number of thinkers of our own time.[7] His point in this famous passage is a purely epistemological one, concerning the limits of our knowledge. To insist that 'we cannot demonstrate that p is false' is not to say that p is true, or even probable. Locke is not setting himself up as a champion of materialism in metaphysics. He consistently writes in terms of substance dualism, which he seems always to have regarded as the more plausible of the rival hypotheses. In the famous chapter of Book Two on personal identity he is quite explicit on this point, agreeing with an imagined critic that 'the more probable Opinion is, that this consciousness is annexed to, and the Affection of one individual immaterial Substance' (EHU II, xxvii, 25, N 345). His point in the notorious 'thinking matter' passage of Book Four is simply that probability is not knowledge. But he must have known that the passage would get him into trouble, and would be seized upon by his critics.[8] In his *New Essays*, Leibniz objects that God in His wisdom will give to His creatures properties and powers that 'can be explained through their natures'. To assume otherwise, that God gave things 'accidental powers which were not rooted in their natures', is to abandon reason and re-admit the 'occult qualities' of the scholastics.[9] The rationalist metaphysician thinks that every property of a substance must be an intelligible modification of its constitutive essence, and Locke's suggestion of 'superadded' powers obviously flouts this requirement.

How broadly might Locke have conceived of these 'superadded' powers? It is clear that he took over from his friend Boyle the vision of a reductive programme for chemistry – this is made explicit in the famous lock and key analogy. If chemistry reduces to physics, there is no need of 'superadded' properties and powers to explain such properties as solubility and chemical affinities. It is equally clear that Locke flatly rejects reducibility for psychology, arguing, as we have seen, that no arrangements and motions of mindless particles could ever give rise to thought and feeling. The interesting questions are going to come in the realm of biology. How many of the characteristic vital powers of plants and animals are reductively explicable in terms of the mere sizes, shapes, motions and arrangements of their parts? We know that Locke was consistently sceptical of the notorious Cartesian thesis that non-human animals are insentient machines – he doesn't explicitly argue against it, but consistently treats it as a joke in his correspondence. If we all believe (*pace*

Descartes) that cats and dogs are sentient beings, we need to say something about animal souls. If thought and feeling can only reside in an immaterial substance, we are going to find ourselves pondering the nature and the fate of all these millions of immaterial souls. What becomes of the souls of cats and dogs after death? Are they all endlessly reborn, as the ancient Pythagoreans and Platonists believed? A more modest hypothesis would be that the animal soul is a sort of collection of powers 'superadded' by God to the organic body, and lost at death. But this is all very speculative.

Locke insists that he is not seeking to weaken our *belief* in the human soul's immateriality when he argues that this is not a matter of knowledge. The crucial point is that we don't *need* a philosophical proof of the immateriality of the soul:

> I think not only, that it becomes the Modesty of Philosophy, not to pronounce Magisterially, where we want that Evidence that can produce Knowledge, but also that it is of use to us, to discern how far our Knowledge does reach; for the state we are at present in, not being that of Vision, we must, in many Things, content our selves with Faith and Probability: and in the present Question, about the immateriality of the Soul, if our Faculties cannot arrive at demonstrative Certainty, we need not think it strange. All the great Ends of Morality and Religion, are well enough secured, without philosophical Proofs of the Soul's Immateriality. (EHU IV, iii, 6, N 541–2)

Metaphysicians have divided into opposite and endlessly warring camps over this issue of the immateriality of the soul. The materialists, 'indulging too much their thoughts immersed altogether in matter', deny altogether the existence of anything immaterial. The dualists, 'finding not cogitation within the natural powers of matter', presumptuously conclude that not even God could add perception and thought to a material thing. But, Locke concludes, neither party can claim to know with certainty the true nature of the soul:

> 'Tis a Point, which seems to me, to be put out of the reach of our Knowledge: And he who will give himself leave to consider freely, and look into the dark and intricate part of each Hypothesis, will scarce find his Reason able to determine him fixedly for, or against the Soul's Materiality. Since on which side soever he views it, either as an unextended Substance, or as a thinking extended Matter; the difficulty to conceive either will, whilst either alone is in his Thoughts, still drive him to the contrary side. (EHU IV, iii, 6, N 542)

What matters, Locke thinks, is that we detach the moral question of the afterlife from the metaphysical question of the soul's immateriality. We need to believe in an afterlife with rewards and punishments in order to live rightly in this life. Metaphysicians from Plato to Descartes have thought that a proof of the immateriality of the soul is needed for the belief in an afterlife. But, Locke will argue, belief in an immaterial soul is neither necessary nor sufficient for belief in an afterlife. It is not sufficient, as we have already seen: the survival after the decomposition of my body of the immaterial thing that is currently having my thoughts and experiences need not amount to *my* survival, if all psychological continuity is lost. And it is not necessary: my body could be rotting in its grave, and God could 'superadd' to some newly constituted body thoughts and experiences continuous with those of my current life. But this is leading us inevitably into Locke's famous discussion of personal identity.

3. Personal Identity

Chapter 27 of Book Two of the *Essay*, entitled 'Of Identity and Diversity', was added to the second edition of 1694, in response to some questions from William Molyneux. At the heart of it is, of course, the famous account of personal identity, which has provided the starting point for so many later discussions of the topic. Even today, philosophers disputing the nature of personal identity can be roughly divided into Lockeans and anti-Lockeans, with both sides drawing on the famous discussion in the *Essay*. Critics of Locke's account will point to weaknesses, apparent inconsistencies and awkward implications; defenders of Locke will try to 'fix' the problems, smooth out the alleged inconsistencies and perhaps defend some of the curious implications. Here Locke sounds astonishingly modern. Although he is obviously addressing an issue of central concern to seventeenth-century Christians – how much metaphysics do we need if we are to understand and accept the doctrine of the afterlife? – his discussion transcends its origins and leads philosophers 300 years later in radically new directions.

In all discussions of identity, we need to distinguish two entirely distinct notions, often labelled 'numerical' and 'qualitative' identity. Qualitative identity is indiscernibility. If two things are indiscernible we would not notice if they were swapped around. They remain, however, two distinct things, even if we have no way of telling them apart. If they are material things, they will occupy distinct places at the same time, and this is sufficient for individuation. Numerical identity is the sort of identity we have in mind when we say 'one and the same', and it generally does not involve qualitative identity. We often find ourselves deploying 'one and the same' judgements to track an object across time, and this is perfectly consistent with striking qualitative changes. As usual, examples may help to clarify the distinction. A pair of monozygotic twins may be qualitatively identical or indiscernible, but they remain definitely two men rather than one. A newborn baby is qualitatively entirely different from an eighty-year-old greybeard, but they may nevertheless be one and the same man at opposite ends of his life. When philosophers discuss identity-questions, it is almost always numerical identity, with judgements regarding what makes something 'one and the same', that is at stake.

Locke's starting point is his insight that identity-judgements fall under sortal concepts. When we ask 'Is A the same as B?', Locke thinks, we always tacitly bring the judgement under an abstract idea of some kind F or G. It is this idea that will provide the grounds or criteria for judgements of identity and non-identity. We must ask, 'Is A the same F as B?', rather than 'Is A the same as B?' *simpliciter*, and the sortal concept F should give us some clues regarding how to proceed. Heraclitus famously claimed that you could not step into the same river twice, because of course the water would be different on your second plunge. An obvious and intuitively correct reply for Locke is to retort that Heraclitus has failed to grasp the concept 'river'. It belongs to the concept of a river that the water flows; if it didn't flow, you would be plunging not into a river but a lake. (Strictly speaking, of course, the contents of a lake change too, but more slowly and less obviously.) So whenever you are faced with the question, 'Is A the same as B?', your first response, for Locke, should be to ask the counter-question 'same what?' In discussions of personal identity, there are three distinct sortal terms that may be relevant: same substance (material or immaterial), same man and same person, and these must be kept sharply separate:

'Tis not therefore Unity of Substance that comprehends all sorts of *Identity*, or will determine it in every Case: But to conceive, and judge of it aright, we must consider what *Idea* the Word it is applied to stands for: It being one thing to be the same *Substance*, another the same *Man*, and a third the same *Person*, if *Person*, *Man*, and *Substance*, are three Names standing for three different *Ideas*; for such as is the

Idea belonging to that Name, such must be the *Identity*: Which if it had been a little more carefully attended to, would possibly have prevented a great deal of that Confusion which often occurs about this Matter. (EHU II, xxvii, 7, N 332)

For simple substances, the conditions of individuation are straightforward. Let us suppose for the moment that the atomic theory is true. Each atom will have been created in a distinct place, and can in principle be tracked through space and time from this 'determinate time and place of beginning to exist'. Whether any finite mind can do the tracking in practice is irrelevant – the atoms will always have perfectly determinate identity-conditions even if we cannot track them. A similar conclusion holds, Locke thinks, for finite spirits, each of which will also have its own 'determinate time and place of beginning to exist'. Here Locke applies his own somewhat idiosyncratic and anti-Cartesian view that spirits have spatial properties such as position and motion, which he had already argued for in chapter 23 of Book Two (EHU II, xxiii, 19–20, N 306–7). It is when we start to consider compound bodies that more difficult identity-questions start to arise.

When discussing compound bodies, Locke draws a sharp distinction between disorganized bodies, such as a heap of bricks, and organized bodies, such as a horse or an oak tree. For a disorganized body, he thinks, the identity of the whole depends strictly on that of the parts: replace one brick and it becomes a different heap. For an organized body, the identity-conditions are entirely different:

> In the state of living Creatures, their Identity depends not on a Mass of the same Particles; but on something else. For in them the variation of great parcels of Matter alters not the Identity: An Oak, growing from a Plant to a great Tree, and then lopp'd, is still the same Oak: And a colt grown up to a Horse, sometimes fat, sometimes lean, is all the while the same Horse: though, in both these Cases, there may be a manifest change of the parts: So that truly they are not either of them the same Masses of Matter, though they be truly one of them the same Oak, and the other the same Horse. The reason whereof is, that in these two cases of a Mass of Matter, and a living Body, *Identity* is not applied to the same thing. (EHU II, xxvii, 3, N 330)

This mass of atoms (in the mature oak) is not the *same mass of atoms* as in the sapling. But the mighty oak is nevertheless *the same tree* as the sapling. The identity conditions for animals and vegetables allow – perhaps even require – the metabolic turnover of their constituent particles. In metaphysical terms, a horse or an oak tree is more like a river than a lake. But the term 'man' functions just like the term 'horse', as the name for a type or species of animal. So we should construe 'same man' or 'same woman' in exactly the same way as 'same horse' or 'same oak':

> This also shews wherein the identity of the same *Man* consists; viz. in nothing but a participation of the same continued Life, by constantly fleeting Particles of Matter, in succession vitally united to the same organized Body. He that shall place the *Identity* of man in any thing else, but like that of other Animals in one fitly organized Body taken in any one instant, and from thence continued under one Organization of Life in several successively fleeting Particles of Matter, united to it, will find it hard, to make an *Embryo*, one of Years, mad, and sober, the same Man, by any Supposition, that will not make it possible for *Seth, Ismael, Socrates, Pilate, St Austin*, and *Caesar Borgia* to be the same Man. (EHU II, xxvii, 6, N 331–2)

Supposing for a moment that thinking requires an immaterial substance, the identity-conditions for this substance are quite distinct from those we deploy when we say that Dr Jekyll and Mr Hyde are the same man. It would be perfectly possible, on the Pythagorean theory of the transmigration of souls, for all those named men (who lived at distinct periods of history) to have numerically one and the same soul. Even if this were the case, Locke insists, they would not be the same man, because there is no continuity of biological organization connecting them. 'A is the same man as B' neither implies nor is implied by 'A is the same substance (material or immaterial) as B'. To say 'A is the same man as B' implies only a continuity of biological organization, which requires a turnover of material components and has no implications whatsoever regarding the presence or identity of any immaterial soul. If there is an immaterial soul, its identity-conditions are not those of the individual biological organism that is the man, as Locke's example clearly shows.

Dr Jekyll and Mr Hyde, we have said, are one and the same man. If the police track a bloody trail from one of Hyde's crimes, it will lead them to Jekyll's house. If Hyde is injured in a brawl, Jekyll will wake up with the wounds, although he will find himself unable to account for them.[10] Are Jekyll and Hyde the same *person*? Should Jekyll be held to account for Hyde's crimes? Such questions, for Locke, are not settled by the fact that Jekyll and Hyde are clearly the same *man*. Each of us, according to Locke, has a sense of self and a special concern for self.

> *Person*, as I take it, is the name for this *self*. Where-ever a Man finds what he calls *himself*, there, I think, another may say is the same *Person*. It is a Forensick Term, appropriating Actions and their Merit; and so belongs only to intelligent Agents capable of a Law, and Happiness and Misery. This personality extends it *self* beyond present Existence to what is past, only by consciousness, whereby it becomes concerned and accountable, owns and imputes to it *self* past Actions, just upon the same ground, and for the same reason, that it does the present. (EHU II, xxvii, 26, N 346)

It is by consciousness of one's own past actions that they are constituted the actions of the same *person*, and this consciousness tells us nothing about its metaphysical grounding. Locke is happy to agree that it is 'the more probable Opinion' that this consciousness is 'annexed to and the Affection of one individual immaterial Substance' (EHU II, xxvii, 25, N 345), but insists that the identity-conditions for this substance ('same soul') are quite distinct from those of the self ('same person'). We have already seen that sameness of soul is not *sufficient* for sameness of person: if my soul was previously that of Hitler, I would still feel no glimmering of guilt or responsibility for Hitler's crimes. If the metaphysical police came knocking at my door, and told me that they had been tracking my soul through space and time, and had discovered that I was answerable for the deaths of millions, I would think they were crazy. Locke also has no difficulty in showing that sameness of soul is not necessary for sameness of person: personal identity, he says, depends only on consciousness, 'whether it be annexed only to one individual Substance, or can be continued in a succession of several Substances' (EHU II, xxvii, 10, N 336). Suppose we have a series of distinct individual souls S1, 2, 3, 4, etc. Then consider a temporally organized sequence of thoughts Ψ1, 2, 3, 4, etc., linked by psychological continuity, so Ψ2 involves memories of Ψ1 and intentions directed towards Ψ3 and Ψ4. If all these connections hold, Locke argues, it wouldn't matter if Ψ1 took place in S1, Ψ2 in S2, Ψ3 in S3, and Ψ4 in S4. From the God's eye point of view of a metaphysician, this sequence of thoughts would be 'skipping' from one soul to another, but from the internal point of view of the subject, everything would be perfectly normal and the sequence of experiences would be indistinguishable from a sequence grounded in a single soul. So even if there is an immaterial soul, which Locke thinks probable, its identity-conditions are not those of the person. Locke doesn't press the more radical line of argument that is available to him here, that we have no access to any identity-criteria for immaterial souls. It doesn't seem to matter in the slightest whether my thoughts go on in one soul, seventeen souls, or ten million souls.[11]

Just as a series of thoughts and experiences could jump from one immaterial substance to another, so they could jump from one organized body to another. Suppose for the moment that the opinion Locke has described as probable is true, and that the thoughts of a single person are in fact affections of one individual immaterial substance or soul. This soul could in principle move between bodies, carrying its consciousness with it. In such cases, we would have the same person but not the same man:

> But yet the Soul alone in the change of Bodies, would scarce, to any one, but to him that makes the Soul the *Man*, be enough to make the same *Man*. For should the Soul of a Prince, carrying with it the consciousness of the Prince's past Life, enter and inform the Body of a Cobler as soon as deserted by his own Soul, every one sees, he would be the same Person with the Prince, accountable only for the Prince's Actions: But who would say it was the same Man? The Body too goes to the making the Man. (EHU II, xxvii, 15, N 340)

In ordinary life, we rarely need to make explicit this distinction between 'same person' and 'same man', but if we are concerned to make sense of the Christian doctrine of the resurrection and the afterlife, such distinctions become all-important. At the resurrection, God may fashion for us new bodies, not necessarily physically continuous with the old ones, or involving any attempt to recombine our previous atoms.[12] So long as the continuity of consciousness is preserved, the person may think of the new body as *his* or *her* body, without worrying about its provenance. The Christian promise of a *personal* afterlife is innocent of metaphysics. It could equally be accepted by a believer in materialism and mortalism and by a believer in Cartesian dualism. The precise metaphysical bearer of the ongoing person's thoughts and experiences is something philosophers remain ignorant of, and perhaps can never hope to know. Whether Scripture contains a clear and unambiguous message on this subject is something Locke was actively researching at his death.[13] Since philosophy cannot penetrate this mystery, our best chance of acquiring knowledge is through revelation.

When Locke speaks of 'consciousness' as linking a sequence of thoughts and experiences and thereby constituting a person, he generally has *memory* in mind. My actions are those I appropriate and ascribe to myself, and as it were take ownership of, through an act of memory. But this emphasis on memory raises an obvious difficulty, spotted by Molyneux. In a common enough type of case, a man gets blind drunk, commits a crime in that condition, and wakes the next morning with a foul hangover but no recollection of his deeds the previous night. When the police come to arrest and charge him he says, sincerely enough, 'I don't remember doing that.' The physical evidence (fingerprints, perhaps) establishes beyond reasonable doubt that this is one and the same man, but by Locke's criterion it looks as if it is not one and the same person. On your theory, Molyneux urges, it looks as if punishing this person is unjust. Locke's reply is not altogether convincing:

> Human judicatures justly punish him, because the fact is proved against him; but want of consciousness cannot be proved for him. (C IV, 785)

But 'the fact' here is proved only of *the man*, in Locke's terms, not of *the person*. It looks as if, on Locke's account, the merely human penal system will necessarily commit numerous acts of injustice against innocent persons. No human penal system could in practice admit 'I don't remember' as an all-purpose means of avoiding punishment, so we will find ourselves establishing that it is the same man who committed the crime, and permitting the inference that it is also the same person. This will lead to occasional injustices, in Locke's terms, but it may be the best we humans can achieve. By contrast, God's justice is absolute and perfect: at the Day of Judgement, no one will be judged for offences he or she cannot recall.

The problem with cases like this is clearly that Locke is placing too much emphasis on a one-off judgement concerning the presence or absence of a recollection of the event in question. The Lockean theory, in its more sophisticated formulations, says that a person is constituted by a system of relations of continuity and connectedness, linking thoughts, feelings and experiences in an ordered temporal sequence. In the case of the drunkard, there will be lots of psychological links connecting his inebriated self to his sober self both before and after the event. The alcohol, for example, may have served only as a de-inhibitor, releasing aggressive impulses that were already an established part of his sober personality. The process of getting drunk isn't like hitting a switch – psychological continuity is maintained here. The man waking with a hangover may still remember going to the pub and meeting his mate Fred, even if he can't recall what happened after the first few drinks. And even the missing memories may not be lost for ever and irretrievably: they might resurface as frightening images in dreams, or be rediscovered by means of hypnosis. So Locke could have replied to Molyneux that so long as there is enough psychological continuity between the sober man and the drunkard, they do still count as the same person, and the sober man is justly punished for the crimes he committed when drunk. The Jekyll and Hyde story raises somewhat deeper problems. Are we to think of Hyde as an entirely different person from Jekyll? If so, punishing Jekyll for Hyde's crimes would be unjust. (He might nevertheless be punished for the risks he imposed on his fellow citizens by taking the drug.) Or is Hyde a sort of dark alter ego of Jekyll,[14] living out in actuality urges that the civilized Jekyll thinks he has suppressed? The answer to these questions will be crucial if we are to settle in our own minds the difficult issue of whether Jekyll is answerable for Hyde's crimes.

If we broaden Locke's theory from its exclusive focus on memory into a more general account of psychological continuity and connectedness, we can also provide the Lockean with a plausible reply to the famous 'gallant officer' objection made by Thomas Reid.[15] The gallant officer, says Reid, was flogged as a boy for stealing some apples, later takes a standard from the enemy in his first campaign, and is made a general in his fifties. The sixty-year-old general can vividly recall taking the standard as a twenty-year-old; the twenty-year-old can still recall the flogging suffered by the ten-year-old boy; but the general has entirely lost all recollection of his boyish crime and its punishment. By Locke's test, says Reid, the general is the same person as the young officer; the young officer is the same person as the boy; but the general is not the same person as the boy. But the identity-relation is transitive: if A = B and B = C, then A = C. Locke's theory entails that A = B, B = C, but A ≠ C, but this is logically impossible. On a simple one-criterion memory theory, Reid's objection stands. On a broader account of psychological continuity and connectedness, there will surely remain enough connections to make the general and the boy the same person as well as simply the same man. A person might be like a rope, the unity of which does not require that any single strand runs the entire length of the rope, but only that each constituent fibre is tightly twisted with its neighbours. For two fibres to belong to the same rope does not require that they directly overlap or are intertwined; it requires only the right sort of connectedness – often indirect – between them.

A striking consequence of Locke's theory, and one that has been much discussed in the modern literature, is that it provides no guarantee of uniqueness. If intelligent beings reproduced by binary fission, with psychological continuity preserved in both offspring, we would have another violation of transitivity. Suppose that A divides into B and C, and that both B and C consider themselves to be A. Both, after all, have full autobiographical continuity with A. It looks as if we have a clear case in which A = B, A = C, but B ≠ C. B regards himself as 'the real A' and C as a strange sort of doppel-gänger, but of course C thinks that he, C, is the real A, and that it is B who is the mysterious double. Neither has any privileged ground for their judgements, which are simply an inevitable consequence of their distinct subjective points of view. If C quickly died, we would come to regard B as the undisputed claimant to being A, but whether B is A or not surely cannot depend on some accident in a sort of metaphysical branch line? Derek Parfit famously argues that our concern should be for survival and not for identity: if my thoughts and experiences continue in some successor or successors, why should it matter, he asks, which if any of these is *me*? Would it matter at all if this were an unanswerable question?[16]

If the psychology of intelligent beings reproducing by binary fission seems so weird that your intuitions fail to get a grip, consider a familiar example from the science-fiction literature. Captain James T. Kirk (Kirk1) of the Starship *Enterprise* steps into the transporter, chief engineer Scott presses a button and a new James T. Kirk (Kirk2) materializes on the surface of a planet thousands of miles away. No viewer doubts that the newly constituted man taking form on the planet is our old friend James T. Kirk, and no Lockean would doubt for a moment that it is one and the same person, even if not one and the same man. Biological continuity is not main-tained, but psychological continuity is maintained, and it is psycho-logical continuity that counts. Kirk1 could start a thought on board the *Enterprise*, and Kirk2 could finish it on the planet surface. But if the transporter retains the pattern or template of the information needed to assemble billions of atoms of carbon, hydrogen, oxygen, nitrogen, phosphorous, etc., into a functioning James T. Kirk, it doesn't matter much if Kirk2 is immediately killed. Mr Scott can just run off a backup copy from the transporter. Now suppose there is a communications failure, and Mr Scott mistakenly believes that Kirk2 has been killed. He runs off a backup copy Kirk3, and then Kirk2 calls from the planet's surface to beam him up. Mr Scott does so, and a new Kirk (Kirk4) materializes on the *Enterprise*. We now have two copies of James T. Kirk on the *Enterprise*, each with an unanswerable claim to be numerically one and the same person as the original Kirk1. Kirk1 = Kirk2, Kirk1 = Kirk3, Kirk2 = Kirk 4, but Kirk3 ≠ Kirk4, which violates the logic of transitivity.

Such examples, although undeniably anachronistic, are by no means irrelevant to Locke. After all, on one possible account of the afterlife, there is no continuity of substance (material or immaterial) between the person in this life and in the afterlife. A human body decomposes in the grave; its 'superadded' mental powers simply lapse; at some future moment God creates a new human body, and gives it thoughts and experiences continuous with those of the original person. If God can do this once, He could do it any number of times, and each of these new men will be the same person as the original, but not numerically the same persons as one another. Insisting on continuity of substance does not help, for the reasons Locke has already given: it is *my* future experiences I care about, not the future experiences of *this soul*. I have no more reason, Locke will say, to care about the future experiences of this soul (supposing that they are not continuous with my own in the ways that count) than I have to care about the future fates of the carbon atoms that currently make up my body. The problem of personal identity, as discussed by modern philosophers, is still the problem Locke set for us in chapter 27 of Book Two, added to the second edition of the *Essay* in response to some questions from Molyneux. But it cannot be said that either the modern Lockeans or their opponents have come up with a theory that satisfies all our intuitions.

4. Immortality Revisited

We have already quoted from Locke's irate response to his long-suffering friend Tyrrell, when the latter dared to raise some difficulties regarding the moral law of nature. At the heart of Tyrrell's worry is the question of sanctions, that is, rewards for virtue and punishments for vice. You do not, Tyrrell writes, tell us where to find the moral law, if not in the Scriptures, and it is 'much doubted by some' whether the existence of appropriate rewards and punishments can be established by unaided natural reason, without revelation. Once again, Locke's response shows him at his most touchy and irritable:

Another thing that stumbles you is that *it is much doubted by some whether the rewards and punishments I mention can be demonstrated as established by my divine law*. Will nothing then passe with you in Religion or Morality but what you can demonstrate? If you are of so nice a stomach I am afraid if I should now Examine how much of your religion or Morality you could demonstrate how much you would have left. (C IV, 111)

Locke goes on to claim that morality might, like mathematics, contain much that is demonstrable but as yet undemonstrated, but this is the flimsiest of promissory notes. We know that in the ancient world, that is, before the advent of the Christian revelation, wise men thought long and hard about whether humans could or could not expect an afterlife, with a wide variety of opinions inconclusively debated. But for Locke the point is absolutely crucial. Can the moral law of nature be truly binding on us, if not backed up by appropriate sanctions? One might attempt to argue that the moral life is inherently the best life, and thus the one most worth choosing for its own sake, but this 'high line' is not going to convince the doubters. As Aristotle says, when we are told that the virtuous man is *eudaimon* (happy, flourishing, leading the good life), even under torture, or when watching his city sacked and his family carried off into slavery, we find ourselves unable to take the claim seriously.[17] The moral law of nature, it seems, will need external sanctions, and these are most plausibly provided by promises of reward and threats of punishment in an afterlife.

So what, for Locke, is the epistemological status of the widespread human belief in an afterlife with rewards and punishments? Metaphysics, it is clear, does not have the resources to demonstrate that this belief is true. Equally, metaphysics provides no grounds to doubt it. Whether materialism plus 'superadded' powers or substance dualism is true, there can be a personal afterlife. Fortunately, Locke explains, what Christians need to understand and accept (the personal afterlife) is entirely independent, in logical terms, of the mysterious metaphysics of the mind–body problem. Belief in an afterlife could have, for Locke, any of three distinct grounds. It could be a matter of *probability*, if the philosophical arguments advanced in its favour are stronger than those against it. This would, of course, be very hard to judge. It could be simply a matter of *faith*, of our reliance on the promises made in Scripture. Or it could be derived from our status as *subjects of the moral law*. Locke could be attempting to argue from morality to metaphysics. If we know that we are subjects of a moral law, and if the moral law could not be binding on us without appropriate sanctions, then it follows that such sanctions must exist. In the fifth of his early *Essays on the Law of Nature*, Locke argues that the moral law requires belief in a law-making God and in the afterlife:

> Even if God and the soul's immortality are not moral propositions and laws of nature, nevertheless they must be necessarily presupposed if natural law is to exist. For there is no law without a law-maker, and law is to no purpose without punishment. (ELN 173)

This argument is not to be found in the published writings of the mature philosopher, but we have no reason to suppose that the Locke of the *Essay* would have rejected it. The problem with this line of argument, of course, is that it will yield at best a conditional as a conclusion. If we are subjects of the moral law of nature, as traditionally conceived, then we are to expect an afterlife with rewards for virtue and punishments for vice. It would remain open to an opponent to accept the conditional and simply deny the antecedent. Must we, if we are rational, think of ourselves as subjects of the moral law? Attempts to resolve Locke's difficulties over this issue point directly towards Kant.

7

The Two Treatises of Government

1. The Context: Locke's Fears of Absolutism

Locke's main work in political theory, the *Two Treatises of Government*, was published anonymously in 1689, shortly after the so-called 'Glorious Revolution' had established William and Mary as joint monarchs after the flight – relabelled an 'abdication' for political reasons – of James II.[1] When Locke refers in his Preface to William as 'our great restorer', and seeks to vindicate his claim to the throne as grounded in the consent of the people, we know that he is making the most of an opportunity provided by the course of events. His insistence on anonymity was, however, perfectly comprehensible: there was no guarantee whatsoever in 1689 that his side would be victorious in the long run. The exiled James still had supporters in England, Scotland and Ireland, and a very powerful overseas backer in the France of his cousin Louis XIV. The ever-cautious and pessimistic Locke would eventually acknowledge his authorship of the work only in his will.

Although published in 1689, with a few late additions to reflect current events, we now know that the bulk of the *Two Treatises* was in fact written during 1680–1, during the fierce debates of the Exclusion Crisis. Setting the work in this earlier context does not, of course, affect the validity of any of Locke's arguments, but does yield three important advantages. In the first place, it helps us to understand why Locke felt the *First Treatise* was needed at all. When Locke was writing, Sir Robert Filmer (*c.*1588–1653) was long dead, but the theory of absolutism defended in his *Patriarcha* was very much alive, and popular among courtiers and clerics. The *First Treatise*, with its curious mixture of scriptural history and natural law theory, seems archaic today, but in 1680 Locke was dealing with living ideas and living opponents. The second advantage of setting the *Two Treatises* in its earlier context is that it helps to correct later representations of Locke as essentially a conservative thinker. There can be no doubt that the *Second Treatise* was, in its time and place, a revolutionary work, defending the legitimacy, under certain conditions, of armed resistance against the reigning monarch. We shall return later to discuss the apparent paradox of representing Locke as both conservative and revolutionary. The third clear advantage of dating the *Two Treatises* to 1680–1 is that it helps to clarify Locke's motivations. To a large extent, the *Two Treatises* are motivated not by the triumphalism of 1689 but by the fears of 1680.

What exactly did Locke fear in 1680? The obvious answer is that Charles II, and his brother James, should he succeed to the throne, would attempt to govern Britain on the model of absolutist France. On an early visit to Paris in 1672, Locke had witnessed with his own eyes the construction of Versailles. His comments, in a letter to John Strachey, are illuminating:

> There I saw vast and magnificent buildings as big almost as others dominions preparing only for one man, and yet there be a great many other two legged creatures, but 'tis not in the way of that country much to consider them.[2]

Louis's famous motto, *L'état, c'est moi*, would have shocked and horrified Locke, son of a Puritan father who had taken up arms against the absolutism of Charles I only a generation earlier. The Sun King was, in essence, plundering the whole country in order to build a monument to his own vanity. And although Louis had not yet revoked the Edict of Nantes (which gave some protection to French Protestants), it was obvious that he was increasingly intent on enforcing religious uniformity across his extensive – and expanding – domains. The plight of the Huguenots, whether at home or later in their various places of exile, would become a recurring theme in Locke's correspondence.

The fear of the English Whigs was that Charles II and James II would try to govern their realms of England, Scotland and Ireland on the absolutist model of the France of Louis XIV. They would seek to govern without Parliament, calling it only if absolutely necessary to raise money, and promptly dissolving it again if it tried to raise grievances and secure reforms. They would use their extensive powers of patronage to place their cronies in positions of power and influence throughout the land. And they might – darkest fear of all – seek to reconvert their kingdoms to Roman Catholicism, by force if necessary. James was known to be a Catholic; Charles was widely suspected of being secretly of the Roman faith. With French support and French money, it was feared, they might attempt to reverse the Reformation in the British Isles. For the Whig opposition to the policies of the later Stuart monarchs, 'popery' and 'tyranny' were always seen as two sides of the same coin. One had only to point across the English Channel to the frightening example of France.

Were the fears of the Whigs groundless? The publication in 1680 of Filmer's *Patriarcha*, with its elaborate frontispiece of Charles II and its unqualified defence of royal absolutism, was bound both to excite these fears and to fan the flames of opposition. Locke was not the only one to feel the urgent need of a reply: his Oxford friends James Tyrrell and Algernon Sydney both composed replies to Filmer, and Sydney was put to death on a charge of treason in 1683. According to Filmer, kings are the descendants of Adam, and inherit from Adam his absolute powers over all their subjects. On this view, the subjects of Charles II, however much they may call themselves 'freeborn Englishmen', are in fact indistinguishable from slaves. As Locke says in the first chapter of the first *Treatise*, the applause that greeted *Patriarcha* was what prompted him to write against Filmer. 'Truly', he writes,

> I should have taken Sr Rt: Filmer's *Patriarcha* as any other Treatise, which would persuade all Men, that they are Slaves, and ought to be so, for such another exercise of Wit, as was his who writ the encomium of *Nero*, had not the Gravity of the Title and Epistle, the Picture in the Front the Book, and the Applause that followed it, required me to believe, that the Author and Publisher were both in earnest. (TTG 141)

A bad book that teaches dangerous principles can generally be safely ignored. But when such a bad book is extolled as the height of political wisdom, not just by flattering courtiers but even by bishops (who should know better), it may be necessary to expose the weakness of the reasoning used in support of absolutism. The *First Treatise* was necessary, in Locke's eyes, to clear the ground for the *Second*.

2. Bad Principles Exposed

Filmer's defence of royal absolutism, says Locke in chapter 1 of the *First Treatise*, can be stated very simply, and indeed amounts to little more than the following:

> His System lies in a little compass, 'tis no more but this,
> *That all Government is absolute Monarchy.*
> And the Ground he builds on, is this,
> *That no Man is Born free.* (TTG 142)

According to Filmer, God gave to Adam an absolute power not just over all the Earth, but over all his children and grandchildren, and this absolute power has passed down the royal line from Adam to the existing monarchs of the seventeenth century who, as Adam's heirs, have the same divine right to rule over their subjects. (How he is to reconcile the 'heir of Adam' thesis with the multitude of existing kings, and with the plain fact that many existing kings rule by conquest or usurpation rather than by inheritance, is an obvious difficulty.) His argument for this thesis rests largely on his interpretation of Scripture, with elements of the Aristotelian notion of a natural hierarchy.[3] Locke seeks to show that Filmer's argument confuses three entirely distinct relations: that between a father and his children, that between a proprietor and his lands and material goods, and that between a king and his subjects. To refute Filmer, Locke thinks, it is necessary only to spell out clearly the moral consequences of these three distinct relations.

A father, Locke argues, might be thought to have absolute authority over his children if he were indeed their *creator*. But this is far from being the case. In addition to ignoring the obvious role of the mother in generation, Filmer ignores altogether the role of our true creator, God:

> Can any Man say, He formed the parts that are necessary to the Life of his Child? Or can he suppose himself to give the Life, and yet not know what Subject is fit to receive it, nor what Actions or Organs are necessary for its Reception or Preservation? (TTG 178)

The origin of a human life is for us something utterly mysterious:[4]

> To give Life to that which has yet no being, is to frame and make a living Creature, fashion the parts, and mould and suit them together

to their uses, and, having proportion'd and fitted them together, to put into them a living Soul. He that could do this, might indeed have some pretence to destroy his own Workmanship. But is there any one so bold, that dares thus far Arrogate to himself the Incomprehensible Works of the Almighty? Who alone did at first and continues still to make a living Soul, He alone can breathe in the Breath of Life. (TTG 179)

If creation confers a right of dominion, that right belongs to God, not to parents, who are no more than occasional causes of generation. Whatever rights parents do possess over their children, mother and father possess jointly, as having 'an equal share' in generation (TTG 180).[5] Filmer tries to derive patriarchy from the Fifth Commandment, but this argument, Locke reminds his readers, might equally well be cited in support of matriarchy. After all, Scripture always links father and mother in this commandment, and, as Locke cannot refrain from remarking, 'whom God hath joyned together, let no Man put asunder' (TTG 186). The law of nature may enjoin honour and obedience upon children, but honour and obedience on the one side are the natural and proper return for protection and support on the other, and would thus be owed to a diligent stepparent rather than to a negligent natural parent. And the law of nature, which requires the preservation of mankind, confers a corresponding *duty* upon parents to protect, nourish and educate their children until they reach maturity (TTG 305). This duty is entirely ignored by Filmer.

Locke is thus emphatic that the mere natural act of fathering a child provides no ground, under the law of nature, to suppose absolute dominion on the one side and absolute submission on the other. Granted that there have been and perhaps still are societies in which it is permitted to parents to expose, or castrate, or even butcher and eat unwanted children, any such practices are 'shameful' and 'unnatural', manifestly contrary to 'the main intention of Nature' (TTG 180–2).[6] But even if there were a special authority vested by the law of nature in the person of the biological father, it would not serve Filmer's argument. If this right is grounded in the act of generation, a father can possess such a right over his children. But the elder brother cannot have any such right over his younger brothers, whom he has clearly not begotten. The law of nature gives the eldest son no natural right to the subjection of any of his siblings (TTG 196).

On Filmer's theory, Locke continues, there is but one living man who has the right to call himself king of all the world, the true heir of Adam's royal authority (TTG 216). There would be endless and almost certainly insuperable difficulties in establishing the identity of this person, but, says Locke with a delicious irony, if we could just establish the relevant historical facts, all problems of political authority would immediately be solved:

> if it really be, as our A. says, the true Title to Government and Sovereignty, the first thing to be done, is to find out this true Heir of *Adam*, seat him in his Throne, and then all the Kings and Princes of the World ought to come and resign up their Crowns and Sceptres to him, as things that belong no more to them, than to any of their Subjects. (TTG 217)

In fact, of course, as the historical facts make plain, most existing kings owe their titles as much to conquest or usurpation as to inheritance, so the 'heir of Adam' thesis fails to establish that we owe such usurpers any allegiance at all. If Filmer allows that regal authority can be seized by a usurper or even a conqueror, as in the Norman Conquest of England in 1066, then he 'may make *Oliver* [Cromwell] as *properly King* as any other he could think of', which, for the loyal cavalier Filmer, would surely be the ultimate *reductio ad absurdum* of his thesis (TTG 201).

To assimilate the king–subject relation to the father–child relation is, for Locke, the source of many of Filmer's confusions. He is equally guilty of conflating both these relations with the quite distinct one between a proprietor and his possessions. Suppose that God has given Adam all the Earth and its contents as his possession, to do with as he pleased. It would then follow, presumably, that Adam could deny any or all of his descendants a place to live or food to eat, 'and so at his pleasure starve them, if they will not acknowledge his Soveraignty, and Obey his Will' (TTG 169). But, Locke insists, we know that this is not the case:

> God the Lord and Father of all, has given no one of His Children such a Property, in his peculiar Portion of the things of this World, but that he has given his needy Brother a Right in the Surplusage of his Goods; so that it cannot justly be denied him, when his pressing Wants call for it. And therefore no Man could ever have a just Power over the Life of another, by Right of property in Land or Possessions; since 'twould always be a Sin in any Man of Estate, to let his Brother perish for want of affording him Relief out of his Plenty. (TTG 30)

This passage shows Locke at his most medieval,[7] and needs to be read alongside the (apparent) justification for the modern doctrine of 'possessive individualism' that some scholars find in the *Second Treatise*. Locke is confident that the law of nature could not place the rest of mankind in such subjection to the universal proprietor that they would starve without his consent. Such an arrangement would fly in the face of 'the intention of nature', that is, of God's benevolent plans when He created the human race.

There is a potential difficulty here in reconciling Locke's endorsement of the claim that the surplus of the rich belongs by right to the poor with his known hostility to beggars, reported by Lady Masham.[8] Presumably Locke would invoke something like the notorious Victorian distinction between the 'deserving' and the 'undeserving' poor, between those who are needy as a result of misfortune and those who are needy as a result of idleness or other vices. The former, but not the latter, have a claim of right to the assistance of the well-off. This was certainly Locke's attitude to his tenants in Somerset, as revealed by his correspondence.

3. Better Principles Expounded

Filmer's fundamental error, in Locke's eyes, is that he misrepresents the state of nature as a state of subjection. The moral authority of the state, on this view, is something grounded in nature itself, something I can no more shake off than I can deny my humanity or refuse to recognize my biological parents. If I ask, 'Why should I obey the laws passed by the king who claims dominion over this country?', Filmer's answer is simply 'You were born to it.' The facts of your birth determine your political status and your allegiances and duties – mostly duties of mere unquestioning obedience. To represent the state as the product of any sort of contract or agreement between the citizens is to misrepresent something natural as if it were merely conventional.[9] In Locke's eyes, of course, Filmer's account of the state of nature is deeply mistaken, and the political principles he derives from this account are both false and dangerous. False for reasons we have already seen; dangerous because they will be cited by all manner of servile flatterers of would-be tyrants. But if Filmer's principles are dismissed as erroneous, then we must 'find out another rise of Government, another Original of Political Power, and another way of designing and knowing the Persons that have it, then [*sic*] what Sir Robert F. hath taught us' (TTG 268). This is the project of the *Second Treatise of Government*.

Locke's starting point is his radically different account of the state of nature. By nature, says Locke, men are born equal – not, of course, in their powers, abilities and virtues, but equal in their rights under the law of nature. By nature, Locke argues, all men have rights to *property*. By this he does not simply mean material goods and possessions, although he will famously defend the right to such private property in chapter 5. Your most fundamental property rights are to life and liberty and security from injury. The true end for which men establish governments, Locke explains in chapter 9, is 'the mutual *Preservation* of their Lives, Liberties, and Estates, which I call by the general Name, Property' (TTG 350). By the law of nature, says Locke in chapter 2, 'no one ought to harm another in his Life, Health, Liberty or Possessions' (TTG 271). Students sometimes miss this crucial point, and think that Locke's defence of property rights is fundamentally a vindication of the interests of the rich against the poor. Locke would reply that *everyone* has the right not to be murdered, raped or assaulted as he or she walks down the street, and that these are his or her most fundamental *property rights*, in his use of the term. No human being could be without property, or without an interest in defending their property rights. We have these rights as human beings, not as citizens of this or that state, and these rights cannot be taken from us, although of course we sometimes forfeit them through our own misdeeds and become liable to legitimate punishment.

The defence of my natural rights to life, liberty, bodily integrity and possessions gives me also, in the state of nature, a right to punish actual or intended transgressors of those rights.[10] The execution of the law of nature is left in the hands of individuals, who may, either individually or by voluntary and ad hoc groupings, exercise retribution on transgressors. (In cases where the aggressors are powerful or numerous, the victim may of course find it difficult to gather volunteers for punitive action.) Such acts of retribution are justified, says Locke, but only 'so far as calm reason and conscience dictates', and 'so much as may serve for *Reparation* and *Restraint*', and may make the transgressor 'repent the doing of it, and thereby deter him, and, by his Example others, from doing the like mischief' (TTG 272). There are obvious problems here. If someone has stolen two of my sheep, I may properly use force to recover my lost sheep, or demand their equivalent in natural or use-value if I find they have already been killed and eaten by the thief. But if I want an effective *deterrent*, I clearly need to do considerably more than this, and the law of nature seems to supply no clear measure of what additional punishments are appropriate for what crimes. A utilitarian like Jeremy Bentham would say that the punishment must be the minimum that will serve as an effective deterrent, but the natural law theorist cannot employ any such measure. He must claim that the natural law gives us insight into the right punishment for a crime that is independent of the empirical measure of effectiveness, but this is far from clear.

Worse still, in the state of nature, each individual is the judge of the severity of his or her injuries, and thus the assessor of retribution. But we know that no man is a good judge in his own case. Consider a situation that is common enough in sub-Saharan Africa. A settled tribe cultivates its crops in the river valley, while a nomadic tribe needs from time to time to drive its flocks and herds to the river for water. The flocks and herds of the nomads do considerable damage to the fields of the farmers. The farmers seek retribution, and seize a number of sheep and goats by force, regarding this as proper compensation for the damages they have suffered. The pastoralists regard the damages exacted from them as grossly excessive, and as warranting retribution on their part. It is easy to see how the state of nature can become a state of family feuds and vendettas, or even one of inter-tribal conflict. It is possible, of course, that such conflicts could be averted, even in the state of nature: the elders of the two tribes could sit under a baobab tree and arrive at an agreement that, say, six goats are appropriate compensation for an acre of trampled millet. But without any of the machinery of government, it is always highly probable that such agreements will be precarious and unstable. Men in the state of nature are subject as rational beings to the law of nature, but there will be an ever-present tendency to 'confusion and disorder'. Although men have rights in the state of nature, they are never secure in their enjoyment of them (TTG 350). The establishment of civil government, says Locke, 'is the proper Remedy for the Inconveniences of the State of Nature' (TTG 276). Rational individuals in the state of nature will see the need both for an established system of rules and for some appointed person or persons to enforce those rules with appropriate and agreed sanctions. To protect their *natural* rights, rational individuals will agree to establish the *artificial* institutions of the state.

Locke's account of the formation of the state involves two distinct phases. In the first phase, a group of men agree with one another to form themselves into a single *community*. This, we are told, requires an act of consent on the part of the contracting parties:

> MEN being, as has been said, by Nature, all free, equal and independent, no one can be put out of this Estate, and subjected to the Political Power of another, without his own *Consent*. The only way whereby any one devests himself of his Natural Liberty, and *puts on the bonds of Civil Society* is by agreeing with other Men, to joyn and unite into a Community, for their comfortable, safe, and peaceable living one amongst another, in a secure Enjoyment of their Properties, and a greater Security against any that are not of it. (TTG 330–1)

Each of the contracting parties agrees, we are told, to be bound by the decision of the majority on all points of difference and dispute. Without this concession, the community could only act by universal consent, which 'is next impossible ever to be had' (TTG 332). We all therefore agree to be bound by the decision of the majority, and consider this to be a more desirable state of affairs than the state of nature. We must first all agree to establish a government of some kind before we can discuss what type of government we think best for our circumstances. Once a political community has been formed by this first act of association, its members can begin to assign legislative (law-making) and executive (law-enforcing) powers to some citizens or groups of citizens. The citizens of the newly formed political entity then agree with one another to surrender their executive powers (the power to punish wrongdoers) to the executive power thereby established. This enables them to escape many of the 'inconveniences' of the state of nature.

Locke is very clear that it takes a real act of assent to turn the natural man (subject only to the law of nature) into a citizen of a state, subject to the laws of that state. However, most of the subjects of seventeenth-century England had never given any explicit assent to the institutions of that state. Here Locke needs to invoke his notoriously problematic notion of 'tacit consent' (TTG 347). There are, of course, circumstances in which by explicitly consenting to X I can be taken to have tacitly consented to Y. If I exercise my vote in a modern democratic state, I might be held to be tacitly consenting to the use of voting as a method of resolving disputes, and thus to consider myself bound by the majority decision. (This perhaps explains why democratically elected politicians worry about very low turnout rates.) But, of course, very few people in Locke's England had the vote: it would be hundreds of years before all adult citizens of both sexes obtained voting rights. Locke also thinks that in inheriting a property from his father, a son might properly be deemed to have tacitly consented to the system of laws that protects that property right. So the sons of the landed gentry are not born subjects of their father's country: rather, they face a choice, when they reach maturity, of either accepting the duties of citizenship or forfeiting their inheritance (TTG 348). By this means, Locke can plausibly claim that the children of the landed classes tacitly consent to become citizens when they explicitly lay claim to their inheritances. But this binds only the landed classes, and has only a limited and dubious application to the poor. It seems hard for Locke to establish that there is anything the poorest day-labourer or maid-servant actually does that constitutes his or her assenting to the system of government.

His response to this difficulty is not, it has to be confessed, entirely convincing. He thinks that the conditions for tacit consent are very weak indeed:

> And to this I say, that every Man, that hath any Possession, or Enjoy-ment, of any part of the Dominions of any Government, doth thereby give his *tacit Consent*, and is as far forth obliged to Obedience to the Laws of that Government, during such Enjoyment, as any one under it, whether this his Possession be of Land, to him and his Heirs for ever, or a Lodging only for a Week; or whether it be barely travelling freely on the Highway; and, in Effect, it reaches as far as the very being of any one within the Territories of that Government. (TTG 348)[11]

This looks far too easy. Suppose I am a pacifist seeking to avoid being drafted into the army to fight what I regard as an unjust war. I seek to flee from such perceived injustices by taking refuge in a foreign land. To that end, I walk or ride on 'the king's highway' to make my way to the nearest port. Have I, by such an act, tacitly consented to the very injustices I am attempting to flee? Surely not. Locke's notion of tacit consent is in itself intelligible and defensible, but his application of it to difficult and contested cases leaves a great deal to be desired. His theory seems to leave no room for the sub-jects of a badly governed state to choose exile, as with the Pilgrim Fathers quitting England for America or the French Huguenots fleeing France for Britain or Holland. And it seems to leave no room for peaceful opposition and civil disobedience within the oppressive state. There must, surely, be some accepted means for the members of a political community to simultaneously reaffirm their allegiance to the community while challenging the decisions of its established government. Locke's theory seems seriously deficient at just this point.

The end or purpose of political organization, for Locke, is the protection of the natural rights of its members. To remedy the many and obvious 'inconveniences' of the state of nature, the parties contract with one another to live in accordance with a system of established laws. To that end, they need to establish a legislative or law-making body, generally a Parliament of some kind, and an executive or law-enforcing body, often but not necessarily a king and his ministers. The distinction of roles here is fairly straightforward. The legislative body need not always be in session – indeed, it may be important that it not always be in session, if, for example, its members represent distant constituencies and need frequently to visit and consult their constituents. By contrast, the laws must always be executed, so the executive branch of government needs to be in continuous and uninterrupted operation. The executive may also be required to make day-to-day decisions that cannot wait for legislation: to that end, it may be allowed a certain measure of latitude in its actions, and may occasionally bend or break laws for the public good. This, for Locke, is the true notion of the prerogative that may be invested in the executive power (TTG 374–80). The public authorities, to give a timely example, may be permitted to pull down perfectly good town houses in order to prevent the spread of a fire. The Great Fire of London took place in 1666, when Locke was in his thirties, and he would have seen its devastating effects on his visits to the capital, and witnessed the efforts of Christopher Wren (a friend from his Oxford days) to rebuild the churches of the city.

The crucial point for Locke is that both branches of government should be regarded as operating on the basis of a trust and not a further or second contract. The parties to the original contract, that is, 'the people', entrust one group of men with the making of laws and another man or group of men with the enforcement of the laws thus made. If the relationship between the people and the government was itself a contract, we might find ourselves facing a regress problem if asked to judge whether the terms of that contract had been broken.[12] Do we need to appoint a further judge to adjudicate between the people and their MPs or their king? But if the relationship is in the form of a trust, it is for the givers of that trust – that is, the people – to decide whether the trust-holders have fulfilled the conditions imposed on them. This point is fundamental to Locke's defence of the right of rebellion. How exactly 'the people' are to make their judgement known is a difficulty Locke sees, but fails to resolve. The views of the people, he says, are expressed by their representatives – but of course the Parliaments of Locke's day were notoriously unrepresentative. It might be argued that the best solution to this problem is to shift Locke's theory much closer to that of a modern democracy. Locke's *Second Treatise* contains no explicit argument for democracy, but a serious and sustained attempt to solve the problems implicit in his theory may force us to embrace a greater measure of democracy than Locke himself would have endorsed.[13]

4. The Case for Private Property

Under the law of nature, says Locke, God has given all things to all men in common, without distinction of mine and thine. But of course if a human being is to survive, he or she needs food, water, warmth (fuel for burning and cooking), clothing suitable for the prevailing climate, and shelter from the elements. If God wills that we survive, He wills also whatever is necessary for our survival, and this includes the acquisition of private property – at least in those things necessary for life itself. Such acquisition of goods must therefore be permitted under the law of nature, without violation of anyone's rights. In chapter 5 of the *Second Treatise*, Locke sets out his famous account of the conditions under which property rights may legitimately be acquired in land and in material goods. Given that God created men equal, and gave the fruits of the Earth to men in common, how has it come about that some men claim possession of great estates, while others are destitute? Were the radical 'Diggers' of the Civil War period right to argue that the private possession of land is always the product of force or fraud, and that all titles to land should revert to the community? Or is it possible for one man to acquire land and goods without violating any of the rights of other men? Locke aims to show, in this famous chapter, both *that* this is possible and *how* this is possible.

The starting point of Locke's account is his famous claim that each and every human being has property in his or her own person:

> Though the Earth, and all inferior Creatures be common to all Men,
> yet every Man has a *Property* in his own *Person*. This no Body has
> any Right to but himself. The *Labour* of his Body, and the *Work* of his
> Hands, we may say, are properly his. (TTG 287–8)

Does Locke think that every human being has a full property right
over his or her body in something like the modern sense? If a thing
is my property, I may destroy it, consume it, sell it or give it away
to whomsoever I please, without committing any wrong. But Locke
flatly and emphatically denies the right to suicide. The state of
nature, he insists, is still subject to the law of nature, which tells us
clearly that a man 'has not Liberty to destroy himself'. This would
be a crime against God: men and women are 'his Property, whose
Workmanship they are, made to last during his, not one another's
Pleasure' (TTG 271). It looks, then, as if each of us should be seen
as *trustees* over our own bodies, rather than their absolute owners.
The same principle will presumably apply to the sale of body parts
– not of course an issue for Locke, but very topical in the twenty-
first century. If the fundamental intention of the law of nature is that
mankind be preserved, it looks as if I do no wrong in donating a
kidney to a fellow human who needs it for his or her survival, but
I do wrong if I put the kidney up for auction, because its eventual
destination is then determined by economic demand rather than by
human need.[14]

Can Locke consistently claim both that we are God's property
and that we are self-owners? He presumably thinks that the self-
ownership thesis has a restricted scope, and concerns only our
dealings with our fellow men. My rights over my own body, on this
view, amount to restrictions on what my fellow humans can do to
me without my consent. The problem still remains, however, of the
relation between the law of nature and criminal or statute law.
Should the state make laws prohibiting suicide and the sale of body
parts? Or should we say, 'This is between each individual human
being and his or her maker', and leave any punishment to God? A
social conservative might argue that the criminal law should mirror
the law of nature; a social liberal might argue that the function of
the criminal law is to provide sanctions to prevent citizens infring-
ing the rights of *others*, not to coerce them into leading the life God
intended us to lead. It looks as if Locke has the beginnings of an
argument for the liberal position,[15] although he might not have been
happy to see this line of argument taken to its conclusion by later
liberals such as John Stuart Mill.

If a man owns his own body, Locke continues, he also owns the fruits of his own labours:

> Whatsoever then he removes out of the State that Nature hath provided, and left it in, he hath mixed his *Labour* with, and joyned to it something that is his own, and thereby makes it his *Property*. (TTG 288)

Locke qualifies this claim by two important provisos. The first requires that in my act of appropriation of something out of the common stock, I leave 'enough, and as good left in common for others' (TTG 288). If I live in a village half a mile from a river, I can carry my bucket to the riverbank in the morning, fill my bucket and return with it to my home. My labour, Locke thinks, gives me property rights in this particular bucketful of water. If anyone wants to take it from me, I can point in the direction of the river and say 'go and get your own'. (A richer and lazier fellow-villager might of course make me an offer to acquire 'my' bucketful of water by means of purchase or barter.) So long as 'enough and as good' is left in the common stock, Locke argues, no one has been wronged by my small act of privatization. The second proviso is that I cannot acquire more goods than I can use (or exchange) before they spoil. According to the law of nature, 'Nothing was made by God for Man to spoil or destroy' (TTG 290). If I have laboured to pick plums from a tree, I can't claim a property right over my mound of plums if they are only going to rot. I might legitimately consume them, sell or barter them, or find some means of persevering them, but I may not let them spoil. Once money has come into being, much of the original moral force of the 'spoilage' proviso lapses, because I can then exchange my mass of plums for pieces of gold and silver, which do not spoil.

What about the acquisition of private property in land? The same principles, Locke thinks, apply to this case too:

> But the *chief matter of Property* being now not the Fruits of the Earth, and the Beasts that subsist on it, but the *Earth it self*; as that which takes in and carries with it all the rest: I think it is plain that Property in that too is acquired as the former [material goods]. *As much Land as a Man Tills, Plants, Improves, Cultivates, and can use the Product of, so much is his Property.* He by his Labour does, as it were, inclose it from the Common. (TTG 290–1)

So long as the first proviso continues to hold, and the would-be encloser of land leaves 'enough and as good' for others, no one's rights have been violated. The first European colonists in America might claim that their small enclosures left ample space both for the Native Americans and for later groups of settlers – Locke had a deep interest in these colonial ventures, and helped draft a Constitution for the new state of Carolina.[16] There is evidence that he was engaged in redrafting the *Fundamental Constitutions* of Carolina in 1682, a probable date for the composition of chapter 5 of the *Second Treatise*.[17] Part of the intended purpose of this chapter might very well have been to provide a justification for the European settlers in the New World.[18] God, Locke insists, has given us the Earth and its fruits in common, but 'it cannot be supposed he meant it should always remain common and uncultivated. He gave it to the Industrious and Rational (and *Labour* was to be *his Title* to it;) not to the Fancy or Covetousness of the Quarrelsome and Contentious' (TTG 291). So the Native Americans, on this account, are merely 'quarrelsome and contentious' if they resent – and resist – the arrival of the first European settlers. So long as 'enough and as good' land remains for them, they should merely shrug and move on to new hunting grounds. They might even gain by trading with the newcomers. But as more and more Europeans flood into America, it is inevitable both that the Native Americans will be driven from their best hunting grounds, and that later European settlers will have to settle lands further from the coast, less fertile, or more subject to attack from the now *rightly* resentful Native Americans. It is debatable whether the 'enough and as good' proviso can strictly be said to hold for any finite resource.[19] In some cases, perhaps, it is a tolerable approximation to the truth, and very small injuries might reasonably be overlooked,[20] but for resources as obviously limited as land and water we need to take seriously the possibility that any act of appropriation harms the interests of others, and may call for some sort of compensation.[21]

Even if the privatization of land is morally permitted under the law of nature, Locke's theory still faces serious problems. His most powerful argument for private property in land is that the 'improvement' of land by agriculture vastly increases the production of food. There is little reason to doubt that this is true, but as an argument for private property it leaves a host of questions unanswered. Suppose that farming multiplies the food production of a given acre of land tenfold. Is the farmer entitled, under the law of nature, to all ten units of food from this acre of land, or just to the added value (nine units) produced by his labour? What if the farmer leaves the enclosed land uncultivated for a year or two – does he retain his property rights? Does his right to the fruits of his own labour give him even a right to exclude others from 'his' land? (Maybe he should provide a public footpath or a right of way.) Can he bequeath his land to his children, who would thus acquire holdings in land without any labour at all? We tend today to think of property rights as forming a sort of bundle, but the items in this bundle can and arguably should be unpacked and treated separately.[22] A right of original appropriation need not involve also rights of transmission and inheritance.[23] If it is taken to do so, then God has given land not just to the 'industrious and rational', but to all the descendants of the industrious and rational, however idle and vicious.

Consider that stock character of so many English novels, the young gentleman of good family, who, on coming into his inheritance, promptly heads for the fleshpots of London, and squanders the family fortune – derived, of course, from the labours of the tenants on his estates – in the taverns and brothels and gaming-houses of that great city of sin. Is he acting within his rights, and committing no injustice? On modern theories of property rights, the answer has to be 'yes': he has inherited this property by due process of law, and no man has any claims of justice against him. He is no doubt unwise and uncharitable, but he is not unjust. Locke's theory lends itself to development along these lines, and he has been seen by some commentators as an early advocate of the doctrine of 'possessive individualism'.[24] But this is the same Locke who, echoing Aquinas and the medieval tradition of natural law, argued that the 'surplusage' of the goods of the rich belongs by right to the needy. If our young gentleman finds himself flush with money, should he not use it to alleviate the poverty of the neediest of his tenants? Locke might reply that this is a matter of conscience, a matter on which the young gentleman is answerable to God but not to man. This would enable him to say that no other man has any claim of right against the young spendthrift, and that he must be moved to mend his ways by prayers and exhortations rather than by any acts of confiscation and redistribution of his goods. His tenants must continue to pay their rents, even if they know they are only supporting the London taverns and brothels.

The deep problem facing Locke is that he has not two but three distinct – and sometimes incompatible – theories of rights running in parallel. There is (1) the medieval theory of the natural law, which regards us all as ultimately God's property, and treats all human holdings (whether in our own bodies or in land or external goods) on the model of a trusteeship. There is (2) the modern theory of possessive individualism, which regards us as absolute owners of our own bodies, and as having the right – under specified conditions – to gain equally absolute property rights over land and material goods. On this theory, what counts is the legitimacy of the process of acquisition: once legitimately acquired, a man can do whatever he pleases with his goods. I could stand in front of a crowd of starving people with a big bag of rice and set fire to it before their eyes, without committing any injustice. We know that Locke would have firmly rejected any such theory, but the germs of it have been found in his work. And there is (3), the theory of rule-consequentialism, which is arguably the position Locke should have adopted.[25] On this theory, we start with a goal provided by the 'intention of nature', that is, that mankind survives and prospers. But which system of rules will best serve that end will depend on lots of details of local circumstance, and will not be the sort of thing that we should attempt to spell out from first principles.

Are there grounds in the *Second Treatise* to suspect that Locke's political theory might be 'morphing' into a form of consequentialism? There is his clear statement of the fundamental intention behind the law of nature in terms of consequences. God wills that men multiply, thrive and prosper; He therefore wills that we establish rules and institutions that serve this end. There is his explicit admission that the public authorities have a certain latitude (sometimes called by the controversial name of 'prerogative') to depart from existing property laws in times of need or emergency. He gives the example of pulling down town houses (without consulting their owners) to prevent the spread of a fire. Another example would be the civic authorities in a city under siege commandeering all food supplies and establishing a system of rationing. The corn-dealers have to accept a promissory note to the effect that their losses will be refunded if and when the siege is lifted and the economy returns to normal. And there is his explicit endorsement of the Roman maxim *salus populi suprema lex* in chapter 13. In times of emergency, Roman jurists would say, existing rules and procedures may be (temporarily) abandoned in the name of public safety. Locke nods his approval:

> *Salus Populi Suprema Lex,* is certainly so just and fundamental a Rule, that he, who sincerely follows it, cannot dangerously err. (TTG 373)[26]

On a rule-consequentialist theory, to say that A has a right to property in X is to say that the optimum system of rules (or perhaps the best system we know) gives A the right to X. What makes one system of rules better than another is to be judged in terms of their consequences for human flourishing. On this view, both the older medieval theory and the modern theory of property rights err in the direction of excessive and implausible determinacy. Both theories attempt to derive detailed and fully determinate accounts of who has a right to what from their respective first principles. The rule-consequentialist has a simple explanation for why this cannot work. God wills that humans thrive and prosper. He therefore wills that we are sufficiently rational to abandon the state of nature, with all its manifest inconveniences, for an ordered society governed by rules. But precisely which rules will have the best consequences is heavily dependent on local circumstances. A system of rules that is optimal in one place or time may not be so in another, for any number of reasons. To take an obvious example, liberal thinkers have tended to assume that every adult human inhabitant of our planet has a right to jump on a plane and fly wherever they like, or to consume whatever food they like at any time of year, even if flown thousands of miles from the tropics to the temperate zones in their winter. Acknowledging such unrestricted rights may have been optimal in the past, but may have ceased to be optimal in the twenty-first century. I think Locke would have seen the force of this argument and modified his position accordingly.

5. The Conservative Revolutionary

The *Second Treatise*, we have said, was written to justify the right of rebellion of the subjects against their king. But Locke hardly fits the usual stereotype of the revolutionary, and he has generally been dismissed by Marxists as a 'bourgeois' writer, a defender of the rights of the property-owning class against the labouring poor. He was himself, of course, a country landlord, albeit on a small scale, and he spent much of his life at the country homes of the nobility and gentry. He writes in defence of an established order of property rights, and seems to have had few qualms about the great divisions of wealth between rich and poor. He may write of a duty of the wealthy to give succour to the needy, but he seems to have regarded this as a moral appeal to the consciences of the rich rather than a political argument for reorganizing institutions in such a way as to redistribute wealth. He was very much a member of the 'political establishment' of his day, both in his early years, working for Lord Ashley, and in the years after the Glorious Revolution when he accepted a position on the Board of Trade. By the end of his life, some shrewd investments had made him a wealthy man. If Locke is a revolutionary, he is a revolutionary of a very conservative type.

The resolution of this apparent paradox gradually becomes clear to any attentive reader of the *Second Treatise*. In both theory and practice, Locke argues, it is the later Stuart Monarchs, Charles II and James II, who were the innovators, and William of Orange is hailed as 'our great restorer'. The theory of absolute monarchy, Locke argues, was unknown to our ancestors, who always thought in terms of a limited or constitutional monarchy. He is fond of quoting lengthy passages from 'the judicious Hooker', Anglican divine and author of *The Laws of Ecclesiastical Polity*, to reinforce this historical claim. Attempts by Charles and James to seize more power than accepted custom and precedent permitted them were therefore, in Locke's eyes, truly revolutionary acts. It was therefore the king's party who were violating the terms of their trust and threatening the social fabric. Under such circumstances, it is within the rights of the members of the political community to resist encroachments upon their lives, liberties and estates. This resistance will no doubt start out as peaceful protest, but if peaceful protest is ineffective, force may properly be used against 'unjust and unlawful *Force*' (TTG 402).

Under what circumstances may force be used against a king and his officers? The answer to this question, of course, depends on the purposes for which the state was set up in the first place. Men agree to form a civil government, and to establish the legislative and executive branches of government, in order to better protect their rights under the law of nature. So, if either the law-makers or the law-enforcers start to threaten those natural rights, the purpose of government is undermined. If a sufficient number of the citizens feel that their rights are threatened or denied, they will resist, by force if necessary. In the final chapter of the *Second Treatise*, on 'The Dissolution of Government', Locke makes it very clear that the blame for the resulting political crises lies with those who have abused the trust placed in them. Governments, he writes, are often dissolved from the outside, by invasion and conquest – such cases are sufficiently familiar to any student of history. But governments are also dissolved from within, either when the legislative body is altered without the consent of the people, or when either branch of government abuses the trust placed in it.

Under what circumstances can the legislative body be altered without the consent of the people? Locke lists five types of case: their application to the political crisis of 1688–9 would have been blindingly obvious to his readers:

1. When the prince 'sets up his own Arbitrary Will in place of the Laws, which are the Will of the Society, declared by the Legislative, then the *Legislative is changed*'.
2. When the prince 'hinders the Legislative from assembling in its due time, or from acting freely, pursuant to those ends, for which it was Constituted, the *Legislative is altered*'.
3. When, 'by the Arbitrary Power of the Prince, the Electors, or ways of Election are altered, without the Consent, and contrary to the common Interest of the People, there also the *Legislative is altered*'.
4. The 'delivery also of the People into the subjection of a Foreign Power, either by the Prince, or by the Legislative, is certainly a *change of the Legislative*, and so a *Dissolution of the Government*'.
5. 'When he who has Supream Executive Power, neglects and abandons that charge, so that the Laws already made can no longer be put in execution. This is demonstrably to reduce all to Anarchy, and so effectively to *dissolve the Government*.' (TTG 408–11)

Under such circumstances, when the old government is dissolved, the people are at liberty:

> to provide for themselves, by erecting a new Legislative, differing from the other, by the change of Persons, or Form, or both, as they shall find it most for their safety and good. For the *Society* can never, by the fault of another, lose the Native and Original Right it has to preserve it self, which can only be done by a settled Legislative, and a fair and impartial execution of the Laws made by it. (TTG 411)

Importantly, the people can reassume this right pre-emptively, that is, rid themselves of an oppressive tyrant, or a king who will sell them to a foreign power, before he has fully achieved his evil aims. As in medicine, so too in politics; prevention is better than cure:

> To tell *People* they *may provide for themselves*, by erecting a new Legislative, when, by Oppression, Artifice, or being delivered over to a Foreign Power, their old one is gone, is only to tell them they may expect Relief, when it is too late, and the evil is past Cure. This is in effect no more than to bid them first be Slaves, and then to take care

of their Liberty; and, when their Chains are on, tell them, they may
act like Freemen. This, if barely so, is rather Mockery than relief; and
Men can never be secure from Tyranny, if there be no means to escape
it till they are perfectly under it: And therefore it is, that they have
not only a Right to get out of it but to prevent it. (TTG 411)

In addition to changes without proper consent in the form of the
legislative, there is a second way in which governments are dissolved, and that is when either the legislative or the executive acts
contrary to the trust invested in them (TTG 412). Since the purpose
for which governments are established is the preservation of the
property of the citizens – and by 'property' here, Locke clearly
means lives and liberties as well as lands and goods – the legislative
body forfeits its trust if it makes laws that violate these natural
rights, and the king violates the trust placed in his hands if he 'goes
about to set up his own Arbitrary Will, as the Law of the Society'
(TTG 413). In both types of case, either when the legislative is
altered without proper consent, or when either the legislative or the
executive breach the trust placed in them, 'those who are guilty are
guilty of Rebellion' (TTG 416). In the eyes of Locke and the 'Whig'
opposition, it was Charles II and James II who were guilty of rebellion against the established – if largely unwritten – constitutions of
their kingdoms, and political resistance against their aggressive
absolutism was actually a form of conservatism. The paradox of the
conservative revolutionary is resolved. Locke defends rebellion
against the Stuart monarchs in order to *conserve* what he takes to be
an earlier status quo.[27]

The final objection Locke feels himself obliged to answer is that
his theory 'lays a ferment for frequent rebellion', that is, could be
used as a justification for launching endless rebellions against established governments on trivial and inadequate grounds. Widespread
acceptance of Locke's principles would, according to his critics,
subvert all governments and speedily restore mankind to anarchy.
Locke replies with three counter-moves:

(1) His account of the origins and basis of government, he responds,
    is no more liable to this objection than any other hypothesis. On
    any theory of government, people who feel oppressed by the
    'ill usage of Arbitrary Power' will seek deliverance from such
    bondage.
(2) Great revolutions are not brought about by 'every little misman-
    agement in publick affairs'. Observation of human affairs shows
    that people will put up with quite a lot of bad government

before they rebel.[28] But once they discern a clear design and concerted efforts to reduce them to slavery, who can blame them for taking up arms to resist such sinister designs?

(3) In fact, the establishment of a power in the people to provide for a new legislative 'is *the best fence against Rebellion*, and the probablest means to hinder it'. (TTG 414–16)

There is no need, then, for 'our great restorer', William of Orange, to sit uneasily on his newly acquired throne, or to feel vulnerable to the threat of internal revolt in his new kingdoms of England and Scotland. If he agrees to rule according to custom and precedent, and doesn't attempt to set himself up as an absolute monarch, his throne should be secure. There remained, of course, the serious threat that James II would attempt to regain his lost kingdoms with external support from France, but that was an entirely separate matter. The contract theory of government is not, for Locke, inherently anti-monarchical. It is opposed only to those kings who deny that their authority to rule rests ultimately on a public trust, and can be forfeited if they breach that trust.

If the authority of kings rests upon a trust, who is to judge when a prince has violated that trust? Locke's answer is deceptively simple. 'The people', he says, must be the judge. This follows from the very nature of a trust. For 'who shall be *Judge* whether his Trustee or Deputy acts well, and according to the Trust reposed in him, but he who deputes him, and must, by having deputed him have still a Power to discard him, when he fails in his Trust' (TTG 427)? The proper umpire in a dispute between a prince and some of his subjects is 'the body of the people'. It is the political community established in phase one of the social contract that acts, as a corporate body, to place its trust in the various branches of government, and, 'as long as the society lasts', this power remains with the community. In practice, Locke seems untroubled by the obvious 'democratic deficit' of late seventeenth-century Britain, and by the striking fact that a very small proportion of the community could claim to be acting in the name of the whole. In this respect, too, he is a revolutionary with a distinctly conservative – not to say elitist – political hue.

6. Equality, Women and Slaves

At the heart of the *Two Treatises*, and fundamental to Locke's reply to Filmer, is his doctrine of the moral equality of human beings. We are not all equal, of course, in our talents, powers and virtues, but we are all equal in certain more basic respects. With the exception of a few extreme and pathological cases, we are all *persons* in Locke's 'forensic' sense, able to recognize our own individuality and acknowledge responsibility for our actions. We are all possessors of the lofty faculty of reason, able (unlike the brute beasts) to form abstract ideas, and to come to recognize both the existence of God and our duties towards Him and towards our fellow humans. Human infants are not born *into* this status, but they are all born *for* it, and their parents have a duty under the law of nature to raise them, through proper nurture and education, to the status of independent rational beings.

According to a recent study by Jeremy Waldron, Locke's moral doctrine of the fundamental equality of all human beings is inseparable from his commitment to the Christian religion.[29] We can distinguish here a strictly historical claim from a distinct and more controversial philosophical claim. The historical claim is that Locke thought of his Christianity and his commitment to human moral equality as inseparable parts of a coherent package of ideas and principles. The philosophical claim is that the same commitment to moral equality cannot be detached from the Christian religion and recast in acceptably secular terms for our modern age. With regard to the historical claim, Waldron is surely correct: Locke frequently uses the thought that we are all equal in the eyes of God to 'flatten' merely human hierarchies and challenge the arrogance of self-proclaimed human 'superiors'. With regard to the philosophical claim, his argument appears significantly weaker. He is in effect issuing a challenge to secular liberals to detach the morality from the religion without either distorting its content or undermining its rationale. There seems no deep reason to doubt that this challenge can be met, most probably by drawing on the famous 'end in itself' version of the Categorical Imperative of Immanuel Kant's ethical theory.[30]

But if Locke's most fundamental ethical commitment is to equality, critics will ask, what are we to make of his views concerning women and slaves? Do we not find him endorsing institutions and practices flatly and manifestly inconsistent with his own stated principles? Can a philosopher who firmly believes in equality casually endorse a wife's subjection to her husband, or draft a constitution for a new colony (Carolina) in which slavery was an established part of its organization? Will we find ourselves obliged to charge Locke with partial blindness and inconsistency at best, or outright hypocrisy at worst? Waldron's attempts to address these objections constitute significant parts of his wonderful book.

With regard to the status of women, Waldron has no difficulty in showing that their basic moral equality with men is consistently emphasized throughout the *Two Treatises*, and that Locke would have been seen by his contemporaries as a strong advocate of the moral equality of the sexes.[31] He emphatically denies, against Filmer, that Eve was created in a state of subjection to Adam, or that the 'image of God' thesis applies only to men and not equally to women. He is very remote in his thinking from Milton's infamous 'He [Adam] for God only; she [Eve] for God in him'. He sees no reason why women should not be sovereigns in their own right, own and inherit property, enter into contracts of various kinds, and share fully and equally in the responsibilities of parenthood. There remains, however, the problematic passage in the *First Treatise* where Locke admits 'a Foundation in Nature' for the subjection of a wife to her husband (TTG 174). This passage gives Waldron real difficulties, and he eventually admits that 'he has no tidy solution to offer',[32] beyond reminding his readers of the sheer weight of the textual evidence he has cited in support of Locke's very deep commitment to his thesis of basic equality.

When it comes to slavery, Locke appears to be in even deeper waters. He flatly and emphatically rejects the notion of natural slavery, insisting in the *Second Treatise* that Nature 'has made no such distinction between one Man and another' (TTG 382). Mere differences in race, or differences of opinion over religion, could never justify enslavement. The only justification for slavery that he is prepared to endorse is the 'captives taken in a just war' account (TTG 383). But this account, which permits me to enslave (rather than kill) combatants who are launching acts of aggression against me, is of very limited utility to the defenders either of the North Atlantic slave trade or of the slave-based plantations in the New World. In the first place, it licenses only the enslaving of active combatants, and emphatically not the taking as slaves of non-combatant women and children. Nor can it provide any justification whatsoever for assuming that children are born into slavery, as they of course were on the plantations. Locke cannot have been in any doubt that both the North Atlantic slave trade and the slavery-based colonies of the New World were manifestly contrary to the law of nature as he understood it. Yet we know that Locke drafted (and redrafted) the *Fundamental Constitutions* of the slavery-based colony of Carolina, and that he made money out of companies involved in the North Atlantic slave trade. Here Waldron struggles to reconcile Locke's high principles with his personal involvement in some dark and shabby practices. I shall leave the last word with him:

> So what can I say? Two facts are clear: (1) There is nothing in Locke's theory that lends an iota of legitimacy to the contemporary institution of slavery in the Americas; and (2) African slavery in the Americas was a reality and Locke himself was implicated in it, in the ways that I have described. I prefer to leave those facts where they lie, sitting uncomfortably together, than to try to resolve a contradiction which exists only by virtue of our own late-twentieth or early twenty-first-century ideas about the political integrity of an intellectual life.[33]

8

Problems of Church and State

1. The Problem of Divided Authority

Locke wrote to his father from Oxford in January 1660, at the height of the political crisis that preceded the Restoration of the monarchy, saying that he was considering taking up arms, 'could I be but resolvd from whome I ought to receive them and for whome to imploy them' (C I, 136). The problem of legitimate or rightful authority that was so pressing for the young Oxford don, lamenting the condition of 'this great Bedlam England' (C I, 124), was a problem that continued to vex the mature scholar for the rest of his life. For seventeenth-century thinkers, the problem of authority was greatly complicated by the potential conflict between spiritual and temporal powers. The Civil War of the 1640s had been in large part the consequence of the attempts by King Charles I and Archbishop Laud to impose 'High' Anglican ritual and ceremony throughout England and – still more problematic – even in Scotland. If an English Puritan, or a Scots Presbyterian, is persuaded that the commands of his King are in conflict with the commands of his God, who can blame him for obeying God rather than man? But if the members of each and every religious sect can claim special exemptions from the laws of the land, and cite 'reasons of conscience' for refusing obedience to laws passed by King and Parliament, do we not have a recipe for civil unrest and even anarchy? Can a man serve two masters? If he does, what should he do when their commands come into conflict?

One man who saw this problem clearly was Thomas Hobbes. In his *Leviathan* (1651), Hobbes argued that, to all intents and purposes, the Church should become a branch of the state. Among the powers of the sovereign, we are told, is that of judging 'what Opinions and Doctrines are averse, and what conducing to Peace', and hence of what may be taught in all places of public worship.[1] The civil authorities must take it upon themselves to give licences to certain men to preach, and to control precisely what they preach. Censorship may properly be used to help suppress opinions judged to be dangerous to public peace and security, and any attempts to evade censorship should be met by civil penalties such as fines and imprisonment. A well-run state, Hobbes argues, cannot permit the existence of divided authority. The sovereign is established in order to secure peace and security, but it cannot attain this end if significant minorities of the population feel themselves entitled – or even obliged – to disobey the laws of the land. A Hobbesian sovereign would not be obliged to enforce strict uniformity of worship across its dominions, and might choose to permit some minor variations in 'things indifferent', but the crucial point is that it is for the sovereign to make these judgements. Which doctrine or doctrines may be preached as 'God's word' or 'God's law' within a given state is for the civil authorities to decide, and they will decide on the basis of public peace and security. Any minister of religion telling his congregation that they should disobey their King should expect to lose his living, if not his life.

At the Restoration of the monarchy in 1660, the great issue of religious conformity became once again a hot topic in English politics. Should the newly crowned King Charles II continue the policies that had cost his father his throne and ultimately his life? Should he seek to impose religious uniformity upon his subjects? If so, should he seek to impose a narrowly conceived 'High' Anglicanism, or should he endeavour to include many of the Protestant Dissenters by means of a comprehensive or 'Broad' Church?[2] If not, which religious opinions could safely be tolerated and which must be suppressed by means of civil penalties? Most fundamental of all, does the civil magistrate have the *right* to impose uniformity, or is this always a violation of the rights of conscience? This question was addressed by Locke in 1660 in the first of his early and unpublished *Two Tracts on Government*.[3] The *First Tract*, written in Oxford around the time of the Restoration, shows Locke at his most conservative in matters of Church and state. He places the blame for the Civil War firmly on the shoulders of the Puritans who had used

their zeal in defence of liberty of conscience as a weapon to fan the
flames of rebellion against the legitimate authority of the King.
Religious liberty, he argues, had been used by unscrupulous and
ambitious men as a pretext for political rebellion, with catastrophic
results.[4]

The King has authority, whether by divine right or by his subjects' consent,[5] to protect the peace and security of his subjects. To
this end, Locke argues, he may establish public worship in a state
Church and fix rules for 'things indifferent' such as clerical gar-
ments, or the practice of kneeling to receive the sacraments. Saint
Paul urges us to 'let all things be done decently and in order', but
what precisely counts as decency and order is a matter of local taste
and custom. Since no one can claim that deep issues of theology
turn on the colour of the ministers' gowns, or the posture in which
a Christian receives the sacraments, no one can claim that their
rights of conscience are being violated. Precisely because these
things are in themselves 'indifferent', there can be no principled
case for objecting to the imposition of uniformity, if the civil powers
judge that this would be conducive to peace and order. The argument is restricted to the mere external trappings of religion, and
thus does not go so far as Hobbes in its defence of the powers of
the civil authorities, but it does indicate the distance Locke has
already travelled from the Puritanism he was brought up with, and
his accommodation to the Anglican reaction of the Restoration
years.

The problem with the argument of the *First Tract*, of course, is
that of determining which things are truly 'indifferent' to religion.
Whose judgement is this? If the civil magistrate is deemed the
proper judge of what is and is not indifferent, we have a position
that is consistent but extremely authoritarian in its implications. On
this model, the King first tells his subjects that the choice between
X and Y is indifferent, and then commands them to adopt X rather
than Y. They, however, might grant that the King has authority to
determine matters indifferent, but deny that the choice between X
and Y is one of those things. Locke will later acknowledge this point
in the *Letter Concerning Toleration*.[6] But if the subjects' consciences
are to be the judge of which things are indifferent, the King's power
to establish uniformity is entirely undermined. For any difficult and
contentious issue, someone or other will object that this is for them
a matter of conscience, and thus not one of those indifferent things
that fall under the power of the King to enforce uniformity. Take
the vexed issue of the presence of images in church – stained-glass

windows, works of sculpture, pictures of angels and saints. To the Laudian Anglicans, they were part and parcel of 'the beauty of holiness', aiding the devotions of the illiterate and helping all the congregation maintain the right mood in church. To many of the Puritans, they were a manifestation of idolatry, a clear breach of the Second Commandment, and a certain indication that the High Anglican Church of Charles I and Archbishop Laud was three-quarters of the way to returning to Rome. Locke's own father was probably among the parliamentary army that trashed Wells Cathedral during the Civil War.

It is fortunate that Locke decided against publication of the conservative *First Tract*, since he would soon change his mind regarding the authority of the civil powers in religion. What brought about this change of mind? Three factors spring to mind: the obvious failure of the 1662 Act of Uniformity, the visit to Cleves of 1665, and the influence of Anthony Ashley Cooper (later Earl of Shaftesbury), long an advocate of toleration, at least for Protestant Dissenters. When the Uniformity Act was passed in 1662, it attempted to impose a strict and narrow Anglicanism, and had the immediate effect of excluding a substantial and productive section of the population from large areas of public life. Locke might have continued to believe, as he had argued, that the civil magistrate has the authority to impose uniformity in things indifferent, but he would have been forced to admit that actual attempts to do this had been clumsy and counterproductive. His visit to Cleves in 1665 as part of a diplomatic mission clearly helped convince him that religious uniformity is not necessary to civil peace. If Catholics, Lutherans and Calvinists do in fact live together peacefully, the conservatives must be wrong to argue that religious uniformity is necessary for domestic peace and security. More important even than Cleves, however, was the influence of Ashley in persuading Locke of the harmlessness of religious dissent and religious diversity. When Locke moved his main place of residence from Oxford to London, he fell under a very different set of influences. The Oxford of the years immediately following the Restoration was – not surprisingly – one of Anglican and Royalist orthodoxy. The London of the same period was much more dynamic and diverse in its intellectual make-up, and as a great trading city was always likely to favour a more 'Dutch' attitude to religion.[7] If I am a trader in a great mercantile city like Amsterdam what I want to know of one of my fellow-merchants is not whether he is Catholic, Lutheran, Calvinist, Muslim or Jew, but whether he honours his contracts and pays his debts. Religious toleration,

Ashley was to persuade Locke, was in itself harmless, and was likely to have beneficial consequences for trade and prosperity.[8]

It was in Ashley's household in 1667 that Locke composed his unpublished 'Essay on Toleration',[9] defending a policy of toleration towards all Protestant Christians, and denying it only to Catholics (as agents of a foreign power) and atheists (who altogether deny the foundations of morality). Most of the arguments of the unpublished English 'Essay' are repeated in the Latin *Epistola de Tolerantia*, published anonymously at Gouda in the Netherlands in 1689. What had changed in the twenty-two years between the *Essay* and the *Epistola*? One thing that has clearly changed is that Locke has made the argument for toleration very much his own. The change of mind between 1660 and 1667 perhaps reflects the very different external influences of Restoration Oxford and the Ashley circle in London. But by 1689 Locke is a fully mature thinker, and he has come to the conclusion that toleration is a mark of the true Christian, as persecution is the mark of something entirely un-Christian in its spirit. In a letter to Limborch of October 1698, Locke makes an important confession of his own Christian faith:

> Learn in a few words what I mean when I say that I am an Evangelical or, if you prefer, an Orthodox Christian, not a Papist. Among those who profess the name of Christians I recognize only two classes, Evangelicals and Papists: the latter those who, as if infallible, arrogate to themselves dominion over the consciences of others; the former those who, seeking truth alone, desire themselves and others to be convinced of it only by proofs and reasons; they are gentle to the errors of others, being not unmindful of their own weakness; forgiving human frailty and ignorance, and seeking forgiveness in turn. (C VI, 495–6)[10]

The influence of Limborch and of the Dutch Remonstrants is another key difference between the early *Essay* and the later *Epistola*: when the anonymous *Epistola* appeared, it was widely regarded as a product of the Remonstrants' workshop. The other important difference is the range of the intended audience. The early *Essay* is written, at Ashley's prompting, to urge King Charles II to adopt a more tolerant attitude towards the English Dissenters. The *Epistola*, written in Latin for a continental audience, is much broader in its scope and ambitions. Although prompted in large part by the revocation in 1685 of the Edict of Nantes and the resulting plight of the French Protestants, it is in effect an attack on religious persecution *anywhere*, and a plea for religious toleration that is intended to be universal in its application. Whether religious persecution is directed from Rome or from Geneva makes no difference. In 1660, Locke had worried that religious diversity might lead to political instability; in 1689, he is convinced that toleration of diversity is both good religion and good politics. Not only is it the attitude of the true 'evangelical' Christian; it is also the mark of wise and enlightened government to permit all religious opinions consistent with public safety. For the mature Locke, religious diversity is in itself not dangerous to the state; what is dangerous is actually the foolish and misguided attempt to impose uniformity by force.

The Latin *Epistola* was quickly translated into English by William Popple, a Unitarian merchant with whom Locke was on friendly terms. There followed an exchange of letters with High Church divine Jonas Proast (*c.*1642–1710), chaplain of All Souls College in Oxford, who argued for the legitimacy of imposing 'moderate penalties' on the Dissenters to compel them, not so much to conform to the Church of England as to consider attentively the arguments on which Anglican belief and practice rested.[11] Locke defended his work under a double veil of anonymity, referring to the author of the *Epistola* always in the third person, writing *A Second Letter Concerning Toleration* (1690), and *A Third Letter for Toleration* (1692). He was composing a *Fourth Letter*, again in response to Proast, at his death in 1704. In the next three sections we shall consider each of Locke's three main arguments for toleration in turn, seeing how he responds to the objections of Proast.[12]

2. Argument 1: Belief is Not Subject to Coercion

This is the simplest and most intuitive of all the arguments for toleration. If the point of compulsion is to make people believe that a particular proposition is true, and if no one can believe anything merely because commanded to do so on pain of penalties, then any attempted compulsion of belief is inevitably futile. If I order you to believe that snow is purple, and you have the evidence of your eyes that it is white, how can you obey my command? Genuine belief is not something you can just turn on or off at will: it should be and generally is a response to evidence. You can of course *say* 'snow is purple', answer 'purple' if asked 'What colour is snow?', and even teach your children to say that snow is purple, but the threat of penalties has produced only outward conformity and no inner conviction. Religious persecution, the advocates of toleration have always argued, can produce only hypocrites and never sincere believers.

The 'care of souls', Locke argues, cannot belong to the civil ruler,

> because his power consists wholly in compulsion. But true and saving religion consists in an inward conviction of the mind; without it, nothing has value in the eyes of God. Such is the nature of the human understanding that it cannot be compelled by any external force. You may take away people's goods, imprison them, even inflict physical torture on their bodies, but you will not achieve anything if what you are trying to do by this punishment is change the judgment of their minds about things. (LT 8)

If you want a man to change his mind, Locke continues, you must offer him arguments and evidence in support of the position you hold to be true, and trust that he is sufficiently rational to understand them and see their force. Threats are of no efficacy here at all:

> To accept a doctrine or form of worship for the salvation of one's soul, one must believe sincerely that the doctrine is true, and that the form of worship will be pleasing to God, but no penalty has any force to instil this kind of conviction in the mind. It is light that is needed to change a belief in the mind; punishment of the body does not shed light. (LT 8)

Proast's response is to grant that force has no 'proper efficacy' of its own to make a man change his mind. From this, however, it does not follow that force may not have benign effects, if only 'indirectly and at a distance' in bringing men to embrace the truth (LT 56). The state might make use of censorship to prohibit the public teaching of certain opinions, while promoting the teaching of others. Who can deny that this might 'indirectly' affect the opinions prevailing among the population? And the state might use force to compel men to undergo religious instruction of an orthodox kind. This cannot, of course, compel belief, but if the evidence for orthodoxy is strong, and men are forced to listen and attend to it, there is a reasonable prospect of bringing all but the most perverse and stubborn of the Dissenters back into the fold. The penalties employed must be 'moderate' and 'duly proportioned' to the end that is being promoted. Extreme punishments (Locke's 'fire and sword') are, Proast concedes, likely to be counterproductive, producing only hatred and resentment of any religion that seeks to employ them

(LT 59–60). But penalties such as the imposition of fines, and exclusion from public office, should not provoke any comparable resentment, and might have benign effects. He shall not, Proast continues, attempt to lay down strict limits on the use of force by the civil authorities.

> It may suffice to say, that so much force, or such penalties as are ordinarily sufficient to prevail with men of common discretion, and not desperately severe and obstinate, to weigh matters of religion carefully and impartially, and without which ordinarily they will not do this; so much force, or such penalties may fitly and reasonably be used for the promoting of true religion and the salvation of souls. (LT 60)

Locke's response, in his *Second Letter*, is to grant that force may, indirectly and at a distance, bring about all manner of benign effects, but to deny that it follows from this that the state has any authority to exercise force in this area. There are lots of situations, he argues, in which an individual or an institution does not have the authority to do all the good they are capable of doing. A doctor might know that his patient will die without a particular operation; it does not follow that he can operate without his patient's consent. But this response would take us into the second main argument for toleration, based on the authority of the state. Returning to the issue of using force to make men consider the grounds for their religious beliefs, Locke asks Proast why he thinks this compulsion should be directed only against the Dissenters. Why does he suppose that the Dissenters are all stubborn and prejudiced, needing to be forced to receive instruction in Anglican orthodoxy, whereas none of the orthodox is in need of comparable instruction? Given the civil penalties attached to dissent, and the corresponding advantages of conformity, might there not be reason to suspect that the conformists will contain a higher proportion of the thoughtless and indifferent? You tell us, Locke writes, that all the Dissenters are to be punished.

> Why? Have no dissenters considered of religion? Or have all conformists considered? That you yourself will not say. Your project therefore is just as reasonable, as if a lethargy growing epidemical in England, you should propose to have a law made to blister and scarify and shave the heads of all who wear gowns: though it be certain that neither all who wear gowns are lethargic, nor all who are lethargic wear gowns. (LT 93–4)

What if one of the Dissenters has received the state-sanctioned instruction in Anglican orthodoxy, but still refused to conform to the Church of England? Must force be applied again and again? Must the penalties be increased? Must we regard such an individual as merely wilful and perverse, deserving of further punishment? Or might it not be wiser to admit the variation in the minds and tempers of men, and to concede that evidence that strikes Smith as conclusive might strike Jones as insufficient, without either man being clearly unreasonable? If we admit that religion is one of those fields of enquiry in which there is such a thing as *reasonable disagreement*, Proast's argument will fail to justify the existing persecution of the Dissenters.

3. Argument Two: The State has no Authority to Enforce Religious Conformity

This is arguably the most fundamental of Locke's arguments for toleration, resting as it does on his account of the state as coming about for the purpose of preserving and promoting what he calls 'civil goods'. By this expression, he explains, 'I mean life, liberty, physical integrity, and freedom from pain, as well as external possessions, such as land, money, the necessities of everyday life, and so on' (LT 7). The civil rulers or magistrates are empowered by the community to enact and enforce laws protecting its members against the invasion of their natural rights by others. The whole jurisdiction of rulers is concerned, he insists, with 'the protection and promotion of these civil goods and these alone'. It should not and cannot be extended to the salvation of souls. Why not? Because authority over men's beliefs and consciences is not given to the civil ruler either by God or by man:

> First, the civil ruler has no more mandate than others have for the care of souls. He has no mandate from God, for it nowhere appears that God has granted men authority over other men, to compel them to adopt their own religion. And no such power can be given to a ruler by men; for no one can abdicate responsibility for his own eternal salvation by adopting under compulsion a form of belief or worship prescribed to him by another person, whether prince or subject. For no one can believe at another's behest, however much they try to do so; and the force and effectiveness of true and saving religion lies in belief. (LT 7)

On Locke's view, there should be a sharp and clear distinction and separation between Church and state. The state or commonwealth is 'an association of people constituted solely for the purpose of preserving and promoting civil goods' (LT 6). A Church, on the other hand, is 'a free and voluntary association' of people coming together to offer public worship in a manner which they believe will be pleasing to God (LT 9). The members of any given Church can, of course, excommunicate members who violate the rules of their institution, but such excommunication 'does not, and cannot, deprive the excommunicated person of any of the civil goods that he previously possessed; they belong to his civil status and are subject to the ruler's protection' (LT 12). The civil authorities must judge whether the doctrines and practices of any particular Church are consistent with public order and security, and take measures to close down any Church that fails this test. But any such prosecutions are based entirely on political rather than theological grounds. The state has no duty to promote the true religion. Assuming for the moment that Christianity is true, a Christian King has no authority to attempt to impose the Christian religion by force. The Gospels do not instruct us in state-building, and contain no blueprint for political organization. Although there are many countries that have adopted Christianity, 'there is absolutely no such thing as a Christian commonwealth' (LT 29). Whether inspired by Rome or by Geneva, attempts to devise and construct a truly Christian state are fundamentally misconceived.

Proast's response is that Locke's claim that the state is established only 'for the procuring, preserving, and advancing of the civil interests of the members of it' is simply question-begging. No one, he writes, would deny that the state should promote such civil ends.

> But if there be any other ends besides these, attainable by civil society and government; there is no reason to affirm that these are the only ends for which they are designed. Doubtless commonwealths are instituted for the attaining of all the benefits which political government can yield. And therefore, if the spiritual and eternal interests of men may in any way be procured or advanced by political government, the procuring and advancing of those interests must in all reason be reckoned among the ends of civil societies, and so, consequently, fall within the compass of the magistrate's jurisdiction. (LT 62)

In addition to the 'fraternal care of souls' which belongs to all Christians to take care of each others' spiritual welfare, and which is generally exercised by prayer and exhortation, there is, according to Proast, 'an indirect and more remote care of souls', which is committed to the civil magistrate and which authorizes him to promote the true religion by means of appropriate sanctions. Why might force be necessary to bring men to embrace the true religion? Because men, when they come to embrace one religion rather than another, are 'so much swayed by prejudice and passion' that they are likely to choose on the basis of bad reasons. Once we acknowledge the force of passion and prejudice in our own minds, we will see that there are good reasons to embrace a form of paternalism:

> it is in every man's true interest, not to be left wholly to himself in this matter, but that care should be taken, that in an affair of so vast a concern to himself, he may be brought even against his own inclination, if it cannot be done otherwise (which is ordinarily the case) to act according to reason and sound judgment. And then what better course can men take to provide for this, than by vesting the power I have described in him who bears the sword? Not that I think the sword is to be used in this business (as I have sufficiently declared already), but because all coactive power resolves at last into the sword; since all (I do not say, that will not be reformed in this matter by lesser penalties, but) that refuse to submit to lesser penalties, must at last fall under the stroke of it. (LT 64)

According to Proast, it appears, the contracting parties establishing the state might reasonably establish a form of benign paternalism, in which decisions pertaining to their own salvation are taken out of the hands of the citizens and entrusted to the public authorities. We humans, it seems, are forever in the condition of naughty children, needing external coercion even to act for our own good. Just as we might authorize the state to ban sales of alcohol or cream cakes on grounds of public health, rather than issuing guidance to its citizens on the health hazards involved in their consumption, so we might authorize the state to establish the 'true' religion and enforce it by means of penalties. Proast's argument reveals a deep 'Augustinian' pessimism about human rationality and about our capacity to steadfastly pursue even what we recognize to be our own good.[13] Once we recognize this permanent weakness in human psychology, we will see that it is rational for us to erect fences to guard against future abuses of too much freedom. We shuffle off on to others – ultimately, on to the state – the responsibility for our own future actions.

The nature and extent of Proast's paternalism is most evident in his response to Locke's medical example. Locke tells us that a surgeon has no right to operate on a patient without his own consent, even if the operation is necessary to save him from suffering or the risk of death. We have not authorized the members of the medical profession to take these decisions out of our own hands. Proast replies that, as things now stand, Locke is right about this. But, he adds,

> if the magistrate should by a public law appoint and authorize a competent member of the most skilful in that art, to visit such as labour under the disease, and cut those (whether they consent or not) whose lives they unanimously judge it impossible to save otherwise: I am apt to think you would find it hard to prove that in so doing he exceeded the bounds of his power. And I am sure it would be as hard to prove that those artists would have no right, in that case, to cut such persons. (LT 119)

Proast's deep pessimism about human rationality is by no means crazy, and there are, of course, instances in which one man may reasonably authorize another to take charge of his decisions. From antiquity, we have the famous example of Odysseus binding himself to the mast of his ship to hear the Sirens' song, and ordering his crew (who have their ears blocked) not to release him even if he begs them to do so. In our modern world, a drug addict undergoing cold turkey might authorize his minders to take control of his life for some limited period. But in both these cases, the rational agent foresees some *temporary* period of dangerous irrationality, and takes steps – with the aid of others – to avoid harmful consequences. Both Odysseus and our drug addict look forward to resuming their rational autonomy in the course of time. Pursuing these analogies would only give Proast a case for compulsory Sunday school for children, but no compulsion of adults. The other obvious problem is why Proast should think that the *state* should have any special authority in matters of faith. The King of England is *ex officio* head of the Church of England, but this is a mere historical accident – no one in Charles II's England thought that their notoriously worldly monarch was a man of deep spiritual insight. And if Charles II in England has this coercive power, then the same power belongs to Louis XIV in France and to the hard-line Muslim mogul emperor Aurangzeb in India, ruler over many millions of Hindus. But this would take us into Locke's third argument.

Locke's response, in his *Second Letter*, is to accuse Proast in turn of begging the question (LT 102). 'Doubtless', Proast tells us, civil society is established for other than merely civil ends. But what is the force of this 'doubtless'? Is it meant to convey any sort of argument? Let us grant that an organization can, and often does, serve ends other than those it was established to serve. Does it follow that it was established for the purpose of serving those further ends?

> Now nobody can in reason suppose that anyone entered into civil society for the procuring, securing, or advancing the salvation of his soul, when he, for that end, needed not the force of civil society. (LT 104)

The parties to the social contract, Locke insists, desire protection against encroachments on their natural rights by others. This is why they feel the need to establish laws enforced by punishments. The contracting parties do not imagine that their spiritual interests are best served by giving the state the authority to coerce them into a national Church against their will and against their own better judgement. We do not establish laws to protect us against ourselves. What could make the parties to the social contract agree to give the state authority in spiritual matters? If the civil government is indeed authorized to establish a state religion and impose it by force, Locke asks, will the interests of true religion be furthered or frustrated? Proast's argument for religious conformity, Locke argues, will be used by Catholics in Rome, Calvinists in Geneva, and Muslims in Constantinople and Delhi. Religious *conformity* will be advanced, but at the cost of religious *truth*. But this leads us into the third argument for toleration.

4. Argument Three: Toleration Does and Coercion Does Not Serve the Cause of Truth

Mutual toleration among Christians is, Locke tells us at the start of the *Epistola*, 'the principal mark of the true church' (LT 3). Toleration is in itself 'so consistent with the Gospel and with reason that it seems incredible that people should be blind in so plain a matter' (LT 6). Forms of Church government are of secondary importance. When Christ says 'Where two or three are gathered together in my name, there am I in the midst of them', he tells us plainly that the precise forms of Church government, and the local details of worship and ceremony, are matters of secondary importance (LT 10).[14] The message here is the same as that of the *Reasonableness*: to be a Christian is to follow Christ, not man. If we are to take our Saviour at his word, no one sect or congregation has any exclusive right to call itself the only true Christian Church.

As for the cause of truth, in religion as in other matters of speculation, it is not advanced by the use of force: 'For truth would certainly have done very well, if she were ever left to herself. She has received little help, and never will, from the dominion of the powerful, to whom the truth is rarely known and seldom pleasing' (LT 31). Christian writers have long argued that it is a mark of the truth of the Christian religion that it spread rapidly throughout the Roman Empire in the face of vigorous attempts to suppress it; now Christians such as Proast are arguing that the true religion cannot stand on its own merits without the backing of force. If they claim that Christianity is true, but people cannot be brought to embrace Christianity except by force, they contradict their own reading of history.

Locke and Proast are in agreement that there can only be one true religion, so that if one religion is true, it follows that the others are false. (Neither of them seriously addresses the logical possibility that all religions are false.) Let us suppose not just that Christianity is true, but that the Anglican version of Christianity is true. If so, it would surely be desirable to have Anglican Christianity taught in Rome, and India, and China – this would aid more men to find the true path to salvation. But this would require the rulers of those countries to permit Anglican missionaries to preach and seek converts. So should the Pope in Rome (temporal as well as spiritual ruler of the papal states), and the mogul emperor Aurangzeb in India, permit Anglican missionaries freedom of operation in their domains? These rulers will use arguments similar to those employed by Proast to justify suppression of Anglican doctrine, and punitive measures against both missionaries and converts. In their own eyes, they will be serving the cause of truth against error. As Locke reminds us, 'Every church is orthodox in its own eyes': to say that only the orthodox have a right to employ compulsion is 'to use big, plausible words to say nothing' (LT 14). In the *Second Letter* he makes the universalism of his approach fully explicit. Referring to himself in the third person, he sums up a key part of his case against Proast:

The author's letter pleased me, because it is equal to all mankind, is direct, and will, I think, hold everywhere, which I take to be a good mark of truth. For I shall always suspect that neither to comport with the truth of religion, or the design of the Gospel, which is suited to some one country or party. What is true and good in England, will be true and good at Rome too, in China, or Geneva. (LT 95)

Proast insists that authority is given to the civil magistrate not to bring men to embrace 'the religion of the court' but only to 'the true religion' (LT 65). Locke will reply, of course, that to tell a king that he may use force to bring men to the true religion is inevitably going to mean, in practice, that he may use force to bring them to the religion he believes to be true. When Louis XIV is taking punitive measures against the French Protestants, he doubtless believes he is serving the cause of the true religion. Your way of applying force, Locke argues against Proast in the *Second Letter*, 'will as much promote popery in France as Protestantism in England' (LT 79–80). If religion were a matter of knowledge in the strict sense, Proast's position would be defensible: once the evidence has been properly presented, only the wilful and perverse could refuse to accept it. But this is manifestly not the case for a revealed religion such as Christianity, which rests largely on trust in the testimony of the Apostles. For Locke, as we have seen, belief in testimony never counts as knowledge. I *know* that there is an active volcano in Sicily because I have climbed Etna and seen for myself that it is still smoking and spewing out rock; if I tell you that Etna is still active you may trust my report and come to believe this, but you acquire only belief and not knowledge. Now the testimony of the Apostles is sufficient to convince Christians that Christ is the promised Messiah, but people who are not obviously perverse or wilful deny this. For the orthodox Jew, Christ was not the Messiah, whose coming is still awaited. For the Muslim, Christ was only the second of the three great historical prophets of monotheism. Must Proast say that all those who have seen the evidence for Christianity and rejected it, are guilty of some terrible moral fault, making them deserving of punishment?

Proast's response is to accuse Locke of a form of religious scepticism. Your argument, he contends, rests on the assumption of 'the equal truth, or at least the equal certainty (or uncertainty) of all religions' (LT 111). If this assumption is true, enquiry into matters of religion is vain, as no man can have good reason to think he is more likely to be on the right road than his neighbour. Holding the correct religious views will merely be a matter of luck. If such scepticism is correct, then 'without more ado the cause is yours'. But, Proast retorts, it is sufficient for his purpose to suppose:

> that there is one true religion, and but one, and that that true Religion may be known by those who profess it to be the only true religion, and may also be manifested to be such, by them to others, so far at least as to oblige them to receive it and to leave without excuse if they do not. (LT 112)

For Proast, a man is left without excuse for his unbelief in the Christian religion if he is presented with sufficient evidence of its truth, but obstinately continues to reject it. Such men are rightly liable to punishment for their perversity (LT 113). The punishments should continue for as long as the offence continues. This is in Proast's eyes perfectly proper, as 'it is impossible for any man innocently to reject the true religion so tendered to him', that is, with the evidence of its truth (LT 115).

Locke denies that his argument relies on the assumption that all religions are equally true or equally certain. In the strict sense, of course, Christians cannot know that Christianity is true, because their belief requires trust in the reports of witnesses who lived almost two thousand years ago. The evidence that convinces Christians of the truth of their revelation depends on testimony regarding 'particular matters of fact, whereof you [Proast] were no eyewitness, but were done many ages before you were born' (LT 157). Christians can nevertheless have a firm conviction that the evidence for their belief is *good enough*. What they should not take it upon themselves to say is that evidence that is good enough to convince them is good enough for any man:

> Whatever gains any man's assent, one may be sure had sufficient evidence in respect of that man. But that is far enough from proving it evidence sufficient to prevail on another, let him consider it as long and as much as he can. The tempers of men's minds; the principles settled there by time and education, beyond the power of the man himself to alter them; the different capacities of men's understandings, and the strange ideas they are often filled with, are so various and uncertain, that it is impossible to find that evidence (especially in things of a mixed disquisition, depending on so long a train of consequences, as some points of the true religion may), which one can confidently say will be sufficient for all men. (LT 153–4)

You and I, Locke tells Proast, think that the evidence for Christianity is sufficient to convince us of its truth. But you think that what convinces you must convince any sincere seeker of truth, and infer that anyone who rejects Christianity after being presented with this evidence must be merely wilful and obstinate, perversely rejecting the saving truth that is being offered to him, and thus deserving of punishment. But whether another man is sincere in his search for truth is not something either you or I can know: this 'must be left to the searcher of hearts' (LT 155). Given the differences between the minds and tempers of men, and the deep and lasting effects of custom and education, one must expect to observe a wide variation in human beliefs. We may be able to identify people who seem too credulous of testimony and others who seem too mistrustful, without being able to specify a precise Aristotelian 'golden mean'. There is not the least reason to deny, for example, that 'there are many Turks who sincerely seek truth', and honestly believe that it is to be found in the revelation of Mohammed (LT 154).

What Locke needs, here as elsewhere, is the notion that religion is a subject matter that allows of *reasonable disagreement* between men. This is quite distinct from either scepticism or relativism: a Lockean can firmly believe that one religion has better evidence in its favour than another, and certainly need not passively endorse a shallow conformism of the 'When in Rome' variety. The key inference that is rejected is the move from 'Evidence E convinces me that p is true' to 'Evidence E should convince anyone that p is true', and thus to the conclusion that 'Anyone who is provided with evidence E but rejects p is perverse and irrational.' This acceptance of reasonable disagreement concerning many matters of inestimable importance for our lives – such as, for example, comprehensive accounts of the good life – is of course one of the most fundamental features of modern liberal political theories such as that of John Rawls's great *Theory of Justice*.

5. The Limits of Toleration

The civil authorities have a duty to protect citizens against encroachments upon their rights to life, liberty and property. To this end, they are authorized to use force to suppress organizations, including religions, which pose a clear threat to public peace and security. The crucial point for Locke is that the proper justification for the use of force is always political and never theological. The parties to the Lockean social contract have no reason to fear the strange and irrational speculative beliefs of their fellows, unless those beliefs prompt them into courses of action that threaten their own lives and liberties. If my neighbour seeks to bring an end to a prolonged period of drought by praying to his rain god, I can cheerfully regard him as a harmless eccentric. If he thinks that the rain god can only be propitiated by the ritual sacrifice of a virgin, I am likely to fear for my daughters and call the police.

Which opinions are beyond the pale, and so dangerous to peace and security that they should not be tolerated? Locke lists four such categories:

1. I say, first, that a ruler should not tolerate any doctrines which are detrimental to human society and prejudicial to good morals which are essential for the preservation of civil society. (LT 35)

Examples of this kind, he thinks, are rare in any Church.[15]

2. A more subtle but also more dangerous problem for a commonwealth arises from those who claim for themselves and their followers some special prerogative contrary to the civil laws, which is concealed in a form of words intended to deceive. (LT 35)

If a religion teaches that 'promises to heretics need not be kept', or that 'an excommunicated King forfeits his kingdom', its followers may reasonably be regarded as enemies of the state. Here Locke is tapping into a long tradition of anti-Catholic rhetoric in English politics. When Pope Pius V issued the Bull *Regnans in Excelsis* in 1570, excommunicating Queen Elizabeth I, he provided Elizabeth and her spymaster Walsingham with a powerful case for punitive action against all English Catholics, who were regarded and treated as a potential fifth column, agents of a hostile foreign power. If an English Catholic swears an oath of allegiance to Elizabeth, but holds in his heart that this oath is not binding on him, and that the papal bull relieves him of any duty to honour it, he is already a potential traitor. English Catholics attempted to rebut this charge,[16] but it would be hundreds of years before they could resume a full role in public affairs.[17]

Toleration must also not be extended to any group that refuses to reciprocate, that is, that rejects the principle of toleration. Again, Locke obviously has Catholics in mind,[18] but the principle applies equally to Protestant Dissenters who preach toleration when they find themselves in the position of a persecuted minority, but quickly forget the case for liberty of conscience if and when they come to power.

3. A church can have no right to be tolerated by a ruler if those who join it transfer their loyalty and obedience to another prince simply by joining. Any ruler who granted such toleration would be giving a foothold in his own territories and cities for soldiers to be conscripted from his own citizens against his own country. (LT 36)[19]

Locke's illustration of this point is the supposed allegiance of Muslims to 'the mufti in Constantinople', himself supposed to be 'completely submissive to the Ottoman emperor'. His readers would not have been misled for a moment: in its original context, this is clearly another anti-Catholic thrust.[20] In the late seventeenth century, the papacy still played a significant role in European power politics: the Pope was not merely the secular ruler of the Papal States, but also took it upon himself to meddle in international disputes. If James II were to re-invade England, with the backing of French troops and the explicit support of the Pope, would English Catholics take up arms to resist him?[21]

The example of Muslims living in a non-Muslim land is much more difficult and controversial for us than it was for Locke. In his time, there would have been very few such people, and their political allegiances might simply be overlooked. Today, of course, there are many millions, and their loyalties are a matter of acute concern for the governments of the West. Do they honour the sura of the Qur'an, ordering that Muslims in a non-Muslim country should obey the laws of the land? If so, Locke would defend toleration. When the Iranian supreme leader Ayatollah Khomeini ordered the killing of a British citizen (Salman Rushdie) for writing *The Satanic Verses*, British Muslims should have refused to do so, if they expected to be treated in turn as bona fide British citizens. If they hold that the Ayatollah has the authority to override the usual duties of citizenship, they must expect to be regarded and treated as enemy aliens.

4. Finally, those who deny that there is a Deity are not to be tolerated at all. Neither the faith of the atheist nor his agreement nor his oath can be firm and sacrosanct. These are the bonds of human society, and all these bonds are completely dissolved, once God or the belief in God is removed. (LT 37)

The moral law of nature is for Locke the law of God, an expression of God's will and His commands for His creatures. An atheist can swear an oath of allegiance to a monarch, or swear an oath on the Bible in a court of law, without fearing any dire consequences if he breaks his oath. The obvious problem, as John Stuart Mill would point out in *On Liberty*, is that this rule will only encourage atheists to lie. Mill thought it an anomaly – and an anomaly that needed correcting – that an atheist who was a liar could gain redress for injuries in a court of law while an honest atheist could not.

Attentive readers may have noticed a possible inconsistency at this point. In Book One of the *Essay* Locke used the atheism of the Thais (a civilized and highly cultured people) as an argument against the claim that the idea of God is innately stamped upon all human souls at their creation. The Thais, presumably, have moral and political virtues broadly comparable to those of European Christians. There seems not the least reason to suppose that 'the bonds of human society' were dissolved in Thailand. Locke might retort that the Thais are Buddhists, and that followers of the Buddha, even if they do not believe in God, still believe in a moral order with rewards and punishments in future lives. It might even turn out, from Locke's point of view, that an erroneous conception of personal identity is what makes it possible for these people to believe in a moral law backed up by sanctions!

But is there any reason to think that belief in a god is essential for morality? Locke clearly thinks so, regarding the moral law as an expression of God's will. The overwhelming majority of his contemporaries would have agreed: 'atheist', in the period, was frequently used as a term of abuse and opprobrium. If you called a man an atheist, it would be assumed that you regarded him as a scoundrel. One contemporary of Locke who dared to challenge the consensus on this point was Pierre Bayle, who in his *Pensées Diverses sur la Comète* (1682) denied the existence of any clear link between a man's speculative opinions and his moral virtues.[22] Bayle even floated the possibility of an entire society of virtuous atheists, but this was a possibility beyond the grasp of his English contemporary. Given his principles, Bayle can argue for a more complete and thoroughgoing toleration than the more conservative Locke.

6. Toleration After the 'Glorious Revolution'

The so-called 'Glorious Revolution' of 1688–9 brought Locke's friends to power in both Church and state. A Toleration Act was passed in 1689, giving freedom of assembly and worship to Protestant Dissenters, but not to Catholics and anti-Trinitarians. Dissenters continued to be excluded from the universities and from various public offices. From Locke's point of view, the Toleration Act would have appeared a clear step in the right direction, but by no means enough to satisfy his principles. As we have seen, Locke himself was inclined to anti-Trinitarian views, and had argued in the *Reasonableness* that belief in the Trinity was not a necessary part of the Christian faith. Is there even the slightest reason, he would have asked, to believe that a man's views on such a remote point of speculation could or should disqualify him from full citizenship? And the continued exclusion of the Dissenters from public life would have been, in Locke's eyes, beyond the legitimate authority of the civil government.

Within the Church of England hierarchy, the balance of power shifted, after the Revolution, in the direction of the so-called 'latitudinarians'. John Tillotson (1630–94) was Archbishop of Canterbury from 1691 to 1694, when he was succeeded by Thomas Tenison (1636–1714). Both men favoured a 'broad' and relatively undogmatic Christianity, and both were inclined to be advocates of toleration. But would the bishops in the House of Lords vote in favour of increasing toleration of the Dissenters, or would they continue to cast their votes as their predecessors had generally done, in favour of repressive measures? An interesting test case is provided by Gilbert Burnet, who had served as chaplain and propagandist to William of Orange and had been appointed Bishop of Salisbury in 1689. Burnet was familiar with Locke's friend Limborch during his period of exile in Holland, and Limborch clearly expected his old friend, now in a position of power, to live up to his stated principles. When a Blasphemy Act was debated in the Lords in 1698, Limborch was shocked to find Burnet speaking in favour of the Bill, which demanded punishments for anti-Trinitarians. Limborch writes to Locke to say that he fears that this edict may be 'the beginning of a new persecution', and adds that he has written to Burnet urging him to rethink:

> I replied [to Burnet] roundly and candidly, and pointed out what kind of zeal should be shown in defence of the truth: that is, not the fiery sort that strives to stop the mouths of gainsayers by the severity of edicts; but that which convinces them of the truth by the weight of arguments. I am doubtful whether my freedom of speech was welcome. I wrote what I believed it was my duty to write. (C VI, 460)

To be fair to the Anglican bishops of William and Mary's age, some of them at least had embraced Locke and Limborch's central claim that persecution is contrary to the spirit of the Gospel. In debates in the House of Lords, the bishops were often to be found among those speaking and voting against coercive measures against the Dissenters. Limborch, however, remained pessimistic regarding the bigger picture. Toleration can come about in Europe, he writes to Locke in October 1700, in either of two ways. The hierarchies of the various Christian Churches might come to embrace our principles and cease to press for coercive measures against Dissenters. Alternatively, the civil authorities might simply decide to deprive the clergy of any powers of persecution. The former route to toleration is, of course, the ideal for which Locke and Limborch are jointly striving; the latter is much more realistic. As Limborch writes:

> But we owe the quiet that we now enjoy not to the more moderate counsels of the clergy but to the prudence and benignity of the magistracy; if that did not restrain the clergy's fiery zeal the same tempest as formerly overwhelmed our predecessors would overwhelm us today. (C VII, 168)

Although some Christians have embraced the message of Locke and Limborch, the best hope for the systematic implementation of policies of toleration lies with the civil magistrates. If they are wise, they will not trust the clergy with any power to impose coercive measures, and they will be deaf to appeals from the pulpit for any such measures, threats of excommunication levelled against tolerant rulers, or attempts by the clergy to engage in political agitation. The verdict of history is that clerics are not to be trusted with political power.

Locke's case for toleration became, of course, one of the central documents of Enlightenment political thought. It is hard for modern readers to see it as a radical document, challenging most (but not all[23]) of the orthodoxies of its age. Reading Locke's exchanges with Proast, we get the sense that Locke wins most rounds of their debate, at least on points, but there is an obvious worry that any such judgement would be anachronistic. We judge from the viewpoint of our own times. At the end of the seventeenth century, the judgement would have been less clear-cut: there must have been any number of social conservatives who would have defended Proast's paternalistic vision of the state against the proto-liberal ideas of Locke. Even the verdict of history is equivocal: most citizens of

modern Western states are liberal on most issues, but political voices
calling for paternalist measures have by no means been silenced,
and paternalist measures are sometimes enacted. Perhaps there are
occasions when we do indeed need to be protected against ourselves. Locke would not have been in the least surprised at this
course of events. Although he is often hailed as one of the prophets
of the Enlightenment, Locke's thought tends to be cautious and his
outlook fairly pessimistic. A Lockean Enlightenment[24] would always
be a slow and gradual affair of humans groping individually and
collectively slowly towards the light, making small piecemeal
advances in both natural and moral knowledge, but forever vulnerable to the powerful forces of passion and prejudice.

Notes

Introduction: The Unity of Locke's Thought

1 Gilbert Ryle, 'John Locke', in his *Collected Papers*, volume 1, 147.
2 See Peter Alexander (1985) Introduction, 1–12, for the importance of setting Locke's philosophy in the right context – that provided by Boyle and Newton rather than by Berkeley and Hume.
3 For a sharp and incisive statement of the recent attack on the rationalist–empiricist distinction, see Loeb (1981).
4 David Hume to Michael Ramsay, 26 August 1737. Quoted from Mossner, 104.
5 Cottingham (1988), 10–11.
6 For an illuminating discussion of this theme, see Edward Craig on what he calls 'the insight ideal': Craig (1987), chapter 1, 'The Mind of God', 13–68.

Chapter 1 Life, Contexts and Concerns

1 The most recent biography of Locke is Roger Woolhouse (2007). A brief *Life* is provided by Mark Goldie in *The Continuum Companion to Locke*, edited by S. J. Savonius-Wroth, Paul Schuurman and Jonathan Walmsley, 1–46.
2 For this period of Locke's life, see J. R. Milton, 'Locke at Oxford', in G. A. J. Rogers, ed. (1994), 29–47.
3 My aim, says Locke in the famous letter to Pembroke, has always been 'to pass silently through this world with the company of a few good friends and books' (C II, 663).

4 See *The Debate at Large* for the contemporary records of this extraordinary crisis meeting of the two Houses of Parliament. Its precise constitutional status was unclear at the time (and remains so to this day), but it took the only practical decision in agreeing to confer the Crown on William of Orange.

5 See Sarah Hutton's 'Damaris Masham, née Cudworth', in *The Continuum Companion to Locke*, 72–6.

6 Strictly, Anthony Ashley Cooper did not become the Earl of Shaftesbury until the next year (1672).

7 See Jonathan Walmsley's helpful account in *The Continuum Companion to Locke*, 234–5.

8 See W. Von Leyden, ed., *John Locke: Essays on the Laws of Nature and Associated Writings* (ELN).

9 This view of the Catholics as a potential fifth column was obviously defensible in the England of Elizabeth 1 and her spymaster Walsingham. Whether it was still defensible in 1667 is much more debatable.

10 A ninth volume of the *Correspondence* is imminent, edited by Mark Goldie.

11 See John Harrison and Peter Laslett, *The Library of John Locke* (Oxford, 1971).

12 See De Beer's comment in C I, xxxv, to the effect that 'there is very little to show any interest on Locke's part in current politics before the Revolution'.

13 See Popkin, chapter 1, 'The Intellectual Crisis of the Reformation', 3–16.

14 Locke, *Essay*, Frontispiece. Cicero, *De Natura Deorum* (P. H. Nidditch translation), 1, 84.

15 Ecclesiastes 11:5.

Chapter 2 The Theory of Ideas

1 For Malebranche's doctrine of the Vision in God and his arguments in its support, see Pyle (2003), chapter 3, 47–73

2 For commentary on this dispute, see Nadler (1989 and 1992), and Pyle (2003), 74–95.

3 The controversy runs to four volumes of Robinet's edition of Malebranche's *Oeuvres Complètes*, and strays far from the initial topic of ideas. Although Locke did not have copies of these exchanges in his library, he could well have followed them by means of the *comptes rendus* of commentators such as Jean Le Clerc and Pierre Bayle.

4 See Yolton (1984), chapter 5, 'Locke and Malebranche', 88–104.

5 *Essay* IV, xxi, 4. For the interpretation of this passage, and its use against Yolton, see Ayers (1991), 60–1.

6 In his unpublished '*Remarks upon some of Mr Norris' Books*' (WJL, vol. X), Locke attacks the occasionalism of Norris and his master Malebranche, arguing that God can delegate powers to subordinate causes.

7 For discussion, see Yolton (1996), chapter 2, 26–71, and Samuel C. Rickless, 'Locke's Polemic against Nativism', in Newman, ed. (1997), 33–66.

8 Descartes, 'Third Replies', in Cottingham, Stoothoff and Murdoch, eds, *The Philosophical Writings of Descartes*, vol. 2, 132.

9 Descartes, *Comments on a Certain Broadsheet*, in Cottingham, Stoothoff and Murdoch, eds, *The Philosophical Writings of Descartes*, vol. 1, 304.

10 Rickless (44 n.vii) points out that there is no reason why a dispositional innatist about mathematics should baulk at this point, if consistency requires them to say that the theorems as well as the axioms are innate. Leibniz (*New Essays*, 78) is happy to grant that 'any truths which are derivable from primary innate knowledge may also be called innate, because the mind can draw them from its own depths, though often only with difficulty'.

11 Gottfried Wilhelm Leibniz, *New Essays on Human Understanding* (1981), 81.

12 Locke, ELN, 136–45.

13 See his irate reply of 4 August 1690 to his friend James Tyrrell, who had passed this line of objection on to Locke (C IV, 110–13).

14 Whether Locke thinks that complex ideas of sensation are presented as such, or whether he conceives of sensation as presenting a miscellany of ideas that are then combined into complexes by the mind, is a point of some difficulty and controversy.

15 See Ayers (1991), 38–9.

16 Ibid., 44–51.

17 Ibid., 48.

18 For an interesting discussion, and some objections to Ayers's defence of imagism, see David Soles (1999).

19 Berkeley, *Principles of Human Knowledge*, 6–17, in Berkeley's *Philosophical Writings*, 46–55.

Chapter 3 Human Knowledge and Its Limits

1 Lex Newman, 'Locke on Knowledge', in Newman, ed. (2007), 333–43.

2 Jonathan Lowe (1995), 172.

3 Newman (n.i), 331–3.

4 We have no conclusive textual evidence for this, and of course Locke always sought to play down his reliance on previous philosophers, but the resemblance is too striking to be a mere coincidence.

5 Descartes, *Regulae*, Rule Seven, in Cottingham et al., eds (1985–91), vol. 1, 25.

6 The issue will come up in a revised form in evolutionary epistemology. Modern discussions of colour vision show clearly that the crucial relation is one to many (the things we call yellow form a pretty mixed group), but we still use our colour experiences to group things in ways that are practically useful.

7 See Hume's *Enquiry* (ed. Tom Beauchamp, 1999), section 4, 'Sceptical Doubts Concerning the Operations of the Understanding', 108–18.
8 See David Chalmers (1996) for the label of 'the hard problem' of consciousness and for serious and in-depth discussion of why it remains the hard problem for neuroscience.
9 Locke wrote a lengthy essay *On the Conduct of the Understanding* (CU) on just this topic, and gave serious consideration to its inclusion in the later editions of the *Essay*. It was reprinted by Thoemmes Press of Bristol in 1996, with a new introduction by John Yolton.
10 For a modern discussion of the epistemology of testimony, see Coady (1992).
11 See especially Matthew Tindall, *Christianity as Old as the Creation* (London, 1730). The most famous of the deists – John Toland, Matthew Tindall and Anthony Collins – were all familiar to Locke.

Chapter 4 The Material World

1 See George Berkeley, *An Essay Towards A New Theory of Vision*, in Berkeley's *Philosophical Writings*, 274–348.
2 David Hume, *Treatise on Human Nature*, Book One, Part Four, section 2, 'Of Scepticism with Regard to the Senses', 187–218.
3 Thomas Reid, *Essays on the Intellectual Powers of Man*, in the *Works of Thomas Reid*, ed. Sir William Hamilton, Essay Six, chapter 5, 'The First Principles of Contingent Truths', 445b. It is, says Reid, a first principle that 'those things do really exist which we distinctly perceive by our senses, and are what we perceive them to be'. For the best recent discussion, see Philip de Bary (2002), chapter 3, 'The First Principles of Contingent Truths', 32–48.
4 See, for example, Alan Goldman's *Empirical Knowledge* (1988).
5 Descartes, *Principles of Philosophy*, in John Cottingham et al, eds, *The Philosophical Writings of Descartes*, Sections 11–20, vol. 1, 227–32.
6 For the best modern discussion of Gassendi's natural philosophy, see Antonia LoLordo (2007).
7 Robert Boyle, *Works*, vol. 3, 7, reprinted in Boyle (1991), 7.
8 Leibniz was no mean judge of the history of philosophy, and he suggests in his *New Essays* that Locke is a follower of Gassendi and his disciple François Bernier, with whom Locke was on friendly terms during his stay in France. See G. W. Leibniz, *New Essays*, 69.
9 For both texts, see Boyle (1991), 1–96, 138–54.
10 For a dissenting opinion, see Alan Chalmers (1993). For a reply to Chalmers, see Pyle (2002).
11 For discussion, see Robert Boyle's *New Experiments and Observations Touching Cold*, in his *Works*, vol. 2, 462ff.
12 For a classic discussion of this problem, see Laudan (1966).

13 See Pierre Bayle, *Historical and Critical Dictionary*, article Pyrrho, 197. 'For if the objects of our senses appear coloured, hot, cold, odoriferous, and yet they are not so, why can they not appear extended and shaped, in rest and in motion, although they are not so?' For Berkeley, see his *Principles*, 9–15, pp. 64–6. 'In short, let any one consider those arguments which are thought manifestly to prove that colours and tastes exist only in the mind, and he shall find that they may with equal force be brought to prove the same thing of extension, figure, and motion' (*Works*, 66).

14 The pivotal work in this area is Peter Alexander's magnum opus, *Ideas, Qualities and Corpuscles: Locke and Boyle on the External World* (Cambridge University Press, 1985), which corrects the misunderstandings of Berkeley and others and sets straight our understanding of the Lockean project.

15 Boyle, 'Of the Positive or Privative Nature of Cold', in *Works*, vol. 3, 733ff.

16 For more depth and detail, see Peter Alexander (1981).

17 Locke's list of primary qualities is not always consistent. Number seems out of place on this list, as it is not a first-order property of particular bodies.

18 See Peter Alexander (1977).

19 Several of Locke's examples can be found in Boyle's *Experiments, Notes, etc about the Mechanical Origin or Production of Divers Particular Qualities*. See Boyle, *Works*, vol. 4, 230–73.

20 See Boyle, *Origin of Forms and Qualities, Works*, vol. 3, 28.

21 For helpful commentary, see Lowe (1995) 78–83, and Jolley (1999), 150–4.

22 For the suggestion that Locke might have pre-refuted Kripke, see P. Kyle Stanford.

23 For a very perceptive account, see Hilary Kornblith (1995), chapter 2, 'Locke and Natural Kinds', 13–34.

24 Kripke, *Naming and Necessity* (1972).

25 Leibniz, *New Essays*, 354.

26 See Putnam, 'The Meaning of Meaning', in his *Philosophical Papers*, vol. 2, *Mind, Language and Reality* (1975), 215–71.

27 Boyle, *Works*, vol. 3, 306ff.

28 See EHU II, xxiii, 13, N 303–4, in which Locke suggests that God may have provided the angels with suitable organs to enable them to gain knowledge of the inner constitutions or real essences of bodies.

Chapter 5 God and Religion

1 Descartes, dedicatory letter to the Sorbonne, *Philosophical Writings*, vol. 2, 3.

2 Ibid., 4.

3 So long as the philosophical arguments for mortality fall short of evident demonstrations, this need not lead us into the notorious doctrine of double truth, or to the conclusion that Pomponazzi must have been guilty of insincerity.

4 This is not an anachronistic thought. The power of the imagination was a stock topic of Renaissance medicine, and the medical schools were notorious – as far as the theologians were concerned – as hotbeds of materialism.

5 EHU IV, xix, 11, N 702–3. For more detail, see Nicholas Wolterstorff, 'Locke's Philosophy of Religion', in Vere Chappell, ed. (1994), 192–5.

6 Newton's anti-Trinitarian tract on 'Two notable corruptions of Scripture' was sent by Locke to Jean Le Clerc with a view to publication in the *Bibliotheque*, but the cautious Newton later withdrew it. See Newton's letter to Locke of 14 November 1690 (C IV, 164–5).

7 Here Locke sets himself in strict opposition to the deism of John Toland, as argued in his *Christianity Not Mysterious* of 1696. Toland argued in that work that we should not accept any proposition in religion that cannot be confirmed by reason – a doctrine Locke explicitly rejects. Toland claimed to be a friend and follower of Locke, but Locke was at pains to disown his self-proclaimed disciple.

8 For Descartes' trademark argument, see *Meditation* 3 in his *Philosophical Writings*, vol. 2, 35. For theological opposition to Locke's denial of innate ideas, see Yolton (1996), chapter 1, 48–64. There is an interesting exchange between Locke and Molyneux on this subject. Molyneux writes on 26 September 1696 that anyone preaching, even ten years ago, that the idea of God is not innate would have been denounced as an atheist; but now it is explicitly taught by divines such as Richard Bentley and William Whiston (C V, 702). Locke's reply on 22 February 1697 was that some divines remain unconvinced, and that Sherlock is planning to preach against him on this very topic (C VI, 5).

9 See EHU II, xxiii, 33–6 N 314–16 for the empiricist account of how we come to possess an idea of God. Locke's account clearly owes a debt to Gassendi's critique of Descartes' innatism in the *Fifth Objections* to the *Meditations*.

10 See Leibniz, *New Essays*, 436.

11 An anonymous critic raised just this objection to Locke in a letter of April 1703. See C VII, 765.

12 See David Hume, *Dialogues Concerning Natural Religion*, in J. A. C. Gaskin, ed., *David Hume: Principal Writings on Religion*, Part 9, 91.

13 ELN *Essay* 4, 151–3. The visible world, says Locke, is 'constructed with wonderful art and regularity', from which we may confidently infer that 'there must be a powerful and wise creator of all these things'. This is a perfectly standard and conventional statement of the argument to design such as could be found in any number of contemporary sources.

14 He justified his exclusion from the *Reasonableness* of the Epistles of St Paul on the plausible ground that Paul was writing to people who were

already Christians. Although the Epistles are fundamental to Christian theology, their teaching cannot be necessary to make a man a Christian.

15 A modern edition of the *Reasonableness and its Vindications*, with a new introduction by Victor Nuovo, was published by Thoemmes (Bristol, 1997). For a good selection of the responses to the *Reasonableness*, see also Victor Nuovo, ed. (1997).

16 See John Edwards, 'Some Thoughts Concerning the Several Causes and Occasions of Atheism', in Nuovo, ed. (1997), 180.

17 The thirty-nine Articles of the Church of England can very easily be found online. It is striking that the very first Article is an explicit affirmation of the Athanasian formula of the Trinity ('three Persons, of one substance, power, and eternity; the Father, the Son, and the Holy Ghost').

18 Extracts from the famous 'Racovian Cathechism' of the Socinians can be found in Nuovo, ed. (1997), 25–46. Jesus Christ, we are there told (p. 31), was a man, albeit a special and unique one. That he had a divine as well as a human nature is flatly denied (p. 32) as 'repugnant both to right reason and to the Holy Scriptures'.

19 Edwards' second attack on the *Reasonableness* is entitled *Socinianism Unmasked* (1696). Extracts can be found in Nuovo, ed. (1997), 209–35.

20 John Marshall (1994), 416. For an opposed view, see Victor Nuovo's introduction to his edition of the *Reasonableness*, xxvii.

21 For more depth and detail concerning Locke's difficulties in accounting for the normative force of the law of nature, see Harris, 78–107 and 264–77.

Chapter 6 The Soul and the Afterlife

1 The *Epistolary Discourse* (1706) of Henry Dodwell the elder (1641–1711) argues that the human soul is naturally mortal and made immortal supernaturally at baptism. The *Discourse* prompted a very lively debate, not just about the metaphysics but about the roles of faith and reason within Christianity.

2 Descartes, Sixth Meditation, *Philosophical Writings*, vol. 2, 54.

3 See Malebranche, *Oeuvres Complètes*, vol. 6, 160.

4 The clear and distinct idea of mind or thinking substance is, Malebranche thinks, not revealed to us by God. But the argument for dualism can still go through if the clear and distinct idea of matter (three-dimensional extension) excludes thinking. This suffices to prove that no material substance can think.

5 EHU II, i, 14, N 111. For a defence of the Cartesian thesis against Locke's objections, see Leibniz's *New Essays*, 113. For Leibniz, the soul is never without 'petites perceptions', even if these are generally below the threshold of consciousness.

6 What exactly Locke has in mind in his talk of 'superadded' powers is difficult both textually and philosophically. For more depth and detail, see Margaret Wilson (1999) and Michael Ayers (1981). If Newtonian gravity turns out to be inexplicable in mechanical terms, it may turn out, Locke thinks, that it is another 'superadded' property.

7 For modern expressions of similar views, see Thomas Nagel, 'What is it Like to Be a Bat?', in his 1979 collection, *Mortal Questions*, 165–80, and Colin McGinn (1989). According to Nagel, it is not that we have good reason to think that physicalism is false, but that we simply cannot understand how physicalism could be true. According to McGinn, there is a true theory of mind and body, but we humans cannot grasp it.

8 For a history of the ensuing controversy, see John Yolton (1983).

9 Leibniz, *New Essays*, 382.

10 It turns out that I was thinking of the film and not the book. In the original RLS story there is enough psychological continuity between Jekyll and Hyde for us to say with confidence that they are the same person and not just the same man.

11 A more radical anti-metaphysician than Locke might have pressed the Quinean slogan 'no entity without identity', and stated that this is an argument against the very existence of immaterial souls. Locke's theism no doubt prevents him taking this radical Quinean line. Even if we can't provide identity-criteria for immaterial souls, God presumably can count and discern them.

12 This was always a subject for irreverent speculations and not a little mirth, not least concerning the consequences of cannibalism.

13 He was working at his death on a paraphrase of the *Epistles* of Saint Paul.

14 In the original story, it is perfectly clear that this is exactly what RLS intended.

15 For a collection of classic texts on the problem of personal identity, see John Perry, ed. (1975). Reid's critique of Locke can be found at pp. 113–18.

16 See Derek Parfit (1984), Part Three, Personal Identity, chapter 12, 'Why Our Identity is Not What Matters', 245–80.

17 Aristotle, *Nicomachean Ethics*, Book 1, chapters 8–10.

Chapter 7 The Two Treatises of Government

1 For details of the ensuing one-off debate of both Houses of Parliament, see *The Debate at Large, between the House of Lords and House of Commons*. It was obvious that public peace and security required Parliament to confer the crown on William of Orange as well as on his wife Mary, but the constitutional basis for doing this was deeply problematic, to put it mildly. Locke's patron, the Earl of Pembroke, played a prominent role in the debate.

2 Letter to Strachey, October 1672, C I, 366–9.
3 For more on Filmer, see Ian Harris's entry in *The Continuum Companion to Locke*, 57–61.
4 Note the striking thematic link here between the *Two Treatises* and the frontispiece of the *Essay*.
5 TTG 180. If anything, Locke suggests, the mother could reasonably be said to have the greater share, 'as nourishing the child a long time in her own body out of her own substance'.
6 TTG 180–3.Locke quotes from a Spanish account of the inhabitants of Peru to the effect that the killing and eating of children was one of their native customs. The story may of course be entirely apocryphal, but it does illustrate Locke's abiding love of the travel literature.
7 The thesis that the excess goods of the rich belong by right to the needy is clearly set out in Thomas Aquinas' statement of the law of nature. How exactly the doctrine should be articulated and applied is, of course, deeply problematic.
8 See Cranston, 426.
9 For an illuminating discussion of 'natural' versus 'conventional' accounts of the state in early modern political philosophy, see A. John Simmons's 'Theories of the State', in *The Cambridge Companion to Early Modern Philosophy*, 250–73. It is worthy of note that the theory of natural subjection is still a target for Rousseau in his *Social Contract*.
10 There are real difficulties regarding the nature and scope of this executive right of punishment in the state of nature. For an illuminating discussion and partial defence of the doctrine, see Simmons (1992), chapter 3, 121–66
11 For criticism, see Lloyd Thomas, 34–42.
12 This regress argument forms an important part of Hobbes' case for absolutism. Locke's insistence that the relation is one of a trust rather than a contract enables him to evade Hobbes' argument.
13 For this line of argument, see Lloyd Thomas, 83–7.
14 A good puzzle case for students is to ask them for their intuitions on the following type of case. A desperately poor man A puts a kidney up for auction, perhaps to raise money for an operation to save his wife's life. Another poor man B needs a kidney of just this type in order to survive. A rich man C has the fancy to breakfast on a human kidney. A puts his kidney up for auction; C easily outbids B and gets his breakfast; B dies soon afterwards. Has A done anything wrong?
15 This liberal tendency in Locke becomes clearest, as we shall see in the next chapter, in Locke's defences of his *Letter on Toleration* against the objections of Jonas Proast.
16 See Woolhouse, 90–1. The *Fundamental Constitutions* date from Locke's period working for Lord Ashley while he was still Lord Chancellor (1669–70). Although the document is sometimes listed among Locke's works, it is more probable that he drew up a manuscript that reflected the deliberations of a committee than that he was its sole author.

17 See the recent article on this subject by David Armitage.
18 See Tully (1993), who argues that Locke systematically devalues both the levels of political organization of the Native Americans and their skills and industry in making use of the natural resources of their lands. If the Native Americans are represented as still in the state of nature, it is easier for the European colonists to justify appropriating their lands.
19 For critical discussion, see Nozick, 174–8.
20 We still regard the air of the atmosphere, for example, as effectively a limitless resource: no one seriously claims that a man drawing a breath (extracting oxygen and exhaling carbon dioxide) is doing an injury to his neighbours. But it is not hard to imagine situations in which such a thought might become pressing.
21 For more on the topic of compensation, see Nozick, 178.
22 For the 'unpacking' of this bundle of rights, see Sreenivasan, 10.
23 Does Locke think that having a right to a property involves having a right to alienate it, i.e., to give it away at will? Tully (1982), 113–14, thinks not; Simmons (1992), 231, questions Tully's reading, and cites evidence suggesting that Locke does think of rights in land and goods as alienable.
24 See Macpherson (1962).
25 For the tendency of Locke's theory to shift in the direction of rule-consequentialism, see Simmons (1992), chapter 1, especially 46–59.
26 TTG 197. It is worth noting that the maxim was explicitly invoked in the great debate of February 1689 between the two Houses of Parliament, and it was invoked to justify setting aside some constitutional niceties and bestowing the crown on William of Orange, as public safety required.
27 The political rhetoric here is more important than the historical reality. Whether in fact the theory of absolutism was a seventeenth-century innovation is a question for the historians. For the Whigs, what counts is that they can portray themselves as defenders of the liberties of 'freeborn Englishmen' and the Tories or court party as attempting to import a fashionable but dangerous absolutism from across the channel.
28 American readers will discern a very clear echo of Locke in the famous *Declaration of Independence*. Scholars disagree about the depth and extent of Locke's influence on the *Declaration*, but on this particular point the influence is immediately obvious at first sight to any reader of the two passages.
29 Waldron (1992). See particularly chapter 1, 'Introduction', 1–20.
30 For a sketch of an attempt to do this, see Simmons (1992), 36–46.
31 Waldron (2002), chapter 2, 'Adam and Eve', 21–43.
32 Waldron (2002), 40.
33 Ibid., 206.

Chapter 8 Problems of Church and State

1 Hobbes, *Leviathan*, Part 2, chapter 18, 233.
2 The Act of Uniformity of 1662 imposed a dogmatically narrow Angli-canism, and thus excluded many of the king's subjects from full par-ticipation in public life, such as occupation of public offices.
3 For the *Two Tracts*, see Woolhouse, 38–43, and Marshall (1994), 12–21.
4 Marshall (1994), 13.
5 In the *First Tract*, Locke is content to leave this question open as not essential to the point at issue in his argument.
6 Things indifferent in religion may be imposed by the civil power, we are told. But 'as soon as they enter into religious ritual, they cease to be indifferent' (LT 24). The religious worshipper must believe that his form of worship is pleasing to God, so if he is ordered to do something he believes offensive to God, he cannot believe that obedience to any such human command will earn him God's favour.
7 René Descartes had earlier noticed and remarked upon the individual freedom to be experienced in the cities of the Netherlands. In a letter to his friend Balzac of May 1631, he remarks that 'I take a walk each day amid the bustle of the crowd with as much freedom and repose as you could obtain in your leafy groves.' See his *Philosophical Writings*, vol. 3, 31.
8 For this argument, see Marshall (1994), 69–71.
9 The definitive edition of the early *Essay Concerning Toleration* (ECT) is that of Milton and Milton for the Clarendon edition of Locke's works.
10 Locke to Limborch, 4 and 18 October 1698 (C VI, 495–6). Limborch responds approvingly (C VI, 517) that by Locke's definitions there are both 'evangelicals' and 'papists' in every Christian denomination.
11 For Proast, see Jean-Fabien Spitz, in *The Continuum Companion to Locke*, 105–7.
12 For more on the Locke–Proast exchange, see Mark Goldie, 'John Locke, Jonas Proast, and Religious Toleration 1688–92', in John Walsh, ed. (1993).
13 The label 'Augustinian' refers of course to Augustine's famous *Confes-sions*, and to the vivid picture it paints of a young man mired in the paths of sin, able to see the better life he feels called to lead but unable (without the gift of grace) to choose the better life and abandon the worse.
14 LT 10. The quote is of course from Matthew 18:20.
15 Perhaps the ancient cult of Bacchus might count as an example?
16 For a defence of the Catholics against this charge, see John Gother's 'Roman Catholick Principles, in Reference to God and the King', in Victor Nuovo, ed. (1997), 100–10. See especially p. 104, where Gother denies that it is Catholic doctrine that the Pope has any temporal

authority over princes, or can release the subjects of a prince from their oaths of obedience.

17 The Catholic Relief Act of 1829 relieved most of the political disadvantages for British Catholics, although they are still debarred to this day from the line of succession to the throne.

18 A letter to Locke of 1679 from his Huguenot friend Henri Justel expresses precisely this worry: that the Catholic clergy always seek domination, and therefore cannot themselves be tolerated (C II, 40–3).

19 LT 36. See also a letter to Henry Stubbe of 1659 (C I, 111).

20 Waldron (218–23) challenges this standard reading of the 'mufti' passage, but I think he is straining a point to do so. Readers both contemporary and modern have seen this as a transparent gibe directed against the Pope.

21 Actually, this was an extremely unlikely scenario, as the Pope and King Louis XIV were in opposite political camps at the time of the Glorious Revolution.

22 Pierre Bayle, *Pensées Diverses sur la Comète* (1682; reprinted Paris, Droz, 1939, 2 volumes), vol. 2, 5, 'Que L'Athéisme ne conduit pas nécessairement à la corruption des Moeurs'. Our actions, Bayle argues, stem from our passions and our habits, not from our speculative opinions in metaphysics and theology.

23 Locke continues to hold that belief in God is essential for morality, and that atheists should therefore remain beyond the pale of toleration.

24 For Locke and the Enlightenment, see Marshall (2010).

Select Bibliography

References to Works of Locke Used in This Volume

C   *The Correspondence of John Locke*, edited by E. S. De Beer, 8 volumes, Oxford: Clarendon, 1976.

References are to volume and page, as VI, 356.

CU   *Of the Conduct of the Understanding*, with a new introduction by John Yolton, Bristol: Thoemmes, 1996.

ECT   *An Essay Concerning Toleration, and Other Writings on Law and Politics, 1667–1683*, edited with an introduction and notes by J. R. Milton and Philip Milton, Oxford: Clarendon Press, 2006.

EHU   *An Essay Concerning Human Understanding*, edited with an introduction by Peter H. Nidditch, Oxford: Clarendon, 1975. References are to book, chapter, and section, as IV, ix, 17. Page references are to the Nidditch edition.

ELN   *Essays on the Law of Nature and Other Associated Writings*, edited by W. von Leyden, Oxford: Clarendon Press, 2007.

LT   *Locke on Toleration*, edited by Richard Vernon, Cambridge Texts in the History of Philosophy, Cambridge: Cambridge University Press, 2010.

PW   *Posthumous Works of Mr John Locke*, edited by Peter King, London: Churchill, 1706.

RC   *The Reasonableness of Christianity, as Delivered in the Scriptures*, with a new introduction by Victor Nuovo, Bristol: Thoemmes, 1997.

STCE   *Some Thoughts Concerning Education*, Dover Philosophical Classics, New York: Dover Press, 2007.

TTG *Two Treatises of Government*, edited with an introduction and
     notes by Peter Laslett, student edition, Cambridge: Cambridge
     University Press, 1988.
WJL *The Works of John Locke*, 10 volumes, London: Tegg, 1823.

Electronic Resources

The *Digital Locke Project* of Dr Paul Schuurman of Erasmus University Rotterdam is a large and expanding body of Locke's texts and manuscripts, with helpful editorial material. See: <http://www.digitallockeproject.nl/>.
There is a very helpful *Locke Resources* website at: <http://www.libraries.psu.edu/tas/locke/>.
Readers who find Locke's somewhat archaic English difficult or off-putting might usefully consult Jonathan Bennett's *Early Modern Texts*, which has renderings into modern English of the texts of the *Essay*, the *Second Treatise of Government*, and the *Letter on Toleration*. See: <http://www.earlymoderntexts.com/>.

Books

Alexander, Peter. 1977. 'The Names of Secondary Qualities', *Proceedings of the Aristotelian Society* 77: 203–20.
Alexander, Peter. 1981. 'The Case of the Lonely Corpuscle', in Richard Healey, ed., *Reduction, Time, and Reality: Studies in the Philosophy of the Natural Sciences*, Cambridge: Cambridge University Press.
Alexander, Peter. 1985. *Ideas, Qualities and Corpuscles: Locke and Boyle on the External World*, Cambridge: Cambridge University Press.
Aristotle. 1985. *Nicomachean Ethics*, translated T. Irwin, Indianapolis: Hackett.
Armitage, David. 2004. 'John Locke, Carolina, and the "Two Treatises of Government"', *Political Theory* 32: 602–27.
Ashcraft, Richard. 1986. *Revolutionary Politics and Locke's Two Treatises of Government*, Princeton, NJ: Princeton University Press.
Ayers, Michael. 1981. 'Mechanism, Superaddition, and the Proof of God's Existence in Locke's *Essay*', *Philosophical Review* 90: 210–51.
Ayers, Michael. 1991. *Locke: Epistemology and Ontology*, London and New York: Routledge.
Bayle, Pierre. 1939. *Pensées Diverses sur la Comète* (1682), reprinted in 2 volumes, Paris: Droz.
Bayle, Pierre. 1965. *Historical and Critical Dictionary*, translated with an introduction and notes by Richard Popkin, Library of Liberal Arts, Indianapolis, IN: Bobbs-Merrill.

Bennett, Jonathan. 2001. *Learning from Six Philosophers*, 2 volumes, Oxford: Oxford University Press.

Berkeley, George. 1965. *Philosophical Writings*, ed. David Armstrong, New York and London: Collier Macmillan.

Boyle, Robert. 1744. *Works*, 6 volumes, ed. Thomas Birch, London.

Boyle, Robert. 1991. *Selected Philosophical Papers*, ed. M. A. Stewart, Indianapolis, IN: Hackett.

Chalmers, Alan. 1993. 'The Lack of Excellency of the Mechanical Philosophy', *Studies in the History and Philosophy of Science* 24: 541–64.

Chalmers, David. 1996. *The Conscious Mind: In Search of a Fundamental Theory*, Oxford: Oxford University Press.

Chappell, Vere, ed. 1994. *The Cambridge Companion to Locke*, Cambridge: Cambridge University Press.

Chappell, Vere, ed. 1998. *Locke*, Oxford Readings in Philosophy, Oxford: Oxford University Press.

Cicero. 1972. *On the Nature of the Gods*, translated P. H. Nidditch, London: Penguin.

Coady, C. A. J. 1992. *Testimony: A Philosophical Study*, Oxford: Clarendon Press.

Cottingham, John. 1988. *The Rationalists*, Oxford: Oxford University Press.

Craig, Edward. 1987. *The Mind of God and the Works of Man*, Oxford: Clarendon Press.

Cranston, M. 1957. *Locke: A Biography*, London: Longmans Green.

The Debate at Large, between the House of Lords and the House of Commons. 1972. Shannon: Irish University Press.

De Bary, Philip. 2002. *Thomas Reid and Scepticism: His Reliabilist Response*, London and New York: Routledge.

Descartes, René. 1985–91. *Philosophical Writings*, ed. John Cottingham, Robert Stoothoff, Dugald Murdoch and Anthony Kenny, 3 volumes, Cambridge: Cambridge University Press.

Dunn, John. 1969. *The Political Thought of John Locke*, Cambridge: Cambridge University Press.

Goldie, Mark. 1993. 'John Locke, Jonas Proast and Religious Toleration 1688–1692', in John Walsh, ed., *The Church of England c.1688–1833*, Cambridge: Cambridge University Press.

Goldman, Alan. 1988. *Empirical Knowledge*, Berkeley, Los Angeles and Oxford: University of California Press.

Harris, Ian. 1994. *The Mind of John Locke: A Study of Political Theory in its Intellectual Setting*, Cambridge: Cambridge University Press.

Harrison, John and Peter Laslett, eds. 1971. *The Library of John Locke*, 2nd edn, Oxford: Clarendon Press.

Hobbes, Thomas. 1968. *Leviathan*, London: Penguin.

Hume, David. 1978. *Treatise on Human Nature*, ed. L. A. Selby-Bigge, Oxford: Clarendon Press.

Hume, David. 1998. *Dialogues Concerning Natural Religion*, in J. A. C. Gaskin, ed., *David Hume: Principal Writings on Religion*, Oxford World's Classics, Oxford: Oxford University Press.

Hume, David. 1999. *An Enquiry Concerning Human Understanding*, ed. Tom Beauchamp, Oxford: Oxford University Press.

Jolley, Nicholas. 1999. *Locke: His Philosophical Thought*, Oxford: Oxford University Press.

Kornblith, Hilary. 1995. *Inductive Inference and its Natural Ground*, Cambridge, MA: MIT Press.

Kripke, Saul. 1972. *Naming and Necessity*, Oxford: Blackwell.

Laudan, Larry. 1966. 'The Clock Metaphor and Probabilism: The Impact of Descartes on English Methodological Thought, 1650–1665', *Annals of Science* 22: 73–104.

Leibniz, Gottfried Wilhelm. 1981. *New Essays on Human Understanding*, translated and edited by Peter Remnant and Jonathan Bennett, Cambridge: Cambridge University Press.

Lloyd Thomas, D. A. 1995. *Locke on Government*, London and New York: Routledge.

Loeb, Louis. 1981. *From Descartes to Hume: Continental Metaphysics and the Development of Modern Philosophy*, Ithaca, NY: Cornell University Press.

LoLordo, Antonia. 2007. *Pierre Gassendi and the Birth of Early Modern Philosophy*, Cambridge: Cambridge University Press.

Lowe, E. J. 1995. *Locke on Human Understanding*, London and New York: Routledge.

Lowe, E. J. 2005. *Locke*, London and New York: Routledge.

McGinn, Colin. 1989. 'Can We Solve the Mind–Body Problem?', *Mind* 98: 349–66.

Mackie, John. 1976. *Problems from Locke*, Oxford: Clarendon Press.

Macpherson, C. B. 1962. *The Political Theory of Possessive Individualism*, Oxford: Oxford University Press.

Malebranche, Nicolas. 1958–78. *Oeuvres Complètes*, ed. André Robinet, 20 volumes, Paris: Vrin.

Marshall, John. 1994. *John Locke: Resistance, Religion and Responsibility*, Cambridge: Cambridge University Press.

Marshall, John. 2010. *John Locke, Toleration, and Early Enlightenment Culture*, Cambridge: Cambridge University Press.

Mossner, Ernest. 1980. *The Life of David Hume*, Oxford: Clarendon Press.

Nadler, Steven. 1989. *Arnauld and the Cartesian Philosophy of Ideas*, Manchester: Manchester University Press.

Nadler, Steven. 1992. *Malebranche and Ideas*, Oxford: Oxford University Press.

Nagel, Thomas. 1979. 'What is it Like to Be a Bat?', in his *Mortal Questions*, Cambridge: Cambridge University Press, 165–80.

Newman, Lex, ed. 2007. *The Cambridge Companion to Locke's 'Essay Concerning Human Understanding'*, Cambridge: Cambridge University Press.

Nozick, Robert. 1974. *Anarchy, State and Utopia*, Oxford: Blackwell.

Nuovo, Victor, ed. 1997. *John Locke and Christianity: Contemporary Responses to the Reasonableness of Christianity*, Bristol: Thoemmes.

Nuovo, Victor, ed. 2002. *John Locke: Writings on Religion*, Oxford: Clarendon Press.

Parfit, Derek. 1984. *Reasons and Persons*, Oxford: Oxford University Press.

Perry, John, ed. 1975. *Personal Identity*, Berkeley and Los Angeles, CA: University of California Press.

Popkin, Richard. 2003. *The History of Scepticism from Savonarola to Bayle*, Oxford: Oxford University Press.

Putnam, Hilary. 1975. 'The Meaning of Meaning' in his *Philosophical Papers*, volume 2, *Mind Language and Reality*, Cambridge: Cambridge University Press, 215–71.

Pyle, Andrew. 2002. 'Boyle on Science and the Mechanical Philosophy: A Reply to Chalmers', *Studies in History and Philosophy of Science* 33: 175–90.

Pyle, Andrew. 2003. *Malebranche*, London: Routledge.

Reid, Thomas. 1994 [1863]. *Essays on the Intellectual Powers of Man*, in *The Works of Thomas Reid*, ed. Sir William Hamilton, 2 volumes, Edinburgh, 1863; reprinted Bristol: Thoemmes, 1994.

Rogers, G. A. J., ed. 1994. *Locke's Philosophy: Context and Content*, Oxford: Oxford University Press.

Ryle, Gilbert. 1990. *Collected Papers*, 2 volumes, Bristol: Thoemmes.

Savonius-Wroth, S.-J., Paul Schuurman and Jonathan Walmsley, eds. 2010. *The Continuum Companion to Locke*, London and New York: Continuum.

Simmons, A. John. 1992. *The Lockean Theory of Rights*, Princeton, NJ: Princeton University Press.

Simmons, A. John. 2001. *Justification and Legitimacy: An Essay on Rights and Obligations*, Cambridge: Cambridge University Press.

Simmons, A. John. 2006. 'Theories of the State', in *The Cambridge Companion to Early Modern Philosophy*, Cambridge: Cambridge University Press, 250–73.

Soles, David. 1999. 'Is Locke an Imagist?', *The Locke Newsletter* XXX: 17–66.

Sreenivasan, Gopal. 1995. *The Limits of Lockean Rights in Property*, Oxford: Oxford University Press.

Stanford, P. Kyle. 1990. 'Reference and Natural Kind Terms: The Real Essence of Locke's View', *Pacific Philosophical Quarterly* 79: 78–97.

Stanton, Tim. 2011. 'Authority and Freedom in the Interpretation of Locke's Political Theory', *Political Theory* 39: 6–30.

Tindall, Matthew. 1730. *Christianity as Old as the Creation*, London.

Tipton, I. C., ed. 1977, *Locke on Human Understanding*, Oxford Readings in Philosophy, Oxford: Oxford University Press.

Toland, John. 1997. *Christianity Not Mysterious*, ed. Philip McGuiness, Alan Harrison and Richard Kearney, Dublin: Liliput.

Tully, James. 1982. *A Discourse on Property: John Locke and His Adversaries*, Cambridge: Cambridge University Press, 2nd edn.

Tully, James. 1993. *An Approach to Political Philosophy: Locke in Contexts*, Cambridge: Cambridge University Press.

Waldron, Jeremy. 2002. *God, Locke, and Equality: Christian Foundations in Locke's Political Thought*, Cambridge: Cambridge University Press.

Walsh, John, ed. 1993. *The Church of England c.1688–1833*, Cambridge: Cambridge University Press.

Wilson, Margaret. 1999. 'Superadded Properties: The Limits of Mechanism in Locke', in her *Ideas and Mechanism*, Princeton, NJ: Princeton University Press, 196–208.

Wood, Neal. 1983. *The Politics of Locke's Philosophy: A Social Study of An Essay Concerning Human Understanding*, Berkeley and Los Angeles, CA: University of California Press.

Woolhouse, Roger. 1983. *Locke*, Philosophers in Context, Sussex: Harvester Press.

Woolhouse, Roger. 2007. *Locke: A Biography*, Cambridge: Cambridge University Press.

Yolton, John. 1983. *Thinking Matter: Materialism in Eighteenth-Century Britain*, Minneapolis, MN: University of Minnesota Press.

Yolton, John. 1984. *Perceptual Acquaintance from Descartes to Reid*, Minneapolis, MN: University of Minnesota Press.

Yolton, John. 1985. *Locke: An Introduction*, Oxford: Blackwell.

Yolton, John. 1996. *Locke and the Way of Ideas*, 1st edn, Oxford: Clarendon Press, 1956; reprinted Bristol: Thoemmes.

Index

Subject Index

revelation 101, 104–5, 106, 107, 119, 121, 122, 140, 144
revolutionary 165–6, 169
revolutions *see* rebellions
Roman Catholics 18, 19, 27, 177, 190–1
  English 190
  freedom of worship 192–3
Roman Catholicism 148–9
royal absolutism 19, 26, 149, 150
Royal Society 9, 72
rule-consequentialism 164–5
Rules for the Direction of the Mind (Descartes) 60–1

Salus Populi Suprema Lex 164–5
sanctions 26, 27, 120, 122, 160
  external 123, 145
  moral law 123, 192
  wrongdoing 124
sceptical doubts 62–3
sceptics 101–2, 103, 119
scholastics 55, 83, 84, 133
science 97
scientific realism 80
scientists 83
Scripture 26, 29, 107, 115, 116, 120, 140, 144, 145, 150, 151
A Second Letter Concerning Toleration (Locke) 178, 180, 185, 186
Second Meditation (Descartes) 67
secondary qualities 84, 85, 86, 88
  mind-dependence of 86–7, 89–90
self 138–9
self-interest 28, 122
self-ownership 160
sensations 47–8, 49, 51, 64, 67, 70, 77, 78, 84, 85
sense of duty 25
sense organs 78, 88, 90
sensitive knowledge 59, 68, 98
  see also demonstrative knowledge; intuitive knowledge; knowledge

sensory ideas 36, 41, 67, 79, 90
  and pain 78
simple ideas 37, 48, 49, 51, 56, 63, 65–6, 67, 68, 77, 84, 85, 91, 92, 111, 114
  see also complex ideas; ideas
Sixth Meditation (Descartes) 125, 127
slavery 26, 170, 171
social conservatives 160, 194
social contract 24, 26, 185, 189–90
social liberals 160, 194–5
Socinians 20, 117
solidity 99–100
Some Thoughts Concerning Education (Locke) 8, 14, 23
souls 4
  actual thinking 130–1
  animals 133–4
  care of 183
  nature of 134
  sameness 139
  substance of 122, 131
  transmigration of 138
  see also human soul; immaterial soul; immortality of human soul
sound 87–8, 97, 112, 128, 135
spiritual beings 69
state 26, 27, 155–6, 179, 183
  authority of 180, 184
  challenging decisions of 157–8
  and church 181
  religious conformity 181
sub-microscopic particles 49, 80
sub-Saharan Africa 155
subjectivity 33, 86, 88, 89, 90
  see also mind-dependence
substance 50, 51, 57, 63, 65, 66, 83, 91, 94, 128, 129, 137
  material 28–9, 94
  immaterial 140
substance dualism 126, 129, 131, 132, 133
suicide 160